With Literacy and
Justice for All

Series Editor: Allan Luke
James Cook University of North Queensland
Australia

Literacy remains a contentious and polarized educational, media and political issue. What has emerged from the continuing debate is a recognition by many critical researchers and theorists that literacy in education is allied closely with matters of language and culture, ideology and discourse, knowledge and power.

This new series of monographs and anthologies draws together critical, cross-disciplinary work on language and literacy in a format accessible to researchers and students of education. Its aim is to provide competing discourses and alternative practices to the extant technical literature which offers 'state of the art' insights and 'how to' formulae for the achievement of literacy narrowly conceived as individual, psychological skills. Drawing perspectives variously from critical social theory and cultural studies, post-structuralism and feminisms, sociolinguistics and the ethnography of communication, social history and comparative education, the contributors to this series begin a critical interrogation of taken-for-granted assumptions which have guided educational policy, research and practice.

Social Linguistics and Literacies:
Ideology in Discourses
James Paul Gee, *University of Southern California, USA*

With Literacy and Justice for All:
Rethinking the Social in Language and Education
Carole Edelsky, *Arizona State University, USA*

Forthcoming Titles

Knowledge, Culture and Power:
International Perspectives on Literacy as Policy and Practice
Edited by Anthony R. Welch and Peter Freebody, *The University of New England, Australia*

Discourse, Gender and School Literacy:
Studies in the Social Organization of Classroom Knowledge
Carolyn Baker, *The University of New England, Australia*

Word Perfect:
Prospects for Literacy in the Computer Age
Myron Tuman, *The University of Alabama, USA*

The Insistence of the Letter:
Literacy Studies and Curriculum Theorizing
Edited by Bill Green, *Deakin University, Australia*

Texts of Desire:
Essays on Fiction, Femininity and Schooling
Edited by Linda K. Christian-Smith, *The University of Wisconsin Oshkosh, Australia*

Writing Science: Literacy and Discursive Power
MAK Halliday and JR Martin

Morning News: Lessons in Learning How to Learn in School
Francis Christie

A Critical Theory of Public Life:
Knowledge, Discourse and Politics in an Age of Decline
Ben Agger

Television Literacy: Text and Context
David Buckingham

With Literacy and Justice for All:
Rethinking the Social in Language and Education

Carole Edelsky

 The Falmer Press

(A member of the Taylor & Francis Group)
London · New York · Philadelphia

UK   The Falmer Press, 4 John Street, London WC1N 2ET
USA   The Falmer Press, Taylor & Francis Inc., 1900 Frost Road, Suite 101,
      Bristol, PA 19007

First published 1991

**A catalogue record for this book is available from the British
Library**

**Library of Congress Cataloging in Publication Data are available on
request**

 ISBN 1-85000-664-4
 ISBN 1-85000-665-2 (pbk)

Jacket design by Benedict Evans

Typeset in 10/11.5 pt Bembo
by Graphicraft Typesetters Ltd., Hong Kong

Printed in Great Britain by Burgess Science Press, Basingstoke on paper
which has a specified pH value on final paper manufacture of not less than
7.5 and is therefore 'acid free'.

Contents

Contents

for Jay, Gail, and Lynn

Series Editor's Introduction

With Literacy and Justice for All is not simply about the great debate over literacy and language education. It is a debate in itself, one which addresses, interrogates, and engages teachers, teacher educators and researchers. The attempt here to 'rethink the social in language in education' speaks not only to the need to counter 'anti-humane' practices and 'deskilling' curricular technologies — as well it serves to represent one teacher's and one researcher's situated, practical engagement with emergent theories of language and the social.

This volume documents Carole Edelsky's decade-long involvement with socially critical, holistic approaches to the everyday problems and possibilities facing teachers of language and literacy. There are no simplistic pedagogical formulas on offer here. Instead these essays progressively work through differences and tensions in the discourses and practices of sociolinguistics and bilingual education, whole language and critical pedagogy — educational 'fields' whose practitioners and advocates often work in isolation from each other and, at times, at cross purposes.

Edelsky begins by taking up what is arguably the most vexing issue facing schools and educators today: the viability of a humane, socially progressive approach to language and literacy set against a backdrop of 'postmodern' skepticism and disillusionment. Such a project has become doubly important in an educational climate where institutional conservatism and technicism together have become dominant strategies to contend with diversity and difference — whether that difference is construed in terms of contending theories and methods, social subjects and collectivities, demographics and cultures, economic and political formations, dominant discourses and media.

It is indeed Edelsky's forceful commitment to equality of access to literacies, school knowledges and social representations for bilingual minority students which traverses this book. To this end, she provides accounts of classroom frames and practices which generate powerful literacies for bicultural and bilingual children. Other essays here offer an equally valuable lesson for life in classrooms: that daily practice needs to be worked through in light of larger social, cultural and political issues. These range from communities' perceived and real concerns about their children's schooling to teachers' diminishing control over their work, from local school board politics to national debates on ethnicity, testing and language policy.

For those educators who are conversant with what Edelsky here describes as 'whole language' pedagogy, then, this book effectively redefines and widens the field — opening out a constellation of questions regarding social contexts and consequences. It demonstrates how literacy education is inextricably tied up with matters of power and control: with students' power over the shape and intent of their own literacies, communities' and schools' control of children's language and education, and, relatedly, the power of researchers and teachers at times to 'misread' these relations and, at others, to remake them in the interests of learners and communities.

With Literacy and Justice for All exemplifies the kind of dynamic and constructive engagement with teachers, learners and critics which educational writing can be about. It is, in the most constructive sense, a heteroglossic work in progress, one which speaks in many voices and registers, offering ideas and practices and then holding these up to interrogation and critique. Cutting across the 'great debate', it is a significant attempt to build through whole language a socially critical pedagogy capable of addressing the cultural and economic and political aspirations of learners of difference.

Allan Luke
San Diego, California
November, 1990

Acknowledgments

'Writing in a Bilingual Program: It all Depends' is part of a study reported in full in C. Edelsky, *Writing in a Bilingual Program: Había Una Vez*, Norwood, NJ: Ablex, 1986.

Much of the material in 'Not Acquiring Spanish as a Second Language' first appeared in two other publications: 'Acquiring a Second Language When You're Not the Underdog', by C. Edelsky and S. Hudelson, in R. Scarcella and S. Krashen (Eds) *Research in Second Language Acquisition*, Rowley, MA, Newbury House, 1980; and 'Acquisition (?) of Spanish as a Second Language', by C. Edelsky and S. Hudelson, in F. Barkin, E. Brandt, and J. Ornstein-Galicia (Eds) *Bilingualism and Language Contact*, New York, Teachers College Press, 1982.

'Contextual Complexities: Written Language Policies for Bilingual Programs' first appeared as an Occasional Paper (No. 10), by C. Edelsky and S. Hudelson, distributed by the Center for the Study of Writing, University of California, Berkeley, June, 1989. It will also be included in *ESL in America: Myths and Possibilities*, edited by S. Benesch, published by Boynton/Cook-Heinemann, 1991.

Sections of 'The Effect of "Theory" on Several Versions of a Popular Theory' were first published elsewhere, some in 'Semilingualism and Language Deficit' (with S. Hudelson, B. Flores, F. Barkin, B. Altwerger, and K. Jilbert) in *Applied Linguistics*, **4**, pp. 1–22, 1983; others in 'The Effect of "Theory" on THEORY — and Other Phenomena', *Southwest Journal of Linguistics*, **7**, pp. 74–86, 1984.

An earlier version of 'Whole Language: What's New?' appeared under the same title, by B. Altwerger, C. Edelsky, and B. Flores in *Reading Teacher*, **41**, pp. 144–54, 1987. Many of the ideas in the present chapter are discussed at greater length in Edelsky, Altwerger, and Flores, *Whole Language: What's the difference*, Heinemann, 1990.

'Hookin' 'em in at the Start of School in a Whole Language Classroom' originated as a slightly longer article by that title, co-authored by C. Edelsky, K. Draper and K. Smith, in *Anthropology and Education Quarterly*, **14**, pp. 257–81, 1983.

'Risks and Possibilities of Whole Language Literacy: Alienation and Connection' first appeared in sightly different form under the title 'Risks of Whole Language Literacy: Alienation and Connection' in *Language Arts*, **66**, pp. 392–406, 1989. The earlier version was written by S. Harman and C. Edelsky.

Originally co-authored with S. Harman for *English Education*, **20**, pp. 157–71, in 1988, 'One More Critique of Testing — with Two Differences' has been somewhat revised for this volume.

'Resisting (Professional) Arrest' was first printed in slightly different form in *Language Arts*, **65**, pp. 396–402, 1988.

Foreword

Carole Edelsky connects the future of our society with details of interaction we seldom notice and assumptions about language we seldom question. If she is right, efforts to establish an official language in the United States are quite unnecessary; bilingualism has not a chance of threatening the dominance of English. The priority of English is inscribed throughout the experience that children have of the world, and they draw the inevitable conclusion. The difference that official language efforts can make is to further divide us, to set group against group, to limit our resources for coping with a multilingual world.

Again, if she is right, efforts to make the United States a productively literate nation are quite likely to fail; productive literacy has little chance of emerging from deeply embedded ways of teaching and testing and judging results that virtually assign large numbers of children to limited competence in writing and reading. The difference that greater efforts at accountability can make is to measure more precisely our failure.

Why should Edelsky be believed? Not because of statistics and surveys, but, first of all, because of telling examples. Such examples may be dismissed as 'anecdotes', and yet they are the kind of experience to which we turn to interpret statistics and surveys. We supply people for the numbers to be about. What Edelsky does is to offer us people we have not seen, people (children) behaving in ways that are not seen until disciplined observers go to look. One finding from one classroom speaks volumes about inequality:

> For the Spanish speakers in our studies, learning the unmarked language [English] to a high degree of proficiency won them little. They were still considered linguistically inadequate. For the English speakers, however, learning sone number and color words and a few songs in the marked language counted as learning Spanish — it was a cause for celebration, evidence of the children's linguistic strengths.

A second reason is a pervasive analogy, one that appeals to what might be called uncommon sense. It appeals to an experience that is so pervasive and common that we seldom feel need to make sense of it. It is the experience of children learning to speak and to interpret what they hear without benefit of school. Of children mastering the various components of a language, its organizations of sound, of vocabulary, of syntax, and integrating aspects of each into styles suited to situations, without instruction first in the several parts. A complex competence acquired in the course of using it.

As is well known, Noam Chomsky has made this experience a starting point for his theory of language, appealing to it as evidence that children are born prepared to acquire language, to acquire the intricacies of a human language. Learning, in the sense of starting from scratch, could not explain what they achieve in just a few years on the basis of limited acquaintance. Most would grant that there must be an innate basis for human language. Where there is disagreement is as to whether it is particular to language, or more general; as to how much of what is acquired is to be explained as the development of innate properties; and as to the form such properties should be said to have.

Chomsky's view is that there is an innate basis that is not part of general cognitive ability, but particular to language; that is extensive and detailed; and that has a particular kind of form. One could accept his view, yet find it necessary to complete it with Edelsky's. Some might speak in terms simply of exposure to language—a language has to be experienced for a child to interpret and acquire it. Edelsky's claim is stronger. Not simply exposure, but meaningful use as well is key.

None of us are going to separate otherwise equivalent children, allow one set to interact normally, making meaning with speech, while allowing the other set only to hear language, not to interact with it. Many of us would expect the result of such an experiment, if carried out, to show a significant difference between the two sets of children.

The claim about literacy involves yet another step. Assuming, as I do, that Edelsky is right, that meaningful use is an essential source of normal competence in speaking and listening, can we say that the same thing is true for writing and reading? Writing and reading, after all, set obvious limits to the adequacy of a theory such as that of Chomsky. Speech and listening are universal in the species; writing and reading have not been. Languages share many fundamental features in their groundplans, pointing to a common origin and biological base; writing systems notoriously need not. Literacy introduces the very dimensions of historicity, relativity, social specificity, that a universalizing theory of language structure wishes to avoid and ignore. And even if simply hearing speech might result in some kind of acquisition of it, seeing writing is unlikely to result in literacy at all. A theory of human linguistic ability, competence, based only on speech, is indeed anachronistic. Adequate to prehistory, it accounts for less and less of the linguistic competence of an increasingly literate world.

Edelsky's thesis of meaningful use, of making meaning, points, I think, to the essential link. Where linguistic competence involves literacy, what children and others can do speaking and hearing, and can do writing and reading, will depend on experience of meaningful use. And Edelsky again has a telling example, an example which should instruct our interpretation of studies, statistics and surveys (see chapter 7). There is further support from another Goodman, not Kenneth, but the late critic and writer, Paul, who wrote trenchantly about literacy:

There is frantic anxiety about the schools' failing to teach children to read
and write; there have been riots on the street about it; the President of the
United States has called the matter our top priority. (1971: 203)

That was two decades ago. Paul Goodman went on to write:

But so far as I know, none of those who are frantic—parents rich and poor,
nor the President—have pointed out that reading and writing spring from
speaking, our human way of being in the world; they are not tools but
arts, and their content is imagination and truth. Occasionally a sensitive
teacher pipes up that children might learn reading and writing if these
were interesting and sprang from what the children wanted to know and
had to say, if they were relevant to their personal lives and had some practical function. But mostly the remedies that are proposed are mechanical
or administrative ... (*idem*)

Goodman is support as well for Edelsky's emphasis on 'literate-person-as-Subject' as opposed to 'Object'. The remark just quoted is part of a general critique of
what he calls 'format', that is, predefined style and shape that colonize autonomy,
that produce an empty style. George Orwell portrayed governmental control of
speech by lies and propaganda; Goodman argues that the government of a complicated modern society cannot lie *much*.

But by format, even without trying, it can kill feeling, memory, learning,
observation, imagination, logic, grammar, or any other faculty of free
writing. (*idem*)

The dichotomy is crude. It does not allow for pleasure in mastering a provided
form.[1] But its point is evident day after day, as news programs present officers and
officials recounting what had happened in the fractured idiom of their formal
reports, and bystanders strain to speak suitably to a reporter. Not all, of course.
Some speak as they would to anyone, fluently; sometimes one has the chance to
hear the same person speak both ways. And it is likely true that most human communities have had a 'natural' style, and that ours has lost much of its grip on one.[2]
Probably communities without writing, to which speech was central, and spoken
narrative essential for the transmission of experience, had a proportion of skilled
narrators far higher than our own (cf. Hymes and Cazden 1978, and Hymes 1982).
Edelsky's approach makes a difference, not only to the acquisition of literacy in
classrooms, but also to the vitality of language in the society as a whole.

These chapters issue from and are addressed to a community of educators,
psychologists, theorists, critics and others concerned with reading and writing, a
community indicated by the references. In this sense it is local work; therein is its
strength and chance of making a difference. In a further sense, it is work with
resonance of a rich tradition—or what forms itself as a tradition as one looks back
and around for theorists of language whose starting point has been the uses of
language in everyday life, the functions, purposes, fullness of that. The nice attention to particulars of the ways in which social meaning of a language and a style are

built up in the experience of persons in the classroom and community would have seemed to Sapir in his last years a realization of his vision (see discussion in Hymes 1970 and 1974, chapter 10). More than once the vital importance of diverse purposes and acts is conveyed by a serial list, for example, 'informing, persuading, jokings, warning, teasing, explaining, cajoling, and so forth', a series which ineluctably brings to my mind the series through which Kenneth Burke expresses his transition from novelist to critical theorist ('what I most wanted to do was to lament, rejoice, beseech, admonish, aphorize, and inveigh' (1966, pp. xii–xiv). In work known in English only some forty years and a World War after its writing, Voloshinov, in collaboration with Bakhtin, set forth trenchantly the foundation of a linguistics that takes the standpoint of the purposeful user (1973, 1986 [1930]). Paul Goodman's critique, mentioned above, is in a critical spirit akin to Edelsky's, and it is unfortunate that Goodman's engagement with linguistics has gone almost entirely unnoticed by linguists and other scholars of language.[3] And for a contemporary approach to social theory that addresses language as situated and engaged, yet encompasses the general issues of class, economy and power, there stands ready to hand the admirable work of Pierre Bourdieu.[4] More than any alternative, it would articulate Edelsky's critical and observational insight. Finally, it goes without saying that Edelsky's work is grounded in ethnography and a critical conception of communicative competence. One of the books' virtues, perhaps even a reason for optimism, is that such grounding can go mostly without saying.

Let me end with a second thought. Progressive' and 'conservative' are established terms, and terms, indeed, used in the opening epigraph, but on reflection I think it would be better not to label the struggle to which Edelsky calls us one between 'conserving' and 'transforming'. Why demur? In part because, 'conserving' is good, if one thinks of trees, salmon, rivers, native languages. Most of all because the two terms imply an equation between change and good, status quo and bad. But there are forces of change that work against what Edelsky advocates, forces perhaps more dynamic than any which oppose them. Consider the change from production to financial interest as the leading force in American capitalism, the change of much of the economy into a semi-dependent, quasi-colonial status, the steadily increasing power of multinational capital beyond local and even domestic control, the dismemberment of communities through lack of work and affordable housing, the degradation of available employment, excluding more and more of the society from the inner circle of those with health insurance and retirement benefits, the channeling of electoral choice in TV spots. Is not the society being changed in ways that lessen the opportunity for critical literacy and images of its worth? Is not a training in literacy in terms of subskills proper preparation for the kinds of employment envisioned for many Americans, congruent with a recurrent industrial process of separating out and downgrading intelligent competence to routine, readily measured efficiency and skill.

Perhaps radical transformation of the teaching of reading and writing is essential in order to conserve certain things. More exactly perhaps, to conserve and extend certain things–to conserve and extend a role for literacy valued by many 'conservatives' and 'radicals' alike, to sustain and augment a saving remnant of self motivated readers and autodidacts. For the idea of critical literacy is indeed old, as is the goal of its extension throughout society. What works against the idea and the goal is new as well as old. In the struggle, carried on across the country by a variety of individuals and groups, what is new must be assessed as well as what is old. Edelsky herself provides trenchant examples of just this in her chapter on theory (chapter 4). Her critical practice points ahead in a way that reaches beyond the stepping-stone of dichotomy.

Professor Dell Hymes
Department of Anthropology
University of Virginia
1990

Notes

1 Just as Edelsky's strong organicism seems to value parts only when part of their whole. Tennis players and instrumentalists, among others, might argue that there is some value in separate practice, say, of one's volley, or of octaves. It would remain true, of course, that neither practice is the same as playing tennis or music.

2 Our society can probably be described with dimensions McDowell (1983) has used to describe the Kamsá of the Andes of Columbia in South America. He compares three modes of speech. At one pole is an esoteric speech of shaman's and priests; it is the most formal, most efficacious (dealing with spirit powers), least accessible. At the other pole is everyday speech, the most accessible, least formal, least efficacious. Between is a ritual style, formalized, broadly accessible, efficacious in ceremonial relations between people. Ability to produce it varies, some of it is obscure to many, some of its features have entered ordinary style. In these respects Kamsá ritual style would seem analogous to what is considered proper for formal formats in our society.

3 An exception is Langendoen 1973. I confess myself to having failed to finish a review of the book for the *American Anthropologist*.

4 See Bourdieu (1991), which incorporates much of his *Ce que parler veut dire: l'économie des échanges linguistiques* Paris, Librairie Arthème Fayard, 1982, together with other essays, and a valuable introduction to the themes of Bourdieu's work by John Thompson.

References

BOURDIEU, P. (1991) *Language and Symbolic Power*, Oxford, Polity Press with Basil Blackwell.

BURKE, K. (1966) *Towards a Better Life, Being a Series of Epistles, or Declamations*, Berkeley and Los Angeles, University of California Press (first published, New York, Harcourt, Brace, 1932).

GOODMAN, P. (1971) 'Format and Communications', in his *Speaking and Language. Defence of poetry*, London, Wildwood House, pp. 200–223.

HYMES, D. (1970) 'Linguistic Method in Ethnography', in Garvin, P.L. (ed.), *Method and Theory in Linguistics*, The Hague, Mouton, pp. 249–311. (Reprinted in Hymes (1983), *Essays in the History of Linguistic Anthropology*, Amsterdam, John Benjamins, 135–244.

HYMES, D. (1974) *Foundations in Sociolinguistics*, Philadelphia, University of Pennsylvania Press.

HYMES, D. (1982) 'Narrative Form as "Grammar" of Experience: Native American and a Glimpse of English', *Journal of Education* 164(2) (Spring), pp. 121–42. Boston University.

HYMES, D. and CAZDEN, C. (1978) 'Narrative thinking and story-telling rights: A Folklorist's Clue to a Critique of Education', *Keystone Folklore* 22, pp. 21–36. (Reprinted in Hymes, *Language in Education*. Washington, D.C., Center for Applied Linguistics, 1980, pp. 126–38.

LANGENDOEN, D. TERENCE (1973) 'The Problem of Linguistic Theory in Relation to Language

Behavior: A Tribute and Reply to Paul Goodman', in *Daedalus* (Summer 1973), pp. 195–201.

MCDOWELL, J.H. (1983) 'The semiotic constitution of Kamsá ritual Language', *Language in Society* 12, pp. 23–46.

VOLOSHINOV, V.N. (1973) *Marxism and the Philosophy of Language*, translated by L. MATEJKA and I.R. Titunik, New York & London, Seminar Press; Cambridge & London, Harvard University Press, 1986, with translators' preface; first published, Leningrad, 1930.

Introduction

What's a Progressive Book Like You Doing in a Postmodern World Like This?

A once progressive critique has come to function as the defense of an academic élite against intellectual change. Radicals champion a liberal idea to conservative effect (Hymes, 1985, p. vi).

Look, Mom, when the artist is no longer the romantic hero who might transform society but, just like everyone else, takes mass produced shlock and revels in it, when art is no longer about pushing the limits of light or color or space but is about putting 200 toothpaste tubes topped with Howdy Doody heads into a piece of cement, then you know there's an enormous shift in mentality that's going on all over (Shuck, 1990).

In the first quote, Dell Hymes was referring to how the theory of equality of all languages has had double-sided effects depending on the historical setting in which it is used, revealing and also hiding 'social facts' in different proportions. In the second, my son was telling me in a long distance phone call (yes, we really had such a conversation) that postmodernism was not just an intellectual toy of the avant-garde but a new, pervasive mentality to be found in the supermarkets along Main Street as well as the galleries of Soho. These two quotations actually have more to do with each other — and with this book — than merely their juxta-position on the same page.

The idea that progressively intended work in language and education might turn out to be conserving rather than transforming was both the impetus for and remains an implicit warning in many of the essays in this collection. Conservative consequences can be a function of something amiss in the work itself, as Hymes was saying. But a giant shove in the direction of maintaining the *status quo* can also come from the context for the work. That is, aside from the 'ordinary' difficulties in making an institution such as education bite the dominant societal hand that feeds it by transforming that hand (into a foot perhaps?), a growing postmodernist mentality that often smirks at the earnestness of projects of transformation may well exacerbate those difficulties. After all, intellectuals and artists are not debating modernism, postmodernism, post-structuralism, critical theory, feminist theory, or the end of the Enlightenment in a vacuum. Something about what is going on in the milieu, in the heads and in between 'plain folks' is feeding (and is fed by) such

1

intellectual debates. Political projects, in other words, proceed, falter, succeed in history.

The relation of the 'temper of the times' to the transforming aim of these essays, then, is one connection between the two opening quotes. Another is the character of this volume itself. Is there a contradiction between a point of view that highlights point of view — relative position, local sites, particular contexts — and a project aimed at transformative change (transformations, therefore, of many points of view and positions)? In other words, is this a hopelessly modern book in a hope-less postmodern world? My preliminary answer is no; the fuller response comes later. The first discussion, however, must focus on transformation and conservation.

Transforming Aims and Conserving Effects

The view of 'transformative' I want to put forward is tied to various critical theories and discourses (feminist pedagogy, critical curriculum theory, critical literacy, critical educational ethnography, post-structuralist discourse analysis). According to Gitlin, Siegel and Boru (1989), schooling produces (and is produced within) a set of attitudes, skills, understandings, and relationships; i.e., knowledges and human subjectivities. Transformative work in education changes (transforms) what schools produce. When and if other social conditions and constraints are right, such changed products can be part of more fundamental societal change. It is important to remember, however, that critical educators who want their work to be transformative do not harbor naïve beliefs that educational practice alone can change social structure and unseat hegemonic ideology.

Transformative work in language and education in Western and Westernized societies is based on certain assumptions: that these societies are unjust and unequally structured; that the texts, voices and interests of the dominant drown out those of the subordinate; that while educational practices along with their built-in assumptions reproduce social hierarchies, schools are also sites for challenging those hierarchies; that change requires the building of collective identities (e.g., seeing oneself as part of the collectivity of women, Hispanics, laborers, and so on). Along with these assumptions, transformative educational practice is characterized by: concern for the struggles of the oppressed; resistance to educationally-sponsored means of oppressing; direct involvement in specific struggles against repression in particular settings; and interrogation of taken-for-granted assumptions about language, text, knowledge, and learning (Aronowitz and Giroux, 1985; Ellsworth, 1989; Giroux and McLaren, 1986; Simon and Dippo, 1985; S. Taylor, 1989).

Transformative teaching would help people 'extend their own agency' (Britzman, 1988) and would explicitly counter prevailing hierarchies. As Shor (1990) warned,

> if we do not teach in opposition to the existing inequality of races, classes, and sexes, then we are teaching to support it. If we don't teach critically against domination in society, then we allow dominant forces a free hand in school and out (p. 347).

Whether in teaching, research, policy making, administration, or other education work, transformative practice promotes a 'critical consciousness'; skills for finding out *how* perspectives and identities are constructed, *how* knowledge is produced, *how* dominance is maintained; and a vision of alternatives (Britzman, 1988; Giroux and McLaren, 1986; Shannon, 1985; S. Taylor, 1989). The aim is to help students

> build a just and equal society which is at peace with itself and other nations and the environment, which does not wage undeclared war on poorer children by abandoning their needs, which does not power-monger other countries, and which respects ecology (Shor, 1990, p. 342).

A tall order indeed. Even if the designation of 'transformative' is granted on the basis of revolutionary *potential* rather than a revolutionary *fait accompli*, even if one insists only that to be transforming the work must serve both short and long term interests of oppressed groups, it is still a tall order. As just one complicating issue, group interests are not always clear cut, nor are they without self-contradictions. No wonder it is so easy to miss the mark; no wonder it is so unlikely that any one project would have all these qualities or that even an entire body of work taken all together would exhibit all of them in equal measure.

Many scholars have presented insightful analyses to show how their own or others' past work has served unwanted conservative ends. Cazden (1983), and Gitlin *et al.* (1989) make such a case for educational ethnography; Eagleton (1983) critiques a variety of literary theories for the same fault; Pratt (1985) explores the conservative underside in ethnographic writing practices in anthropology. Research and classroom practice in language and education has the same unfortunate potential. It is not only the work intended to preserve hierarchies and exclusions (e.g., that which lauds the superiority of standard curricula, texts, or dialects) or the work which obviously lends itself to such use (e.g., that which 'explains' school failure by locating deficiencies in individuals and their communities) that preserves existing inequalities. Such unwanted consequences can even follow from the work aimed at evening things up, at eliminating or at least diminishing the privilege of one gender, class or race — from agendas which aim towards social transformation.

What has promoted these unwanted consequences? At least three culprits have been at work: unexamined acceptance of prevailing conceptions of language instruction and evaluation, especially written language; distortions in the way progressive research or liberatory principles are used; and a focus on failure, along with a concomitant absence of concrete examples of liberatory practice.

Despite often exquisite analyses of oral or written texts and despite serious efforts to change classroom practice, much well-intentioned work in language and education is conserving because it accepts as givens various assumptions and practices concerning language. For instance, with few exceptions (most of which are taken up in this volume), even progressive educators and educational linguists accept certain hegemonic assumptions about language proficiency and language instruction. One such frequently accepted assumption is that concerning 'skills'. Reading and writing are presumed to consist of separate skills; unlike oral language which is *acquired* as part of an 'identity kit' (Gee, 1989a) through active present-time use with a community of language users, written language (i.e., reading and writing 'skills') is presumed to be *learned* through lessons for *later* use. (See Krashen, 1982 for a discussion of the difference between acquisition and learning.) Closely related is the prevailing assumption that the purpose of schooling itself should be to convert literacy and various competencies into a set of formal and separable skills (Cook-Gumperz, 1986).

An acceptance of these prevailing assumptions seems to be buried in language and education workers' acquiescence in an assortment of other typical educational practices. For instance, though they critique unequal treatment in reading groups, even critical researchers often accept reading groups themselves — and also the related ideas that 'reading' *per se* is an appropriate school subject, that reading must be taught, and that it is best taught through activity whose sole purpose is instructional or evaluative and not communicative. Some progressive researchers look closely at the structure of talk in lessons (portraying children as competent beings who must and do learn complex pragmatic arrangements for language use), but they neglect to analyze what the talk or the lessons are about. In such cases, the typical lesson focus — separate language skills — is simply accepted (with no protest or disassociation) as suitable content. Further, lessons focused on skills (rather than reading and writing for some purpose beyond being instructed about written language) are taken for granted as the events through which such skills *must* be taught. Special instructional materials to accompany lessons for teaching skills are similarly taken for granted. Thus, instead of using elegant analyses of the language of basal texts as evidence for questioning the need for such texts in the first place, these analyses have sometimes been used to argue for the need to prepare children to cope with basal reader language.

Though critical educators do occasionally study the way test responses are interactionally accomplished, revealing the subjectivity and variation hiding within the myth of objectivity and standardization, they rarely question the legitimacy of language performance for no purpose other than evaluation — i.e., the very enterprise of testing itself. Thus, even some critical educators use test scores without comment, referring to them respectfully as though they were legitimate evidence of individual ability or program success. Even though tests are hopelessly biased, even though they are conceptually invalid, even though they are used to support social stratification, tests and test scores are nevertheless appealed to — with a straight face — in work that is supposed to promote change. I argue here that while such work may promote slight reform (e.g., of details in materials, policies, or other practices), it prevents fundamental change. Additionally, it further legitimizes a major instrument of inequality as well as the faulty conceptions about language embedded in that instrument and endemic in educational practice.

To take the endemic without question and, what is worse, to treat 'separate skills' ideas, testing, basal technologies, reading-as-a-school-subject, or artificial language lessons not merely as typical but as intrinsic and therefore necessary to teaching and learning — these moves have conservative effects. It is as though teachers and researchers with an interest in the social dimension of language and education have not taken the 'social' seriously enough. They too operate with the aforementioned hegemonic assumptions about written language; they too do not

Not questioning leads to:

question those assumptions; and so they too make major pragmatic mistakes. Like confusing exercises in reading with other kinds of reading. Like legitimizing curricular and assessment practices that are *a*social in conception (e.g., that fail to account for the social construction of people's interpretations or their abilities). Like being unwitting accessories to testing practices that are *anti*social in their use (e.g., that assault people on the one hand or, on the other, that function to make a structural socioeconomic hierarchy appear natural).

The second push in the direction of conservation rather than transformation comes from distortions in the way transformatively intended research and liberatory principles are used — often by both traditional and progressive-minded educators. An example of a distortion (or perhaps merely an oversimplification) of a liberatory principle appears in the use of the idea of adding previously silenced voices, of making student, Asian, gay, female, poor, etc. voices heard. Each voice within these voices, however, is also a plurality — and not necessarily a harmonious plurality at that. There is great intra-individual conflict among the voices people internalize from a stratified society (Cazden, 1989, citing Bakhtin). Attempting to merely add voices, as Ellsworth (1989) notes, ignores the contradictory, partial, and 'teeth-gritting' nature of each voice. A similar problem, which I begin to address in this volume, occurs when work with a transformative agenda focuses on a liberatory pedagogy for literacy but ignores ensuing contradictions for students.

Another example of conserving distortions in the way some work is used comes from the late 1960s and early 1970s. New understandings in linguistics were offered as aides in putting a stop to victim-blaming practices. The intent, misguided or not, was for educators to learn about linguistics, specifically the major ideas of transformational generative (T-G) grammar, in order to appreciate the complexity and systematicity of poor and minority children's language. What happened instead was that many publishing companies (and their school district customers) turned a usually misconstrued presentation of T-G grammar into a new skill/subject for children to learn. A current example of distortion of research concerns classroom interaction. Analyses of the typical initiation-reply-evaluation (IRE) structure of interaction during lessons are now being used in many teacher education classes not for revealing something about the construction of social relations in classrooms but for training teachers to be sure to include the 'third slot' (evaluation) in their interactional exchanges!

What was and is conserving about statements concerning T-G grammar, class-room interaction and other language and education topics aimed at an educational audience is not only the contorted use. It is also a failure on the part of researchers to clarify appropriate and inappropriate uses of the original work. That omission contributes to the more general myth that research (and science) is politically neutral and that researchers have no responsibility for anticipating the uses of their research.

A third push in the direction of conservation rather than transformation emanates from a frequent focus on failure — failure of children with particular social identities to succeed in school (Trueba, 1988), failure of schools to be sites for those children's success. Much research in language and education provides both summaries and also richly detailed pictures of these failures, so much in fact that it is the 'scientific' mainstay, however unintentionally, of a 'failure industry'. As McDermott (1987, p. 361) has said, millions of people are 'measuring, documenting, remediating, and explaining' these failures. What is conserving about all this activity is that it puts an analytic distance on failure and offers no countering 'language of possibility' (Aronowitz and Giroux, 1985).

Recently, there has been a shift toward studying classrooms where minority students succeed (Trueba, 1988; see Chapter 7, this volume, for an example). What too often counts as success, however, even to educators with an emancipatory agenda, are responses to tasks sedimented with oppressive assumptions about written language. Moreover, the success is usually within curricula that do little to promote a critical consciousness. What is needed are glimpses of 'actual moments of critical pedagogy' (Britzman, 1988, p. 93) or details of 'more vivid utopias' (Cazden, 1983, citing M. Mead). Alex McLeod's (1986) depiction of critical literacy in John Hardcastle's classroom is an exception, as is Sandra Taylor's (1989) action research to help girls reflect on the experiences of women through a Family Photos Project, and Patrick Shannon's (1989a) discussion of teachers' study groups.

If there are few examples and too-brief reports of transformative moments, there are even fewer that deal with the struggles over and resistance to potentially transformative educational practices. There is some acknowledgment of the ways in which whole language, for example, is being coopted (Edelsky, Altwerger and Flores, 1991). And Shannon (1989b, p. 632) discusses the way publishers promise students and teachers a voice but ensure 'they have nothing of social or political consequence to talk about'. But there is far less about struggles within classrooms or within students, far less about how students explain to themselves their prior (and probably their families' continuing) enjoyment of what their new critical consciousness shows them is sexist or racist (S. Taylor, in press), even less about outright resistance to a critical curriculum or a critical pedagogy. As Britzman (1988, p. 93) cautions, 'a critical consciousness cannot be mandated'. Resistance occurs, but there are no analyses to help progressive educators get beyond it.

The view I have presented here of how work in language and education that is meant to be transforming can be inadvertently conserving depends, of course, on an appeal to history. A project is deemed transforming or conserving in relation to the structural conditions, social practices, and ideologies of the time. Research, classroom activity, policies and discourses that start out progressively may end up regressively — not only because of unintended blind spots but also because conditions change. For example, conceptualizing failure as a structural, curricular, and interactional 'accomplishment' rather than an individual flaw and fleshing out that conceptualization with detailed pictures of those classroom accomplishments prodded more radical work in some classrooms. What was (and still is) needed next were: 1) rich images of the mutual accomplishment of success — images to rival those portraying academic failure and images to 'ground' critical theorizing; and 2) a new vision of what that success might be about (i.e., success at what? at doing exercises on tests? at being able to challenge dominant knowledge through sustained critique?). What happened instead, however, was persistence in a focus on failure, conserving today (though not initially) because something else is needed now.

Or consider the example Hymes (1980b, 1985) offered of how a transformative theoretical insight became conservative. The functional equality of all languages, an idea developed through research in linguistics and anthropology, promotes an appreciation of the extraordinary complexity of all languages and, therefore, of the amazing creativity of speakers of any language. In the mid-twentieth century, that idea was progressive in that it shook the foundations of scientific support for ranking languages linguistically in correlation with the socio-political positions of their speakers. But this tenet is now conservative in that it often is used to mask other 'social facts', like the historically-produced inequalities among languages in power, prestige, or function. (Hymes gives the example of decrease in the narrative function in various American Indian speech communities as traditions of myth have been extinguished.).

The potential for transformation is not only tied to socio-historical contexts; it is also limited. Educational practice, by itself, without more fundamental shifts in economics and politics, is unlikely to effect wide-ranging change in an inequitably structured society (Gitlin *et al.,* 1989). Moreover, given particular conditions, all social positions and practices (even transformative ones) have the potential for oppressing (Ellsworth, 1989). And since all viewpoints necessarily both reveal and block out, all understandings, all visions, all projects are necessarily partial and contingent.

Even so, partial and limited potential is still *some* potential. Ideologies have contradictions; social fabrics have holes and uneven seams. On the one hand, then, currently transformative work can make small differences for a few people by exploiting the contradictions within those small openings. On the other, such work can be a necessary (but admittedly insufficient) partner in larger social movements.

In referring to the limits and necessary partialities of transformative projects, I am not letting the essays in this volume off the hook. They too have transformative and conservative potential, though I did not intend the latter. They rely on female pronouns to convey generic meanings; they counter prevailing assumptions; they challenge (and report classroom practices that challenge) educational weapons used against dominated groups; they offer a somewhat detailed picture of educational activity that is at least partly counter-hegemonic; and they present some subtleties that could help fill in a few of the gaps in practice that aims at transformation.

In this volume, however, I have not offered any fine-scale descriptions of, for example, teaching in opposition to sexism or racism. I have admitted errors in my work as well as naïve surprises. But I have done little to problematize my authorship or to discuss how reported or even quoted voices of students, teachers, and other researchers have been invented, reinvented, and inserted into a text of my own construction and used for my own purposes. Thus, like all critical writing in language and education, this volume too, as well as the classroom work it describes, is based on and presents partial understandings.

Yet I intend for it to have transformative potential. In this volume, I have poked away at meanings and assumptions because that is 'my' (actually, it is a socially shaped) inclination. That enterprise, as well as post-structuralist analyses and postmodernist media, has taught me how slippery stable concepts are when examined up close. Yet in these essays I take definite positions, slippery ground notwithstanding. Are these contradictions within the volume? Or are they contradictions between this project and the present historical context?

Modernism and Postmodernism: On the Relationship between Projects and 'the Times'

At the start of this essay, I asked whether this was a modernist book in a postmodern world. That question, with its modernist overtones of attempting to locate and pin down meanings, is not really about how to categorize. It is about whether the times are especially bad now for transformative work and — if postmodernism has become an overarching mentality for generations, as modernism was before it, and not just a fad for a decade — whether they will continue to be bad into the future. That is, does postmodernism hamper or perhaps outright prevent progressively intended projects from achieving their transforming potential? That question presumes another: Is postmodernism the very air we are breathing; is it the all-pervasive mentality through which lived experience in the Western world is filtered?

Modernism (some put the period between the Industrial Revolution and the mid twentieth century; others locate it between the 1840s and the 1920s) was (is?) marked by a belief that people could remake the world by faith in Progress, Reason, and the tenets and methods of Science (Berman, 1989). Modernism's dominant analyses (for defining problems and offering solutions) generally appealed to some underlying, comprehensive system or scheme (e.g., behaviorism, Marxism, Darwinism, Freudianism). A modernist sensibility valued (values?) inquiry and discovery and was (is?) anchored in the idea that there is a reality existing outside of culture — that there are essential, assertainable qualities or natures that pertain even after culture is stripped away (i.e., that's the way women/ the poor/Jews/pieces of literature/great paintings *are*) (Peller, 1987).

The twentieth century brought with it cataclysmic disasters — world wars, chemical warfare, catastrophic pollution. Change as Progress, remaking the world for the better through Science, was no longer such a certainty (Lyotard, 1984). Indeed certainty itself seemed unwarranted (Morgan, 1990b). In its place came a profound skepticism, humbled aims, and resignation. Instead of taking for granted the existence of a transcendent Truth beyond interpretation or culture, a different view developed: everything is culturally defined; all meaning is socially constructed; there is no essence to great art or to women's nature or to anything else. What makes a text 'literature' is the way it is treated, not some characteristic of the text (Eagleton, 1983). There is no *essential* difference, then, between 'high' and 'low' art or even between a President and a media image.

In such a milieu, cynicism is all too easy. Not only do people recognize that public life, for instance, is simply 'politics' (e.g., there are no transcendent rights; the judge *invents* rights according to a particular viewpoint; therefore, it is best to argue for rights based on whose interests given interpretations will serve) and that Presidents are indistinguishable from media images, but they participate in the charade. They are even informed about the particulars of the charade by the media 'spin doctors' (e.g., about 'the making of the President'); yet ever more knowing, they still play their parts in the act. People in postmodern culture also know that they themselves (their subjectivities — their identities and their sense of those identities) are social constructions. Conceivably, such knowledge can liberate, permitting people to be aware of how they are positioned. But that knowledge can also lead to extreme self-consciousness and disconnection — not being fully present, always both participating yet holding back a bit to watch oneself participate. Cynicism and disconnection may lead, in turn, to nostalgia, a deep yearning for a time without self-consciousness and cynicism, a time when what is now smiled at knowingly and condescendingly was taken in earnest innocence (Birkerts, 1989).

Several approaches to analyzing (and effecting) social life have developed within postmodernist times (if these are in fact postmodernist times); e.g., deconstruction, post-structuralism, critical pedagogy, critical ethnography, critical sociology, critical legal studies. Despite great differences among these various critical theories, they share certain premises. For instance, they appeal, with more or less emphasis, to the fundamental instability of meanings, to the way meanings carry their opposites embedded within them. The ground did not shift beneath modernists' feet. In a postmodern world, if one stops to look, the ground turns out to be quicksand. Related to this deconstructionist morass is various critical theories' acknowledgment of the importance of intertextuality (Bloome and Bailey, 1990; Morgan, 1990b); the meaning of any text (print texts, interactional texts, scenic texts) is tied to others that came before and still others yet to come.

Central concerns of these theoretical approaches are issues of knowledge, authority, and power. A shared premise is that what is put forth as neutral (i.e., scientific, factual) knowledge by dominant groups in society supports existing power arrangements and thus is far from neutral. A shared project is to unmask what is hidden within dominant knowledge structures. And a shared position is to remove class as the privileged category for explaining social life and instate a triumvirate instead — gender, race, and class (Morgan, 1990a), followed by various other subjectivities (ethnicity, health, sexual orientation, and so on).

Let us now look again at the two questions I posed earlier: Does postmodernity hinder or even prevent projects from achieving their transforming potential? Has postmodernism, as an all-pervasive mentality, unseated modernism? And let us begin with the second.

It is not at all clear that postmodern qualities have taken over (Fraser, 1989). Yes, there is widespread cynicism and nostalgia. But no, there is not widespread acceptance of the view that all knowledge is socially constructed (witness the arguments in favor of canonical literature and standardized curricula, let alone the arguments over abortion). Yes, there may be general skepticism about what science can accomplish, but no, there is not widespread agreement with the idea that nothing is transcendent; e.g., that rights (to private property, to one's own opinion, to control over one's body) are merely social inventions invoked for political purposes. And there are also counter movements which may not look to Western science for their answers but which still actively cultivate innocence and a faith in total transformation without struggle (e.g., the New Age movement). Scholars too disagree over whether modernist premises and projects must be abandoned and over whether they *have* been abandoned (Fraser, 1989). For example, many literary theorists are currently arguing that elements of modernism are to be found in postmodernism and vice versa and that the two currently co-exist and will probably continue to do so (Morgan, 1990a). The 'times', then, are not entirely postmodernist. Just partially. (Which, of course, is a fitting characterization for an outlook that recognizes the partial nature of all understandings [Ellsworth, 1989].)

Whether complete or partial, postmodernism is more than 'in the air'. Postmodern strategies appear in mass media advertising campaigns that must be interpretable by millions of people. Postmodern premises shape plans in community organizations, become the punchlines of jokes, affect commitments between people. In this light, then, we can ask the first question: Is postmodernism one more barrier (and perhaps an insurmountable one) to educational projects that intend to transform?

It might well be. Since postmodernism rules out single answers that are always true, and instead ties answers to the positions of the various answerers, it can encourage a vacant pluralism (Caplan, 1990) or vulgar relativism (Giroux and McLaren, 1986) — more answers, but no principled basis for choosing among the many. In addition, a postmodern sensibility, marked by increased cynicism and disillusionment (e.g., Baudrillard, 1988), could well retard projects for transformation. After all, if progress is always a sham, why bother? In exposing the futility of trying to make meanings stand still or the non-neutrality in claiming neutral or natural or common-sense justifications for positions, poststructuralist approaches are able to demolish all positions. This relieves them of the obligation to take any position themselves (Eagleton, 1983); and, of course, that throws considerable cold water on advocacy or taking action. If these analyses do not lead to paralysis, if people are still moved to act, postmodern analytic approaches encourage people to shift the sites for action to what critics claim are pale substitutes. Instead of wage differentials and working conditions, there are texts and discourses. Language becomes both the central analytic metaphor and, often, the only terrain worth analyzing or acting on. 'If modernism found both fulfillment and defeat in the streets, postmodernism save[s] its believers the trouble of having to go out at all' (Berman, 1989, p. 83). It does seem, then, that the postmodern mentality wherever, whenever it appears, provides an inhospitable climate for politically progressive projects.

But let us look again. With its appreciation that social life (knowledge, beliefs, attitudes, relationships, identities, economies, political processes, and so on) is constructed rather than given, postmodernism attends more seriously to people's agency as well as their dignity. And with its post-structuralist sensitivity to the ways constituencies are silenced through 'neutral' facts and 'totalizing' explanations, postmodernism may be more likely to seek out subordinate voices. If progressive language educators living in a postmodern world are indeed more willing to solicit previously silenced voices and less inclined to impose their own projects on followers, they may be making things harder for themselves (imposition is always more efficient and therefore easier than dialogue) but they may also be promoting more widespread commitment to progressive projects.

A major postmodern stance is skepticism and uncertainty, suspecting and sometimes analyzing what is taken for granted. Uncertainty can be paralyzing, but when it is linked to the understanding that the *status quo* is a human construction, that there are no out-of-culture, out-of-history principles to justify the way things are (Peller, 1987), then interrogating the taken for granted can open possibilities for transformation (Britzman, 1988). One of those taken-for-granteds now more open for interrogation is the idea that Reason is orderly, unemotional, and unbiased. Postmodern analyses, however, unearth the passion embedded in rationality, the subjugating power it masks, the hierarchy it supports (Peller, 1987). These analyses make space for *non*-rational voices which imbue transforming efforts with a new energy (Ellsworth, 1989). Perhaps postmodernism is not necessarily the drag on transformation it seems it could be.

Many critical theorists would agree. They have found ways to maintain transformative agendas within a postmodern identity, though these projects, by comparison with modernists', are smaller and more local, humbler, 'chastened' (Isaac, 1989). Some deliberately emphasize a language of possibility (not of certainty) to offset postmodern despair (e.g., Aronowitz and Giroux, 1985). Others take a definite position even though their analyses, showing an infinite regress of contradictory meanings, have led them to an impasse. When they adopt their definite position, they do it with full knowledge that it (as well as any other) is full of holes (Morgan, 1990b). The position they take is based on a morality informed by politics (whose interests *should* this serve?). That is, if meaning is constructed and if civil, political, economic, human rights are social inventions, then the transforming postmodernist works to *construct* meanings and to get agreement on *invented* rights that will help equalize rather than stratify relations among people. Such work is political, potentially transformative, and profoundly hopeful.

This introductory chapter reflects my present position as well as the essays collected herein. I have gone back and forth between the various relationships between projects, consequences, and historical contexts because of my own uncertainties about this book and any other, my own sense of cultural foreboding, but yet my stubborn hope. And if I can not resolve these contradictions, I can at least offer a belief in a key activity: rethinking. It is one activity that characterizes both postmodern and critical projects. It has also been the activity most salient to me in working on these essays. Instead of leaving already published essays as is and thus making my own intellectual history a major subtext, I revised (slightly or drastically) and added new essays to fill in old holes only recently noted. The object was not to hide what I now see as inadequacies (the old versions are accessible anyway; the new ones sometimes make the changes explicit). It was to move towards a coherent theoretical, pedagogical, and political position.

Three main sources have made such rethinking possible for me: the opportunity afforded by Falmer Press; the informal 'post-doctoral' education so generously given to me over the last few years from half a world away by Allan Luke and from relatively around the corner by Steve Gelb; and the example of extraordinary classroom teachers. Karen Smith and Chris Boyd, for instance, showed me minute to minute workings-out of general theoretical notions which often provided both the stuff of and the prod for my rethinking.

In this introduction, I present contradictions and admit and imply what is missing from the volume. In the final chapter I analyze what is missing from a major counter-hegemonic movement. The message for language in education, for critical educators, for progressives generally, for you, for me — though it hardly needs saying — is that the work is nowhere near finished, nor should it be.

Part I

Introductory Note to Part I

The essays in this part demonstrate some rethinking concerning the social nature of language in the education of language minority children; they also point out areas that need continued re-examination. Chapter 1 highlights the importance of the political relationships between native and target language when trying to understand second language acquisition. That chapter presents a study of first grade speakers of English learning Spanish as a second language in an ostensibly two-way bilingual program. Their learning — but mostly non-learning — of Spanish reflects a larger political reality played out by 6-year-olds.

Larger societal relationships also had consequences in the study of young bilingual children's writing reported in Chapter 2. This chapter deals with a web of social influences on children's development as writers. Some of these influences are close up and within the classroom (e.g., the teacher's beliefs about children's capabilities). Others seem more distant (e.g., the politics in the school district office) but they too impinge on individual children. Looking at writing by positioning the writers in scenes within scenes within scenes raises a question about whether development is individual and indeed whether development is an appropriate metaphor for changes in young children's writing.

Chapter 3 focuses on what needs to be considered in policies about written language education in bilingual programs. It is a cover-all-the-bases approach, mentioning factors but not exploring them fully. The intent is not only to show the complexities but to argue against homogeneous, top-down language and education policies that fail to account for particularities and that therefore subvert the goals of those who want language education to help even things up for minority language childern.

Evening up, decreasing privilege, has been the aim of much research, practice, and policy concerning minority language children's school careers. Chapter 4 looks at one line of such research and argues that researchers' own unexamined and unacknowledged assumptions about reading and school achievement can, in the long run, end up supporting rather than undermining the *status quo*.

In general, then, what this part argues is the need to rethink the conceptualizations and the boundaries of phenomena in language and education. Bottom-up approaches (e.g., confining one's gaze to activity inside the classroom) fail to show how larger social and political contexts come right into the classroom,

invited or not. Top-down approaches (e.g., developing general educational policies) fail to account for local particularities. What is on the surface (e.g., school failure) must be considered in the light of not only what counts as success or failure but
with an eye on assumptions underlying 'what counts'. And what is underneath (or
is it above or inside or infused within?) needs grounding in live instances. This part
sets up the need for a broader, more inclusive approach to language in education,
premised on the interweaving of layers. One attempt at such a broader approach is
then presented in part II.

Chapter 1

Not Acquiring Spanish as a Second Language: The Politics of Second Language Acquisition

Language is political — nothing new in that statement. Yet it must be admitted right here that when my colleague Sarah Hudelson and I began the studies I will discuss here, we both did and did not understand just how political it is.

To begin at the beginning: In studies of 'naturalistic' second language acquisition (as opposed to studies of the learning of foreign languages through direct instruction in language classrooms, for instance), the political nature of the second language learning situation is largely ignored. Almost always, researchers investigate the 'spontaneous' acquisition of a target language which dominates the native language of the learner — English in the US or the UK or the local majority language in a community where linguist parents do field work and also study their children acquiring the local language. We had been sensitized by Hymes (1970; 1972b) to always consider situational particularities in language use. Certainly, learning a second language would be included in language use. And the relative political positions of native and target languages — and of speakers of those languages — would be an important 'situational particularity'. Thus, we wondered if second language learning would look different if we investigated a situation in which the usual relationship of dominant target language/less powerful native language were reversed. Perhaps what had been presented in other research as characteristics of second language acquisition in general were, in fact, only characteristics of the acquisition of a dominant language by minority language speakers. Perhaps the acquisition of a minority language by dominant language speakers entailed different strategies, followed different trajectories, had different meanings.

We were delighted by our own reasoning, and we carried out a study to investigate this relatively uncharted territory. Unfortunately, we had neglected to consider the larger consequences, for second language learning, of gross political inequality between two languages. That is, by and large, majority language speakers do not acquire the minority languages in their midst. And that, of course, is what happened (or, rather, didn't happen) in the two bilingual classrooms in which we kept trying to study second language acquisition of a non-dominant language. But more interesting than the non-acquisition of Spanish, in this case, is what we came to understand about how the various actors in the classroom played out the larger political conditions of non-acquisition.

How We Started

We began with a school-year long study of three Anglo first graders supposedly acquiring Spanish as a second language in a bilingual classroom near Phoenix, Arizona. Although the goals of that school district did not include explicit attention to mutual second language learning on the part of both Anglos and Chicanos, the teacher expressed that desire and made plans for it to occur. We did limited classroom observations in order to find out who was addressing Spanish to the English speakers, for what purposes, and under what conditions. Every two weeks, with one of us (Sarah Hudelson, subsequently noted as SH) posing as a monolingual Spanish speaker, we audio-taped three children, each paired with a bilingual peer, in language testing and play sessions. We left the room for about ten minutes during those half-hour sessions, leaving the tape recorder on, in order to have samples of completely child-child interaction.

Our findings were: 1) that no Spanish was addressed individually to these children by anyone except us during our biweekly sessions (i.e., that neither Spanish speaking adults nor children took the language teacher role); 2) that during both Spanish-conducted classroom activities when they were part of a large-group 'addressee' and in our taping sessions, the three Anglo children 'tuned Spanish out' (i.e., they did not take the language learner role); and 3) that, with the exception of a few color and number words, no Spanish was acquired (Edelsky and Hudelson, 1978).

Despite what seemed to be a clear set of findings, we hoped that we were wrong, that genuine, mutual second language learning could occur if the conditions were optimal. After all, in that first study, school conditions were *not* optimal. It was not school policy to encourage the Anglos to learn Spanish — only this one teacher held that goal. And Spanish was not used as the vehicle of instruction for anywhere near half the time. Of course, such a state of affairs stemmed from a larger 'condition' — the relative political position of the two languages. While, on the one hand, we were sensitive to that condition (it was, in fact, what prompted the study in the first place), on the other, we still naïvely hoped it could be overridden by more equitable local classroom arrangements. Therefore, we began a second study the next year, still searching for strategies used by dominant language speakers in the acquisition of a *subordinate* language, in what we thought would be a more effective setting for problematic second language acquisition. It was finally through this second study that we were able to see non-acquisition as an activity engaged in by many social actors, rather than as lack of activity or individual failure.

The Second Study

This time we chose a 'better' classroom. It was in a district in which one of the explicit goals of the bilingual program was to produce bilinguals among both

Spanish and English speaking children. To that end, the district had instituted systematic, 'pull-out' second language instruction in each language (not just in English), and it assessed second language proficiency in each language with a test.[1] The language schedule in this first grade was an Alternate Days model, continuing the presentation of content rather than translating it — one day was English Day, the next was Spanish Day. We assumed that there would be more Spanish in this Alternate Days allocation than there had been in the subject-matter allocation of the preceding year.[2]

There were twenty-two children in the class: ten were bilinguals or monolingual Spanish speakers who were bussed in from a barrio. Twelve lived in the neighborhood and were English monolinguals or English dominant children with some limited ability to produce Spanish. Of the neighborhood children, five were Anglos; seven were Chicanos.

Again, SH posed as a monolingual Spanish speaker. Contrived though it was, 'la Señora Spanish' (as one bilingual child named her) assured the Anglophiles of getting at least some Spanish directed to them occasionally on a one-to-one basis. Moreover, if they wanted to interact with SH, the English speaking children would have to attempt to understand her and to accommodate to her monolinguality.

We were classroom volunteers and observers for one-half to a full school day at least three times each month from October through early April. We took special note of code choice, functions of language, and any instances of sense-making or withdrawal by Anglophiles in relation to Spanish interactions. We targeted three of the Anglo children, Kathy, Katie, and Nathan, and two Chicanos, Vince and Anita, for close observation. According to school records as well as our observations and the teacher's, Vince and Anita were very close to being monolingual in English. However, the teacher knew that Spanish was used around them at home occasionally. We reasoned that perhaps some familiarity with the 'tune' or maybe a prior understanding of some social routines would provide the extra push that would result in significant second language acquisition for these two children.

In addition, as in the previous study, we took each of these five children with a Spanish speaking peer to a separate room where we gave them a short comprehension and repetition task (they were asked to show SH the picture of the big boy/ little boy, etc. and to repeat sentences such as *es un muchacho grande*/this is a big boy). After SH tested them, she played with them using playdough, puppets, magic slates, and so on while the other researcher observed. Again, during the play time, we left the children alone for several minutes. The sessions were conducted entirely in Spanish and were audio tape recorded, with one child wearing a lapel microphone.

The Second Language Learning Context

What seemed noteworthy about the context in which the acquisition of Spanish was supposed to occur was: the functions for which the two languages were used; the circumstances under which Spanish and English crept into each other's 'day'; the children's perception of the nature of the systematic second language instruction (ESL and SSL); and the effect of the presence of the 'monolingual' Spanish speaking adult.

'Public Spanish' (the use of Spanish to several people or to one person in front of an audience) was used by children for a wide range of functions — directing, predicting, informing, teasing, threatening, explaining, consoling, and so forth, but only if all present were bilingual. Public Spanish from the teacher and two aides seemed to be restricted to teacherish functions: directing, reprimanding, explaining, entertaining (story-telling), keeping order, providing transitions between activities, establishing social contact, and conducting classroom routines (taking attendance, collecting lunch money).

Spanish directed individually to our target children or to other English dominant children was much more rare than Public Spanish and much more limited in function. Adults used Spanish to individual English speakers for social routines (*buenos días*), reprimands, and directions when they could also signal non-verbally (to get their meaning across). They did not use it for explaining, joking, warning, or 'making conversation', though they did use English for these purposes. With almost no exceptions, children did not address Spanish to individual English speakers at all. The rare exceptions were produced by two Mexican immigrants (Elena and Lily) who were monolingual in Spanish at the start of the school year. Once, Elena gave Anita a short direction in Spanish which she followed without pause with an English paraphrase. During a test session, Lily and Kathy provided the only evidence of any explicit argument over code choice.

Kathy:	What's she doing?
Lily:	Dice tú — (She says you —)
K:	Don't say in Spanish. English.
L:	Que te digo español (That I tell you Spanish)
K:	English.
L:	No.
K:	Say it in English.
L:	No (the argument was ended as we resumed testing).

In an Alternate Days bilingual program, the 'rule' is one language per day. Nevertheless, loudspeaker announcements are made daily in English, Spanish speakers talk to each other in Spanish every day — in other words, no day is 'language pure'. However, the frequency and extent of the other language's intrusion was not symmetrical in this classroom. Spanish was used very infrequently on English days. Except for Spanish reading time for Spanish speakers, adults used no Public Spanish on English day, though they did use Spanish individually to Spanish dominant children only, either as a reprimand or in response to an initiation in Spanish by a child.

The intrusion of English into Spanish Day was another story. English was used publicly to all (not merely to English dominant children) and for the same functions as Public Spanish. Additionally, it was used for insuring the understanding of the Anglophiles. There was no comparable checking, on English Day, with *¿entienden?* (do you understand?) along with a Spanish explanation to the Spanish dominant children. Whenever adults referred to a meaning that could not be pointed to or acted out, they switched to English (Now when you get finished wait for someone to come around and help you; There's going to be a surprise tomorrow). And, not surprisingly, English was used to conduct activities in other rooms in the school and in the presence of nonbilingual outsiders who might come in to make announcements. It was even used by Spanish dominant children to SH, the 'monolingual' researcher.

Another aspect of the second language learning context was the provision of second language, audio-lingual method instruction (both ESL and SSL) and a 'booster' program for development of the weaker language in bilinguals.[3] The children were aware of these divisions in the language teaching program and in the class generally. They referred to 'the kids who come on the bus'; they would name which children went to SSL, to ESL, and to Special English; they sometimes commented on which children were potential after-school playmates (for logistical reasons, at least, it was not those who left on a bus); they knew which children could be used as translators.

Their perception of the special second language lessons also became part of the context. To them, the lessons and the routines learned were to be used as games or performances. Kathy occasionally approached SH with cards showing fruit, articles of clothing, and so on, pointed to the cards while repeating *español*, and tried to elicit Spanish card naming as a game. Unfortunately, the children perceived both SSL and ESL as equally artificial and communicatively useless. Nathan bragged that though he could not speak Spanish, he *had* learned to say *es un (sic) abrelata* (it's a can opener). In one taping session, Kathy told us that what she talked about in the Spanish class was *es un* (it's a, as in it's a sweater, it's a book). And Lily, Kathy's taping session partner, responded to SH's question about what they talked about in ESL with *dicen 'I'm a fireman'. Dicen así.* (They say, 'I'm a fireman'. They talk like that.)

As we have indicated, we deliberately manipulated the context by offering the occasional presence of 'monolingual' SH who persisted in her monolinguality. Not only did this provide English speaking children who wanted to interact with her with a *demand* to accommodate, it also enlarged the range of purposes for which Spanish was used with them. Since SH was not responsible for directing activities or maintaining order, she could engage children in casual conversation, something the teacher and aides never did in Spanish. While 'shooting the breeze', then, SH (but no other adult) used Spanish both publicly and individually in order to get information, to make social contact and open a conversation, to get translations, to joke, to compliment. Because it 'couldn't be helped', SH could avoid switching to English when her addressee showed a lack of comprehension. That is, in these language 'showdowns', it was Spanish speaking SH rather than the English speaking target children, whose language choice prevailed. This was an anomaly we will discuss later. For now, suffice it to say that every other week, the range of functions of situated Spanish directed to the Anglo children was broadened because of SH's presence.

Language Acquisition (?) in this Context

Even if they didn't become Spanish speakers, the Anglo children did respond to the second language learning context. And their responses are instructive as we think about the role of all concerned in second language learning. Their responses can be grouped into four categories: 1) display of metalinguistic awareness; 2) taking the learner role in comprehending; 3) not taking the learner role: and 4) producing Spanish.

Metalinguistic awareness. Even after only two months in first grade, the children appeared to have developed a striking awareness of language as an entity. Sometimes, this awareness was stated neutrally; sometimes with feeling — the positive and negative valences often expressed by the same child. In class, Kathy and Katie were engaged in a bit of competition.

> Kathy: I can speak three languages — English and Spanish and Indian.
> Katie: Well I can speak four — English and Spanish and Scotland and Jewish!
> Kathy: So! I'm gonna learn Flagstaff! (a city about 150 miles away)

Some children thought synonyms might really be translations ('pony' in English is 'horse'. Anita told us). On several occasions, after we had left the room during a taping session, children echoed Vince ('Finally, we can speak English. I hate Spanish.') While school personnel bragged about how well the Anglos were learning Spanish, the children themselves saw it differently.

> Nathan: I don't talk Spanish. I just know the colors.

Taking the learner role.   In order to acquire a second language naturalistically, one must do two things: make sense out of nonsense; and present oneself as a legitimate participant (Fillmore, 1976). Primary aspects of the learner role, then, are to use clues to guess at meanings and to stay in an interaction by taking one's conversational turn.

On occasion, the five English speakers we focused on did indeed act as learners; most often, this happened in the taping sessions with SH. There, they would watch faces intently, matching facial expressions with the speaker, with a split second delay. Frequently, they took their turns non-verbally (nodding their heads or shrugging their shoulders). More interesting was their verbal turn-taking, which often included uncanny guesses at the speaker's meaning. These guesses seemed to be based on various combinations of verbal and visual clues along with clues from their 'real world knowledge' (e.g., knowing that there is a great likelihood that an adult in an interview/testing setting is asking a child a question, that some questions are more likely than others, that topics tend to be maintained across several turns, that certain behaviors are expected in school or testing settings, and so on).

For instance, when SH pointed to 'Grease', printed on Nathan's T-shirt, and asked *Nathan, ¿qué dice?* (Nathan, what does it say?), Nathan answered 'Grease'. Now it could be that he understood that situated *phrase*. Or it could be that what he understood was the *situation*. That is, when adults in school call a beginning reader's name and point at print, they probably want the child to read it. In other words, Nathan could have been 'simply' interpreting a gesture in combination with a name cue and his knowledge of likely situational demands.

Or to take another example. The children were writing on magic slates. Anita's Spanish speaking peer partner told SH in Spanish that she knew how to write her name in cursive.

> SH: ¿Quién te enseñó? (Who taught you?)
> Elena: Mi mamá (My mom)
> SH: Y tú, Anita, ¿quién te enseñó a escribir así? (And you, Anita, who taught you to write like that?)
> Anita: Papa.

Once again, it could be that Anita understood the question and that she meant to say that her father had helped her learn to write. But her answer could just as well have been the result of the following deduction: the topic includes *mamá*. Adults in school often ask a question with many right answers and then expect children to take turns giving answers to the same question. A likely question is what else goes with *mamá*. If that were the case, Anita would have been taking her turn by sliding over SH's words and, instead, by interpreting the single language clue *mamá* in combination with a guess about the likely question.

Many examples of the Anglo children producing appropriate content during their conversational turns make it seem like they had already acquired enough Spanish to understand the *language*-in-context, not only the context. Our contention, however, is that they were, instead, doing what is necessary in order to *begin* to acquire a second language; namely, participate, guess the general gist of an extended exchange, and guess the specific communicative demand of a particular turn. Evidence for our position comes from the children's failure to respond correctly when SH would deliberately withold gestures, from the great number of times when at first they 'looked blank' and then responded appropriately to the same questions translated by one of the bilingual children, from their failure to respond to any 'there'/'then' topic which could not be tipped off by a person's name, and most importantly, from the times when they took a guess but their guess missed the mark. Because these conversational errors can be accounted for by appealing to the same combinations of clues and knowledge that resulted in appropriate responses, we believe a guessing strategy was at work throughout. That is, at least some of the time, the children were taking the learner role, using clues to make sense and to take their turn.

For example, the use of a language clue in combination with knowledge of a likely question resulted in the following missed-the-mark responses. (Our inference about the child's thinking is in brackets.)

> (preceding references have been to Katie's picture of her mother and father and her sister, Cassie)
> SH: ¿Cuántos años tiene? (How old is she?)
> Katie: [I recognize *cuántos* as meaning 'how many'. The general topic has concerned members of my family. The likely question is how

many children are there] Holds up two fingers (Cassie is actually 9 years old)

SH: Dos. Tiene dos años, dos años (Two. She's 2 years old, 2 years)

K: [I understand *dos*. The adult is reiterating my elicited answer that there are two children in my family. I will further elaborate that response] Me and Cassie.

(Katie had told us the month before that her father had hurt his back)

SH: Y Katie, ¿cómo está tu papá? (And Katie, how is your father?)

K: (no response)

SH: ¿Mejor? ¿Se siente mejor? (Better? He feels better?)

K: [I recognize *papá,* which must be the new topic. A likely question concerning my father is: what does he do for a living] Makin' insurance.

Not taking the learner role. These examples show that at least occasionally the children acted as second language learners, guessing and taking their turns. Mostly, this was in interactions with SH who did not honor the political relationship between the two languages but who stubbornly persisted in speaking Spanish and in not understanding English.[4] But there were many more times when the children either failed to take their turn, failed to guess, or outright refused to take part or to comprehend. Non-response was the response when the Spanish speaker asked about there/then topics, initiated new topics which were not accompanied by gestures or supporting context, or subjected the child to a barrage of successive questions.

There were other instances of non-turn-taking and supposed non-sense-making which were more emotionally loaded. When an unfamiliar story was read in Spanish in class without a preceding synopsis in English, the English dominant children would quickly escape through misbehavior or by moving away physically. There were also times when the children played on their monolinguality in order to defy an adult or to express their frustration. For example, Nathan had misbehaved and was being shepherded by one of the aides to another seat, accompanied by her repetition of *siéntate acá* (sit there). He glowered, 'I don't even know what you mean!' Another day, the class was playing Hokey Pokey in Spanish for the first time, but using the same melody, the same sequence of body parts being 'put in and out and shaken all about' that the children were familiar with in English. Nathan wailed, 'I don't understand this'. During our test sessions, Kathy refused to repeat a phrase, maintaining she had already done so 'privately'.

Kathy: I said it. I said it with myself, like this (moves her lips, goldfish style)

SH: Es un muchacho chiquito (He's a big boy — the test phrase)

Lily: Say, Kathy

K: I did. Really (laughs).

Producing Spanish. In class, except for interactions with SH, the only Spanish produced by these five children was color words, number words, *adios,* and song lyrics. Even to the 'monolingual' SH, the English speaking children's rare in-class

Spanish production was mostly single words, uttered in response to an opening gambit initiated by SH.

In the taped sessions, though more Spanish was produced, it was hardly frequent, and there too, it usually consisted of single words. Occasionally, the children used a Spanish color or number word to their peers (*I want dos yellow; Lemme have the rojo*). In response to questions from SH, children switched to the Spanish pronunciation *mamá* and *papá* instead of *mama* or *daddy*. After SH showed she didn't understand, Anita once converted 'this is a hot dog' to the single word 'taco' (another fast food, but not the gastronomical equivalent of a hot dog).

When we left the children alone with the tape recorder on, they produced even less Spanish than when we were present. This is not surprising since our exit removed the peculiar inversion that came with SH's presence, and permitted the 'normal' relationship between the two languages to reassert itself. When we were gone, neither Kathy nor Katie produced even one Spanish word. Nathan used a number and a color word once. And Vince said *tortilla, masa* (cornmeal), and *bruja* (witch) once each, and had one exchange with Hector involving two taboo Spanish words.

The five children, then, used language about language quite frequently. Sometimes, they acted out the second language learner role when receiving Spanish, though mostly from SH rather than from peers or other bilingual adults. And, less frequently, they produced some Spanish when responding to particular people who addressed it to them. As we said at the start, these efforts resulted in no major second language acquisition between October and April. Were there *any* changes?

Changes in the Children's Spanish Performance

When we first met them, these five children already knew some color and number words, a song about the date on the calendar, the names of some letters, and two social routines (*adiós; buenos días/* goodbye; hello). Six months later, each of the two Chicano children had used an additional two or three word Spanish formulaic phrase once or twice. Their performance on the comprehension/repetition tasks had not changed. We can hardly say, then, that being in this bilingual classroom resulted in any significant acquisition of Spanish syntax, morphology, or even lexicon for these two children. More importantly, if the acquisition of syntax, morphology, and lexicon (i.e., a narrowly conceived notion of language acquisition) is dependent on the use of certain discourse strategies (Hatch, 1978), the latter were missing. Neither Vince nor Anita demonstrated any increased inclination to initiate or sustain interactions with Spanish speakers using Spanish. Being Chicano and having a headstart through prior exposure and some already-established routines in Spanish did not result in the great leap forward that we had hoped these children would take.

Of the three Anglos, Nathan showed only one change — he learned the SSL routine about the can opener and used it to show off. Kathy was the only one of the five who (rarely) used Spanish to convey her own intentions over more than one turn — always with SH (e.g., trying to get SH to play an SSL card-naming game by saying her own name in Spanish, pointing to the cards, and repeating *español,*

spañol). Katie's performance did improve on the artificial comprehension task we used during part of the taping sessions, but under less constrained conditions (during class or during the playing part of the taped session), when the input was less predictable, her comprehension seemed no better as the months passed. Essentially, the three Anglos made no greater or lesser improvement than the Chicanos did.

It is important to remember that while these five children were making minimal, if any, progress in Spanish, the Spanish speakers were taking giant steps in English. They produced long English strings, used English to initiate activity and conversation (as opposed to merely responding to others' questions), and attempted to follow extended exchanges and stories which were not augmented by Spanish translations. English was their increasing choice for use with other Spanish speakers, both adults and children (e.g., once, we heard Andres and Hector discussing in English the Spanish reading group's Spanish worksheet). English was the language they used more and more for their labeling of school-taught concepts (rectangle, circle) despite presentation of these concepts in both languages. It was also the language they used increasingly for social routines, even to 'monolingual' SH. This was a repeat of what we had seen in the prior study when, by the end of first grade, the Mexican immigrants had even Anglicized the pronunciation of their own names.

But everything was not a repeat. As we said, there were in fact differences between the two schools in what was done to promote two-way second language learning. Yet despite these in-school contextual differences, there were almost no differences in what was learned. From October through March, the two groups of children seemed to be the same in their (non)acquisition of Spanish. And, of course, despite the in-school differences in efforts to promote second language learning, the second language learning context outside of school was the same in both studies.

The Second Language Learning Context Reconsidered: In-school Reproduction of Out-of-school Inequality

If children were exposed to a second language both in a naturalistic setting and through direct instruction, if others used that second language with them in one-to-one interactions, if the children themselves took interactional turns and tried to derive the meaning of second language utterances, why didn't they make more gains in second language acquisition? We could answer — as so much classroom-centered educational research does — with an appeal to quantity (there wasn't enough one-to-one interaction in the target language; the second language wasn't used for enough functions) or to time (six months wasn't long enough — though it *was* long enough for the Spanish speakers to make great strides in English). We believe, however, that the relative political position of the target and native languages is the more important factor.

It is the phenomenon of markedness — one manifestation of the relative political position of two languages — that figures most prominently in why only one language became a target language, only one group assumed the role of teacher and only one group became second language learners. As Fishman (1976) explained, for particular institutions within particular domains of social life, the use of a particular language may be expected or taken for granted. In that case, it is the unmarked language for that institution or domain. Any other language is marked. A marked language requires some deliberate activity on its behalf before it is used for carrying on the business of the institutions in that domain. An unmarked language, on the other hand, is one which is used 'anyway' without any consciously devised language policy, the one people take for granted is 'naturally' the language of that institution or domain.

Markedness is a dimension that has its source outside the school. It cannot be determined by comparing one language to another in terms of its power in the world at large. A language is marked or unmarked in relation to particular domains in particular speech communities. Theoretically, a politically weak language of low prestige in one speech community could be the unmarked language of education in another, even within one nation's borders. It is our guess, however, that the language of the more powerful speakers — the dominant language — will be the unmarked language in high status, governmentally controlled domains like education. That is certainly the case across the various local speech communities in the US, even those in which non-English speakers are both in the numerical majority and in power in the local government. And it was the case in the two schools in these Arizona suburbs.

Markedness can be artificially upset in a limited way through the establishment of bilingual immersion programs. Indeed, it is because speakers of a dominant language do acquire non-dominant languages to some extent in bilingual immersion programs (but not in two-way bilingual programs in the US, at least, according to both our studies and Fillmore's [1978]) that we can see the importance of the notion of markedness. The difference between an immersion program and 'regular' bilingual programs is that in the former, the marked language becomes an unmarked language *within* that school. Outside the school program, within the wider community, that language is still marked, requiring special policies and activities to justify conducting the daily affairs of the institution in that language. In 'regular' bilingual programs, on the other hand, the marked language remains a marked language, even though it is used as a language of instruction.

Immersion programs are not a second language learning panacea for dominant language monolinguals, however. Other factors besides a program-bound shift in markedness affect whether children learn a non-dominant, marked language. As one example, relative lack of parental support for the Spanish immersion program in Culver City appears to have been related to the limited success of the Culver City experiment, in contrast with more parental support for and greater success of some French immersion programs in Canada (Torres, 1988). And even in the more successful immersion programs in English speaking parts of Canada, because of fewer functional demands for producing the second language (which, we believe, is related to the fact that French continues as a marked language outside the classroom), the Anglophile children do not attain native speaker proficiency in French (Swain, 1985).

Knowing that a language is marked in a particular domain may help predict that it will not be acquired as a second language but it doesn't explain just how that non-acquisition occurs. Our own two studies and Fillmore's (1978) comments offer a beginning sketch of what people are doing that prevents some from learning a second language.

Bilingual code switching (like other language use) not only gives a message; it gives *off* a message (Goffman, 1959). Among bilinguals in many communities, the 'rule' is to address people in their more comfortable, preferred language (Genishi, 1976; Hudelson, 1978; Schultz, 1975). In the classrooms for our two studies, however, bilinguals sometimes used English with non-English speakers. But they did not use Spanish with non-Spanish speakers. That is, there was a double standard for *violating* the rule, depending on whether the addressee's preferred language was marked or unmarked.

Since the unmarked language is the normal, expected, taken for granted language of the institution, it is also normal, expected, and taken for granted that all students will learn it. Students know this at a very young age. They may initially resist (Itoh and Hatch, 1978; Saville-Troike, 1988), but most eventually make efforts to learn, trying to make sense of the babble around them and trying to get into the action in the other language.

There is no mystery in how everyone learns who the second language learners will be — which language *must* be learned (i.e., which is the unmarked language). It is the language one persists in when another doesn't understand, the language whose presence no one comments on, the language one gets lunch in, the language the school secretary uses to answer the phone, the language of classroom management, the language of most of the trade and textbooks. A small child's personal experience with a reading group which, at first, uses mostly Spanish as the instructional language, does not trick the child into thinking that English is merely an option.

The clues mount up quickly over which language must be learned, and the many 'showdowns' over language (they can be compared to contests over who will blink first) soon begin to turn out the same way. The child who speaks the dominant unmarked language holds out longest, refusing to understand the other; the marked language speaker gives in, pretending to understand or using formulaic utterances to get into the action (Fillmore, 1978). In other words, the speaker of the unmarked language takes on the language teacher role (using a modified version of the unmarked language to the minority language speaker); the marked language speaker takes on the learner role, guessing, pretending, trying out chunks of the new language to accomplish social ends. Once a child becomes the learner, it becomes pragmatically difficult to get out of that assymetrical relationship; thus unmarked language speaking teachers stay teachers and the marked language speaking learners stay learners (Fillmore, 1978).

And teach and learn they do. A linguistic 'underdog' in school, then, is not one more likely to 'lose' the second language learning game but rather, one destined to 'win' it. We do not mean to belittle the severe problems both in and out of school faced by these students. Nevertheless, it is their subordinate status that guarantees considerable second language learning, just as it is privileged status that prevents comparable acquisition on the part of non-underdogs.

There is, of course, a subtext to winning the second language learning game. Like learning to read, learning a second language is not an unmitigated, neutral 'good'. Becoming bilingual, like becoming literate, doesn't mean the same thing or have the same consequences in all societies or for all people in any given society (see Graff, 1986, for a discussion demystifying the idea of universal meanings of and benefits from literacy; see Cummins, 1976, for a discussion distinguishing the socio-politically determined categories of additive and subtractive bilingualism). For the Spanish speakers in our studies, learning the unmarked language to a high degree of proficiency won them little. They were still considered linguistically inadequate. For the English speakers, however, learning some number and color words and a few songs in the marked language counted as learning Spanish — it was a cause for celebration, evidence of the children's linguistic strengths.

How can such a state of affairs be changed? If markedness originates outside of classrooms in speech communities, then it is outside of classrooms, in speech communities, where the primary efforts must be directed toward changing this discriminatory language situation. In other words, our analysis implies that people interested in equitable language education must not only work to change programs; they must work to change the political context of those programs. To offset even slightly the power of the unmarked language, those who plan programs aimed at mutuality in second language acquisition will have to seriously understand the wider society's discriminatory arrangements, including critically analyzing the antecedents and consequences of the political relationship between the target and native languages; and they will have to establish strategies (and criteria for assessing the success of their strategies) that account for those arrangements.

In our studies, it was SH's status that gave legitimacy to her sociolinguistically peculiar behavior ('facing down' the dominant language speakers, refusing to take on the learner role and implicitly persisting in 'teaching' the subordinate language). Had she been someone of lesser status (a Chicana, a child, an aide) her rule breaking would, in turn, have been resisted (it was never even commented on). And had she not been deliberate and determined, she would most likely not have been able to maintain her rule-breaking. But as it was, she *did* maintain her violation of politically motivated language norms, and that changed the pragmatic situation in the taping sessions at least. It gave the Spanish speaking peer partners a boost, evening up the usual asymmetry where they were always learners. In essence, SH was a one-person immersion program, giving the usually marked language unmarked status for those taping sessions — and, therefore, letting the Spanish speaking peer partners have a chance to take the teacher role. Even though SH only maintained such sociolinguistic contrariness for short periods of time, it was wearing. We doubt she could have maintained it on a daily basis. And it hardly provides a theoretically adequate or practical model for what schools might do.

The two teachers and some of the school personnel who worked with them to further the goal of two-way bilingualism were also opposing the established order. They bucked speech community norms, even if they saw little reward for their efforts. These two teachers' efforts, as well as SH's, to undo the effects of markedness in the classroom were undertaken seriously and sincerely, but they were — and had to be — ineffective. That is because they either ignored the larger reality or they were not part of any organized (in concert with others) and sustained action.

Establishing a full scale immersion program would have provided some relief

27

in the classroom from the inequities of markedness. However, it would not have completely neutralized the impact on second language acquisition of the out-of-school relationship between the two languages, and it would have done nothing to change the out-of-school language situation which gives rise to markedness and all its consequences.

What we are saying, then, is that in the end, bilingual programs cannot compensate for a discriminatory political context. The gross inequality of power between two languages (and two groups of people) that guarantees that one set of young children will always be language teachers and the other set language learners, that one set will be congratulated for making almost no progress while the other is disparaged for making tremendous (but not 'total') progress — this situation is not one that any program can change.

But just because schools cannot undo existing power relations that profoundly affect language learning does not mean they should continue to conduct business as usual; e.g., maintaining élitist monolingual language policies and exclusionary canons and privileging only certain discourses. After all, schools — and what goes on within them — are not only mirrors and reproducers of societal arrangements; they can also be sites of resistance. That resistance can be both individual and collective, sometimes self-defeating and sometimes transformative (Aronowitz and Giroux, 1985). The question is how, in regard to second language learning, such resistance can be mounted to account for the profoundly political nature of the enterprise.

Notes

1 It is not that we looked favorably on such efforts as pulling children out of class and giving them direct instruction in a second language or testing their second language proficiency with questionable test instruments. It is just that these were signs that the district was willing to take seriously the second language learning of *each* language.

2 It will appear throughout that we are being either covertly or overtly critical of the bilingual adults, especially the teachers, involved in these two studies. On the contrary: We praise them for their motives and their efforts to make bilingual education a two-way street. Especially noteworthy is the extraordinary amount of energy the teacher in the second study must have expended in order to persist in doing what was often followed by signs of incomprehension by her students (just the opposite of what a teacher hopes for!) in the name of a larger principle, to provide the amount of Spanish she did when all around her the push was toward greater English usage, and to maintain her Spanish maintenance desires in the face of contradictory desires from many quarters. These teachers were up against an entire politico-linguistic context — which is the point of this essay.

3 'Special English' was provided for children who scored badly on the English version of the language proficiency test. Actually, some Spanish surnamed children went to Special English who appeared to us to be native English speakers. There were no comparable Special Spanish classes for those who scored badly on the Spanish version of the test.

4 Fillmore (1978) discusses how even young children come to act 'appropriately' in the US in English speaker/non-English speaker interactions. The young English speakers hold out longer, making fewer efforts to understand the other; the Spanish speakers eventually submit and switch to English.

Chapter 2

Writing in a Bilingual Program: It All Depends

Alone in his own room, sitting at his desk, coffee cup rings on crumpled papers, involved only with self and text — that has been the popular image of the writer in the act of writing. It is only recently that this supposedly universal image has begun to be understood as one that ignores the social nature of writing — the remembered voices and texts that people the writer's room, the historically and culturally conventionalized meanings attached to different kinds of texts and different ways of producing them, the ways women as writers are excluded from and contradict such images. (See Brodkey [1987] for a social-practice view of academic writing that critiques this image.)

In thinking about writing as a social practice (Street, 1984; deCastell and Luke, 1986) and the new images of writers such a view would entail, an old question gets a new interpretation. From a social practice perspective, the question 'how do people write?' is interpretated as: how are 'ideological and cultural conditions' a part of the writing that is done in a society (Brandt, 1989, p. 43). Of little interest is the older, cognitivist interpretation of the same question: how do individuals do the minute by minute work of writing? As Brandt says, each interpretation underproblematizes the other perspective; the cognitivist perspective ignores the ways minute by minute work is socially constituted; the social view takes for granted a 'technical ability to produce texts' (p. 43).

But for young children learning to write, that technical ability and knowledge of socially shared conventions cannot be taken for granted. Even while focusing on text production, however, recent research in young children's writing reveals that just as the prevailing asocial/antisocial image of the adult writer is being challenged, so are similar images featuring children learning to write. Dyson (1989) has shown young public school pupils relying on each other as they talked and drew their way into text creations. These children figured out genre conventions, spellings, letter formations — the 'technical ability to produce texts' — as they played with and struggled with what they wanted to say in particular social contexts. Moreover, as they learned and grew as writers, rather than becoming more isolated and creating increasingly decontextualized texts, their writing became more socially 'embedded'.

So the lone child-writer, unfolding as a flower, is clearly a myth. Yet while children's writing is part of a whole constellation of activities that can be considered literacy-as-social-practice, it is also a phenomenon that includes within-the-child activity such as hypothesizing, predicting, planning, and so on. What is especially intriguing is to try to understand the ways this internal activity gets its shape from social forces. Dyson (1989), Graves, (1983), Calkins (1986) and others offer rich descriptions of young writers changing in the midst of social influence through peers and teachers. There has been little investigation, however, of the social influences on young children's writing when that influence emanates from beyond the classroom walls.

A study of children in a bilingual program permitted a glimpse at this web of influences — the local community and school district interwoven with teachers' influences on children's writing activity.[1] Unlike the research of Dyson, Graves, and Calkins, this study did not provide rich descriptions of children as they write. Like the children's writing, our research design was also influenced by that web. In fact, the director of the program and I feared the imminent demise of bilingual education in that school district. Thus we planned the study as a cross-sectional investigation of changes in written products over one shool year, rather than as a several-years-long observational investigation of the same children in the act of writing. If it didn't describe richly, however, the study did connect details of what children produced with teacher's beliefs and activities and events in the school district.

The Study

The study began in 1980 in Duncan School District (a pseudonym), a small district in Arizona that served mostly Hispanic migrant and settled migrant farm workers' children. Since most bilingual programs at that time emphasized reading instruction and paid scant attention to writing, they were not good sites for conducting research on writing. But Duncan's bilingual program was a rarity. It defined literacy to include both reading and writing and devoted considerable time to both.[2]

A research team selected twenty-six children (nine first graders, nine second, and eight third graders) and collected their regular in-class writing (journal entries, letters, stories, reports, etc.) at four times during the school year. Different researchers analyzed the following aspects of the 524 collected pieces: written code switching, spelling, punctuation, segmentation (*habíaunavez* [onceuponatime], *ab re la ven tan a* [o pen the win dow]), quality of the content, sense-of-genre signals, and structural features such as beginnings, endings, and organizational schemes. Pieces produced by children from other classrooms in the bilingual program were collected to augment the systematic analysis. Serendipitously, the year after the study, a third grade teacher gave the program director some of the work done by four of the second graders we had followed during the study year. This unplanned-for, two-year picture of four children will figure later as I present connections between district activity and children's writing. In addition to collecting pieces of writing, we interviewed teachers and aides, observed in classrooms, gathered a variety of demographic data, and made use of a language situation survey commisioned by the district.

The data were analyzed in three main ways. First, we derived coding categories (e.g., types of segmentation, our inferred bases for spelling inventions, and so forth) from the written pieces. Using these codes, we made various comparisons (e.g., English versus Spanish writing, assigned versus unassigned writing, first grade versus third grade writing). Second, we kept dated lists (somewhat like Glaser's [1978] theoretical memos) of insights and hunches about the writing process, acquisition, influences on the writing, and other issues. Third, we deliberately went on a 'myth hunt', searching the data for examples that countered prevailing assumptions about language proficiency, bilingualism, biliteracy, written language learning, and so on.

The main purpose of the study was to plot changes in the written products; i.e., to study development. Our concept of development was a general movement (with the possibility of regressions and spirals) toward adult norms. Now there are other conceptions of 'development'. Vygotsky (1978), for example, saw development as change-in-*action* of some higher order intellectual process (e.g., developing a new way to solve problems). Increased intellectual power-in-the-act, not adult convention, was his sign of development (Jilbert, 1989). However, our fears for the bilingual program's future, as well as our wish to document the rarity of writing in bilingual education that was more than fill-in-the-blank, led us to design a study of products. Moreover, we quite deliberately wanted to study what was/is so common in educational research — change over time, with 'adult-like' as a goal (e.g., this is the focus of studies of beginning versus fluent readers, younger versus older speakers, even — stretching it — novice versus expert teachers). The twenty-six target children were selected because their first writing of the school year seemed to represent a range of quality. We wanted the fullest picture possible of abilities and paths of change. Writing from the three non-study classrooms further enlarged this picture. Because our writing data — even the data from the same grade — came from different classrooms taught by teachers with different beliefs giving different assignments in the midst of different resources during a time when district events were creating different configurations of power, we were able to relate many of the changes in products to these contextual differences.

The Contexts

The Bilingual Program: Rhetoric and Reality

Printed material as well as conversations with program personnel described the program as having certain features: a) a 'whole language' approach to literacy (Goodman and Goodman, 1981); b) initial reading instruction in Spanish, with the introduction of English reading only after first language reading was well established (or at the end of second grade); and c) an emphasis on writing for a variety of purposes to a variety of audiences. I must re-emphasize how unusual such practices were in 1980 — a time when 'back to the basics' was the only voice getting a wide hearing; and how doubly unusual this was in bilingual education in the southwestern US, where programs sometimes lived or died by how well (or how poorly, since funding could be cut off if scores were too high) children scored on tests of 'the basics'.

While this bilingual program in 1980 was clearly honoring at least some of the implications from then new qualitative studies of writing by Graves and his colleagues and was promoting itself rhetorically as a 'whole language', 'writing process' program before such labels became educational buzzwords, it did not reach its aims. In each classroom, practice was idiosyncratically out of step with rhetoric and teachers varied on many dimensions (interactional styles, fluency in Spanish, comfort with leaving textbook-bound teaching, and so on). Still, teachers in each of the three study classrooms *did*:

1   allocate a portion of each day for writing;
2   carry on Spanish reading instruction through second grade (though the vehicle for that instruction was both Spanish and English);
3   permit children to choose the language they wrote in and read in during non-reading group time (in the reading group, Spanish dominant children were assigned to read in Spanish);
4   establish a journal writing time;
5   accept all topics (none were taboo);
6   accept many unconventional forms (e.g., invented spellings or unconventional segments).

But the teachers did *not*:

1   establish a need or demand for children to interact with a great variety of published whole texts in either Spanish or English. According to Smith (1982b), it is wide reading rather than writing that gives access to what is to be learned for writing;
2   publish selected works. Therefore, there was no real need for children to evaluate their own work, no need for content revisions, no need for editing to achieve a conventional final copy;
3   read aloud extensively to children from children's literature written in Spanish. Hearing written language rendered orally is what gives one a feel for its cadence (Smith, 1982a);
4   hold conferences in which peers or adults questioned the writer on the meaning of text in order to help children anticipate reader's needs in relation to writers' intents.

The Communities: Political Grounds for Bilingual Programs

In the same year we were gathering children's writing, opposing forces within the district were gathering momentum. Duncan District's voters comprised three distinct communities: farmworkers, ranchowners, and well-to-do retirees. With her membership in multiple overlapping networks, the bilingual program director had managed over the years to develop ties of affection and loyalty with the farmworkers' community. Through years of one-to-one lobbying, she had encouraged the Hispanic parents to increase their participation in bilingual program activity. By 1980, the farmworker parents were solidly in support of bilingual education. However, they were uninformed about any new curricula, preferring the traditional one they themselves or their older children had failed at or dropped out of.

The ranching and retirement communities did not enter into discussions over curriculum in the bilingual program because they were still arguing about whether there should be a bilingual program at all. And their answer was a resounding 'no'. They were joined in their opposition by some of the local clergy (one minister warned that bilingual education was the devil's idea) and were rebutted by others (a rural priest praised it).

The divisions over bilingual education had ended, on the surface at least, in the Arizona legislature and the State Department of Education, both of which meet just a few miles from Duncan District. Though there were both private opponents and private proponents of even stronger bilingual programs (e.g., programs that would maintain both languages as vehicles of instruction without phasing one out), official policy favored limited transitional bilingual education as a way to get children into an English curriculum as quickly as possible. The state also took a position on curriculum. In this case, their stance was opposite to the direction in which the bilingual program director was moving. Beginning in the mid-1970s, legislative and state agency actions mandating certain materials and kinds of evaluation (of both teachers and students) were pressuring teachers to avoid stepping outside the separate 'basic skills' path.

While Duncan District administrators had given everything from grudging acceptance to public support for the idea of bilingual education, and while they showed off writing samples with pride, they often disapproved of teaching that failed to emphasize skill drills. The bilingual program director, as noted, had a different view of literacy and of education in general. She was designated in charge of the federal monies that funded the program, which enabled her to hire program teachers and to determine the program's in-service education. A key factor allowing the director to maintain her power within the program — to make her view 'stick' rhetorically and officially — and preventing the principals in the program schools from forcing the program to operate according to their own opposing views was the support the director received from the highest Duncan District administrator, the superintendent.

A few months before our study began, the bilingual program parents (with the help of some retirement community members who wanted to be released from obligations to pay school taxes) organized a petition drive for a special election to re-draw district boundaries and exclude the retirement community. During our study year, that election was held and the boundary lines were re-drawn, ensuring majority support for continuation of bilingual education. Concurrently, the Arizona legislature and the State Department of Education established a testing program (in English) to ensure teacher accountability, based on the premise that good teaching requires the instruction of separate skills. The bilingual program director, therefore, spent considerable time reassuring teachers that since she was the one to make personnel decisions about program teachers, their evaluations and tenure would not be tied to student scores on English language tests. Meantime, throughout the year, at school building level meetings (to which the bilingual program director was not invited), principals kept reiterating the importance of high scores on these tests.

Now all of this was also taking place at the start of the Reagan years, when right wing forces would undo past civil rights victories, widen economic disparities, and be increasingly successful in pushing policies for a return to a mythological golden age of harmonious (patriarchal) families, calm (small town, white, Protestant) communities, respectful and patriotic (obedient, unquestioning) citizens.[3] That larger context must be acknowledged; it certainly had widespread effects throughout the 1980s on funding for schools, possibilities for programs, and the very curricular and evaluation emphases that were taking hold in Duncan District. But to connect that larger national climate in 1980–81 with writing in this bilingual program would require a different analysis and additional data. Therefore, I will simply remind readers of this larger context, but I will set contextual borders in the greater Phoenix area.

Connections Between Writing and Contexts

As I said earlier, this study was not designed to show definitive relationships between specific features of texts and classroom, program, or community contexts. Nor was it designed to reveal exactly *how* (by what mechanisms) text-context ties were established. Nevertheless, even if we do not understand exactly how it happened, features of children's writing, at any one time and over time, and class-room or district-wide goings-on seemed closely connected. Some of these connections were direct and intended. That is, by means of certain policies, purchases, materials, room arrangements, uses of print, assignments, and responses to writing or writers, various people intended to have an impact on a particular aspect of the children's writing. Other connections were indirect. Sometimes a teacher or policy maker would be either unaware of the effect of a particular action or intended to have only the most general effect (e.g., 'to make children want to write').

Direct Influences on Children's Writing

Teachers' assignments — shaped by their own beliefs about writing and learning to write, their sense of obligation to state policies, their responses to pressure from principals and counter-pressure from the bilingual program director — had a direct impact on the genres children wrote. At the beginning of the year, when Ms. D, the first grade teacher in our study, thought children could only write their names, she only assigned 'signed' drawings, so their own names were all the children wrote officially. When she thought they could write journal entries, they wrote journal entries. By spring, she saw the children as competent writers and she assigned and received letters, stories, journals, and expository pieces. Third graders, whose range of assignments remained constant throughout the year, appeared not to 'grow' in the genres they tackled.

The planned environment also had its intended effects. In mid-winter, Ms. D 'took the lid off' and set up a Writing Center, stocked with many kinds of paper and writing implements, intending for children to want to write more, about a wider range of topics, and with 'more feeling'. The Writing Center had just that effect (as well as others to be described later). Writing produced at the Center was more often about home and community topics. Moreover, the same child often exhibited a strikingly more poetic style in writing done at the Center. Example 1 is Writing Center writing from late February. Example 2 is a journal entry written by the same child one week earlier.

1 Todos los días cae nieve en todas las partes y también caía lluvia en todas las partes. Y un señor se robó y la policía iba. La policía agarría al señor y lo llevó a la carcel y allí se estuvo todos los días. Era cuando estaba cayendo nieve.
   (Every day snow fell everywhere and also rain was falling everywhere. And a man robbed and the police came. The police grabbed the man and took him to jail and there he remained forever. It was when the snow was falling.)

2 Hoy es martes. Hicimos muchos reportes.
   (Today is Tuesday. We made a lot of reports.)

In one of the non-study second grade classrooms, the teacher had set up mailboxes and had given the children considerable freedom to write letters to others whenever they wanted to. This resource, Mr. M told us, was intended to get the children to become more involved with and to expand their audiences. Actually, the mailboxes did little to expand audiences since the children preferred writing to and receiving answers from their teacher or aide rather than peers, but it did increase the ways in which children related to their audiences in writing. The excerpted letters in example 3 consist of genuine complaints, apologies, excuses, queries, and threats; rarely was writing from the other classes used for any of these purposes.

3 Querido Mr. M,
   ¿Quién son las señoras que vinieron y yo he visto a la Sra. que teniá anteojos en la tienda ...
   (Dear Mr. M,
   Who are the women who came and I have seen the woman with glasses at the store ...)

   Mr. M,
   Se me olvidó decirle mi perro tiene 6 dedos y no estoy diciendo mentiras ...
   (Mr. M,
   I forgot to tell you my dog has 6 toes and I'm not telling lies ...)

   Querido Mr. M,
   ¿Porqué no me ha mandado mi carta? Dígame en la carta cuándo me va a mandar la carta porque si no me dice yo me voy a enojar con Ud ...

(Dear Mr. M,
Why haven't you sent me my letter? Tell me in the letter when you're
going to send the letter because if you don't tell me I'm going to get
angry with you ...)

For different reasons, writing by the second grade children in the study classroom also showed more involvement with the reader than did the writing of first
and third graders in the study. Ms. C did not set up mailboxes but, as a way to promote opportunities for writing and as a way to promote the image of the bilingual
program to administrators whose support was in question, she had children writing
frequent letters to administrators — birthday letters, get well letters, glad-you're-
back letters, thank you letters, come-and-see-us-letters, etc. With so much opportunity for children to address a reader directly and to compare the reader's
condition with the writer's (*y yo estaba mala también y me dieron medicina y me
alivié* .../ and I was sick too and they gave me medicine and I got better ...), it is no
wonder that involvement with the reader seemed to be a characteristic of second
grade writing.

The district had mandated a general curriculum guide as well as a listing and
allocation by grade level of language arts skills (e.g., 'knows third person singular
verb ending'; 'uses '-er' and '-est' appropriately'). The bilingual program director
had convinced the superintendent to exempt program teachers from having to
teach the separate, sequenced list of language arts skills because, she argued, this list
was based on English. (As usual, she was able to win such an argument in 1980–81
by appealing to language bias but not by arguing that the conception of language
and literacy underlying such a list was in error.) While the bilingual program
teachers did not have to teach the list of (English) language arts skills, they did have
to — and they wanted to — follow the general curriculum guide. That meant, for
example, teaching cursive handwriting in third grade.

Not surprisingly, the manifest curriculum (i.e., that which was explicitly
taught) showed up in children's writing, especially in their handwriting and spelling. Third graders learned to use cursive by midway through the year, though a
small percentage of all writing (including that done by first graders) contained connected script in advance of instruction. Since all the teachers believed that spelling
in Spanish was primarily a matter of mapping sound onto letters, they advised children to 'sound it out' and they taught phonics lessons about letters that 'make the
same sound'. Thus children learned that *ll* and *y*, *b* and *v*, *h* and *no h*, *y* and *i* could
be decoded the same way. Their writing reflected that information. Not only did
we find *llo* and *io* for *yo* (1), *abia* and *habia* for *había* (there was), *vien* and *bien* for
bien (well), but when they 'sounded it out', the extra glides they produced were
also spelled with these equivalents — *maeystra* and *mallestra* for *maestra* (teacher).

Teachers' preferences directly affected what children wrote. Through February, Ms. C thought long (over twenty-pages) pieces were a sign of quality.
The children gave her what she wanted, leaving empty spaces, making over-sized
letters, repeating ideas and single words (*bien bien bien bien triste*/very very very very
sad). A member of the research team pointed out to Ms. C that quality was being
sacrificed for length. Two months later, in an interview, Ms. C said she was
starting to think that children could do 'too much writing'. By April, her students

no longer produced twenty-plus page pieces with outsized handwriting, big spaces, and repeated words; their pieces were considerably shorter and contained little or no evidence that the writer was trying to extend the length.

Indirect Influences on Children's Writing

Assignments, environmental resources, the manifest curriculum, and teachers' values also had unintended effects on particular features of children's writing. So did the political activity within the district. Assignments became more sophisticated toward the end of the year (in the first grade the progression was stories at the end versus signatures and then journal entries at the beginning; in second grade, at the end of the year only, children wrote in 'shape books' — e.g., all pages cut in the shape of bones for writing a story about magic bones). And the quality of writing at the end of the year was judged better by raters — more insightful, more organized, more creative.

The teachers had not intended for their assignments to have an effect on the organizational structure of writing, but they did. Many children organized their pieces chronologically (first ... then). But first and second graders also used an organizational principle we called 'big shift', in which there was a sudden switch in topic or function. No third grader made use of 'big shift', but probably not because they had simply 'outgrown' such behavior. The first and second grade teachers sometimes gave assignments that can only be described as 'motley genres' (e.g., write a letter to the program director [letter], tell her about the Creek Indians [report], and invite her to the class party [invitation]). Third grade assignments were not of this type; therefore, third graders did not have 'big shifts' in their writing.

The same resource that was intended to and did encourage more writing and a greater range of topics also yielded several unintended effects. The teacher placed colored markers at the Writing Center to generate interest. The markers also generated color-loaded topics with pieces about colorful objects, lettered with the appropriate pen (*rojo* with red, *azúl* with blue, etc.). When these first graders wrote what they wanted to at the Center, unassigned, they used no punctuation at all. On assigned pieces, they invented punctuation, most of it based on units of paper (e.g., a capital to start every page, a period to end each line, and so on, Edelsky, 1983). But children did not write multiple page pieces on the large sheets of paper at the Writing Center, so there were no inventions such as a period to end each page. Since the paper was unlined, neither were there line-based punctuation inventions in unassigned first grade writing.

Two non-study first grade teachers offer an interesting contrast. One was most anxious to comply with the director's wishes that children should write. She once indicated she was sure children should be taught to read in a structured fashion but she had no training in teaching children how to write. The other teacher believed children had to be able to 'decode' phonetically in order to read and to spell in order to write. Her principal's warnings about the need for high scores on tests of phonics and decoding may well have strengthened her in these beliefs. Each of these teachers exerted very different kinds of control over writing time. The first teacher exercised minimal control. Since writing was the one 'subject' she did not know how to teach, she simply told children it was time to write and then she kept order during that time. As the year went on, the second teacher controlled what letters, then what words, then what sentences the children would write. By the end of the year, children in the first classroom were writing jokes, stories, notes, song lyrics, and grocery lists. When the children in the second classroom had 'free writing time', they produced pieces resembling disconnected phonics worksheets.

4   Es un carro. El niño no iba. La casa de mamá. El carro de papá. Tony
    iba a su casa. Mamá ama a papá. Es una niña. Es una mamá.
    (It's a car. The child didn't go. Mama's house. Papa's car. Tony was
    going home. Mama loves Papa. It's a girl. It's a mama.)

It is not only that the unintended consequence of the year-long differences in children having control versus being controlled showed up in what genres the children wrote. The genre represented by 4 as contrasted with jokes and stories reveal certain notions of 'text-ness'. Children in the first classroom were learning that texts produced in school can (should?) be coherent; children in the second classroom were learning they often are not.

The print environment both inside and outside the classroom is a critical resource for learning where writing is used in a particular community, what it is used for, and how it works. Though the teachers may have brought print into classrooms to instruct children in literacy, shopkeepers, parents and others who brought the great variety of print into this district did not do so to show children how to spell or to teach them which language to use when writing. Even the teachers often used print for something besides instructing. But all the print — from the ditto sheet exercises meant to instruct to the print on the cereal boxes meant to increase sales — instructed anyway. In this district, one of the lessons coming from the print environment was that, despite the ubiquity of code-switching in talk, code-switching rarely appeared in writing. There were even more subtle lessons on code-switching to be derived from contrasts between the Spanish and English print resources. Even though the first and second grades did not offer reading instruction in English, each classroom contained more English than Spanish print. That disparity was repeated outside the classroom. Moreover, of all the printed material in the classrooms, more of the Spanish print was homemade (teacher-made posters, dittos, labels, children's writing), while English print was overwhelmingly commercially produced. Spanish print, thus, could well have looked informal while English print may have looked authoritative and, to children growing up in a print-saturated popular culture, more 'real'.

The children in this study switched very frequently between English and Spanish in their speech, and they did so both between sentences and within sentences. However, they rarely code-switched in writing. If they did, it was only within the sentence (which, by the way, is an intriguing bit of counter evidence to those who maintain that poor bilingual children have a language deficit since 'they don't know English and they don't know Spanish either'). If they code-switched at all in writing, it was in Spanish texts and it was referentially inspired (e.g., nouns, adjectives, verbs, and address terms). The use of a Spanish word in an English text, however, was four times more rare. If it occurred at all, it was more like a slip of the pen; an article like *the* or a conjunction like *and* (not a noun or verb packed with referential meaning) that the children knew in English would 'slip out' in Spanish but would quickly be brought into check ('... *y es* fun, thank you' or '*y el* dinosaur is gonna be ...). Code-switching in Spanish texts thus seemed more deliberate (or at least more semantically motivated); code-switching in English texts seemed accidental — something to be avoided. It was as though these children saw written English, the language that had stronger associations with powerful sociocultural domains like the educational establishment, commercial publishing, and the like, as a language that could not so easily be appropriated for their own voices — as a language one had to be careful of, a language that would not be hospitable to a 'stranger' in its midst.

The most drastic indirect influence from the goings-on in the district became noticeable a year after the study was over. As I said earlier, during our study year (1980–81), as a result of a special election instigated by the bilingual program parents, new district boundary lines had been drawn. The new majority elected a new school board whose members showed only lukewarm confidence in the superintendent. Even though he had been a strong supporter of the bilingual program, the superintendent's ties with the retirement community were not so easily forgiven. As he lost favor, so did those associated with him (e.g., the bilingual program director). During the next school year, it became increasingly clear that his contract would not be renewed. In that 1981–82 school year, then, with an apparently lame duck superintendent, principals were able to overrule the bilingual program director in hiring teachers for the bilingual program and in deciding on the substance of in-service education for bilingual program teachers. They were also coming closer to winning their demand that the bilingual program should teach lists of separate English language arts skills and should evaluate teachers on the basis of children's scores on standardized tests in English. The bilingual program director could no longer protect the teachers or ensure that the program would keep moving, albeit at snail's pace, in a holistic direction.[4]

During that school year, a third grade teacher saved children's writing and gave it to the bilingual program director. In the batch was the output produced by four of the children who had been part of the study when they were in second grade. It is most instructive to look at their writing over two years while keeping in mind the events in the district. There were some changes in spelling and punctuation conventions and a switch to cursive handwriting, but little change in content. Almost all of the pieces seemed to be perfunctory compliances with assignments, offering 'acceptable' responses to the teacher's topics. There was no evidence of the use of writing in new genres for new purposes or new audiences or with new rhetorical means. Where were the touted benefits of writing as a way of learning, the benefits that were to come from using written language to explore new ideas and find the limits of (or make new connections between) old ideas? *Were* the children using writing for such purposes?

It should come as no surprise, given the turn of events in the district office, that the answer is no. During their third grade year, more time was spent on basal readers, more importance attached to spelling and punctuation through direct instruction with worksheets and in evaluation of their narrative output, less importance to making sense or having an impact on a reader. No wonder the children seemed to have turned their attention so completely to matters of form.

To be fair, I must reiterate that this 1981–82 school year does not stand in complete contrast to the preceding year. It is not that all the teachers in 1980–81 were helping children write for their own purposes or that they were causing them to reflect on and revise their writing. In the study year, too, the children were often merely complying superficially with an assignment. The difference is that in that year, ambivalence was in the air. Both protected and goaded by the program director, the teachers were trying to get beyond exercises — and that showed in the children's experimentation with genres, spelling, handwriting, and rhetorical devices. A year later, to accommodate shifting political (and therefore curricular and evaluational) winds, the teachers were embracing exercises — a stance reflected as much in what was missing from children's writing as in what was there.

Another Look at Writing Development

We went into this study assuming that change would certainly occur over time and that these changes would be evidence of development. Though we expected the changes to vary with external conditions, we still imagined that development was somehow a property or activity of the child. Yet the many examples we saw of the way teachers, administrators, and legislators influenced the children's writing put that image in question. People with positivist leanings and those wedded to looking at development from the standpoint of the lone individual would say there was nothing wrong with thinking of development in this way; the problem was our research design. A different study, one in which conditions are controlled so that variables like assignments, resources, and the like would be held constant, would make 'development' unproblematic by sorting out the impact of assignments, teachers' beliefs and so on from the developmental activity the child would have been engaged in without such contextual influences.

Such a solution is no solution, however. In the first place, it would be impossible to 'control' everything involved — from subtleties of teachers' beliefs to children's perceptions of the task and definitions of the situation to children's motives and purposes (according to activity theorists like Leont'ev [Minick, 1985], if motives change, the activity changes). More importantly, in the second place, stripping away (and thereby controlling for) context not only does violence to writing; it distorts human activity in general. As Bateson (1972) said of language, we erroneously think of utterances (or other human endeavor) *in* a context, as though the talk or the activity were a dependent variable and the context were the independent variable. But the talk or activity is actually part of an ecological system (context), not just what remains after the background is removed; nor is the background what is left after the talk or behavior is cut away. Writing always happens in messy, non-reproducible contexts. If we want to study it, we have to study that messy, context-dependent practice, not some neatened-up substitute.

The evidence presented here shows something of writing's context-dependence and, therefore, of the context-dependence of writing development. However, I do not want to imply that writing and writers do not change, that these children did not 'develop' at all, that they simply responded to different demands, made use of different resources, were receptive to different pressures and preferences. Such a message misleads on two accounts: 1) it makes the children look like mere passive responders; and 2) it renders invisible their more progressive changes in writing. First, children were not only surrounded by multiple literacy practices; they were themselves agents in those practices. And their 'practicing' concerned both the social uses of writing and writing as a tool (a system that works to do other work). In fact it is in regard to writing as a tool — how it works, what its parts are like, and how they fit with different social uses — that we have the most obvious evidence that something highly active was going on within the child.

Children must have been actively creating new hypotheses to invent stable unconventional spellings, punctuation patterns and segments. By extension, it is likely they were also hypothesizing about minute details of *all* that goes into creating a text in a context within a context within a context within a context. That is, no matter what close in or far off (and then brought close in) conditions influenced the children's writing, children had to be actively construing those conditions (or their consequences) in order to include them within the hypotheses they made. Given the vast number of possible hypotheses, the narrow range that was actually displayed (along with the fact that we could make sense of them and infer their logic) shows that children must have been not only actively creating as individuals, but creating based on a socially constituted model.

While these socially constrained hypotheses changed depending on assignments, resources, teachers' values, principals' demands, state agency edicts and district politics, many of those changes showed progress. That is, over time or under particular conditions, the children's writing did become more like adult writing. For example, while at first children segmented unconventionally by chunking together major syntactic units (like whole sentences, entire noun phrases, entire verb phrases) or by separating into syllables, later on they wrote in single words and only chunked more minor units (e.g., prepositional phrases). Earlier hypotheses about spelling seemed to be based on phonetic features and manner and place of articulation and some unknown features. Later hypotheses were more 'literate' (i.e., based on phonics generalizations and knowledge of orthographic conventions such as silent *e* in English). The earliest invented punctuation marked units of paper (e.g., periods to end each line; capitals to begin each page). Later inventions were related to units of text (e.g., a capital to start and a period to end an entire story). Writing later in the year, the writing of older children, and unassigned writing was also evaluated by raters as having higher quality content.[5]

I am not saying, then, that there was no development (though I have no evidence or explanation to offer on just how that development occurred). There were indeed these general trends in the direction of adult norms. Yet to understand even this common and elementary conception of development focusing on mere residues of past development (as Vygotsky criticizes), it is necessary to think of the person in a new way. We can not simply envision a meaning-making, hypothesizing, predicting, planning, strategizing being; we have to envision a person who *never* hypothesizes, predicts, plans *without* contexts. Even if we drop the idea of 'development' altogether and think instead only of changes in children's writing, the same requirement would pertain. The various interwoven socio-politico-historical contexts children live through are the contexts that show them what writing is, the contexts *through* which they write, the contexts they change (in).

Notes

1 Because certain conditions of interest to educators generally are often exaggerated in bilingual settings (e.g., political pressures on educational activity), research in bilingual education has much to say to all educators (Edelsky and Jilbert, 1985). Moreover, research in bilingual classrooms can sometimes offer a perspective that can make problematic what is often taken for granted in mainstream language arts education. For instance, bilingual classrooms provide instances of children reading a language before they can speak it, which certainly should cast doubt on taken-for-granted sequences of instruction where all the children come to school speaking the language they will learn to read and write. Unfortunately, because of turf- and status-based parochialism, few articles on bilingual education find their way into journals aimed at an audience of mainstream educators or into the citations of authors who write about mainstream education. The mainstream is missing out.

2 As I look back, I can see that much of what children did when they put pencil to paper constituted writing exercises produced for either compliance or evaluation rather than writing produced for some other purpose and under the writer's control. In Chapter 5, I will be taking pains to distinguish writing exercises from other kinds of writing. Nevertheless, in this chapter, I will refer to the children's work as writing, without qualifying it as writing *exercises*, in order to locate it among other studies of writing and curricular suggestions about writing — even though those studies and suggestions also are mostly about writing *exercises*. That is, while a few teachers (e.g., Atwell, 1987; Giaccobe, 1989) refer to 'real' writing versus writing exercises when they describe their own classrooms, and while teachers who understand the theoretical underpinnings of an orientation to education called 'whole language' are conscious of trying to eliminate exercises and elicit some other kind of writing instead, most researchers do not make that distinction. Thus writing researchers present pictures ('prompts'), ask 'subjects' to produce a description, and then equate that writing done simply to comply or be analyzed with writing done for any other purpose. Or teachers tell children to think of what they might want to persuade someone of, then to think of someone they might want to persuade, and then to produce a persuasive letter — and they call that artificial activity writing. In each case, someone other than the writer is in control of the purpose and consequence of what is produced; the activity amounts to instruction for instruction's sake or is produced only to be evaluated in a classroom or a research study. In other words, print has been produced, but through an *exercise* in writing. Not making the subdivision between exercises and non-exercises in this study allows these children's writing to be compared with other instances of what goes on in school and in research studies that were also labeled *writing*, but which were most often a very special kind of writing — writing *exercises*.

3 The wider context has changed again in the US. The end of the 1980s was bad for bilingual education. Bilingual programs not only lost financial and 'moral' support (Crawford, 1987); they found themselves in a climate in which outrageous proposals for legislating 'English Only' became reasonable topics for discussion and actually won as referendum items in state elections. With increasing frequency, school programs were offered that should have been characterized as English as a Second Language but they were called 'bilingual education'. If Duncan District's bilingual program, with its insistence on holding off literacy instruction in English, was unusual in 1980, it would have been illegal in some locales by 1989!

4 In 1982, the superintendent was replaced. In 1983, the bilingual program director's contract was not renewed. The new program director had been a high school foreign language teacher; one of her first acts was to order phonics and grammar workbooks for all bilingual program classrooms. The days of writing in the bilingual program were over.

5 In an important sense, however, the general trends are misleading. Each child followed a unique path toward adult-like writing. One became more conventional steadily in all aspects; one seemed to make no improvement, then took leaps in both content and form; another improved at first and then regressed. Yet another adopted more conventions in content but not form; for another it was the reverse. One of the second graders, whose writing we had also obtained from his third grade teacher, abandoned his highly unconventional way of segmenting and also the totally conventional spellings he had used for two years in favor of not only unconventional but less literate spellings (he reverted to phonetic-based rather than phonics-based inventions, but only for two sounds — /s/ and /y/). As D. Taylor (1989) argued, there may be predictable global patterns but any local individual patterns are unpredictable.

Chapter 3

Contextual Complexities: Written Language Policies for Bilingual Programs

with Sarah Hudelson

Imagine this situation. You are interviewing for the position of director of bilingual/second language education in an urban school district of almost 100,000 students. Until twenty years ago, the district's student population was 85 per cent Caucasian and 15 per cent black, with a few Mexican–American migrant children. Since that time immigration has resulted in an influx of students from a variety of ethnic and language backgrounds. The largest population of non-English speakers, about 10,000 in number, is Hispanic. The earliest Hispanic immigrants were Cubans, followed by Venezuelans and Colombians, but now most of the Spanish speakers entering the district come from war-torn Central America. Most of the first waves of Spanish speaking immigrant children came from well educated middle class families. Many of the more recent immigrants have not been to school or have had their schooling interrupted by war.

The next most populous group of immigrants (about 1000 students) are of Haitian origin. Their home language is Haitian Creole. The majority of the Haitian students enrolled in this district have not been to school in their own country. The few who did go to school in Haiti were in schools conducted in French, a language the children did not use in their homes. Only after the Duvaliers were overthrown in 1986 did Haiti award Haitian Creole official language status along with French. And only since 1982 has Haitian Creole been permitted to be a medium of instruction.

Another smaller group of immigrants are Southeast Asian refugees from Vietnam, Thailand and Laos. The educational backgrounds (as well as the languages) of these 500 students vary. Most of the more recent arrivals have spent considerable time in refugee camps waiting to come to this country. In these camps, schooling focused on teaching English.

There is also a group of about 110 Russian speakers in the schools, since this is one of the official ports of entry for Russian Jewish immigrants. In addition, there are small numbers of students from more than eighty other language groups, including Afghani, Arabic, Chinese, French, and Portuguese.

Student populations vary tremendously from school to school. Some schools are almost 100 per cent Hispanic or American black and Haitian. Others are almost exclusively white non-Hispanic with a few non-English speakers from different native language backgrounds. And there is every possible combination between those two extremes.

One of the questions posed during your hypothetical interview is the following: Given the situation just described, what kind of a design would you propose for bilingual and/or second language instruction in the school district? More specifically, what would you propose in terms of the language or languages used for non-English speaking students' writing and reading instruction?

From our perspective, the 'ideal' or theoretically preferred answer would be that students' native languages would be used in written language instruction, that students would have an opportunity to develop first as readers and writers in their home languages and then gradually add on English literacy. We base our ideal answer on: 1) the theoretico-political stance articulated by UNESCO (1953) for initial literacy in the vernacular followed by second language literacy; and 2) research evidence which has demonstrated that quality bilingual education programs benefit children in both their academic and English language achievement (Edelsky, 1986b; General Accounting Office, 1987; Hakuta, 1986; Hudelson, 1987; Rosier and Holm, 1979; Troike, 1981).

But while there may be a theoretically 'correct' answer, the educational and noneducational realities that individual communities face — the conditions permitting (or not) — make it impossible to offer one policy regarding written language instruction that will be appropriate for all educational scenes. Therefore, instead of offering a single policy, we will present a general position. Then we will argue against national or state-level policies that are highly specified by pointing out just a few of the complex variations that can exist between any two bilingual programs. We follow that by elaborating some of the issues that must be considered by those making local decisions in order to have sensitive, informed policies that work well in their own localities.

Our position is: For teaching and learning written language use, teachers and students must have autonomy and must be able to account for local conditions.[1] Therefore, upper level governmental policies should be broad, non-specific and linked to appropriate equity-oriented *general* goals. Local program policies should be developed locally to consider (but not always acquiesce to) the details of the local situation while still leaving responsibility for major decisions to individual teachers. We take this position because — as illustrated in the case presented in Chapter 2 — learning to write in school (whether or not in a school with a bilingual program) always happens in multiple co-occuring contexts, because each of these contexts has profound effects on the learning and teaching of writing inside the classroom, and because the contexts are complex in ways that may not be immediately obvious.

Contextual Variation Precluding Uniform Policies

The Languages Involved

Writing occurs during time and group arrangements within classrooms, within schools, within communities, within school districts, within larger geographic and political regions which exist at certain historical times and are brought to life by people with varying interests and beliefs. Although larger contexts influence smaller and vice versa, and although the smaller contexts are tied together at least through membership in the same gigantic political-economic-social-historical context (e.g., the US in 1987), these smaller contexts present a dizzying variety of details.

In the US, the 'other' school language (the marked language [Fishman, 1976]) may not be the student's home language (e.g., the students may speak non-standard Puerto Rican Spanish and be placed in a standard Mexican Spanish bilingual program in Chicago). If the non-English school language *is* the student's home language, it is not simply an uncomplicated 'Other'. Students may come to school speaking a standardized dialect of a world language (e.g., Standard Mexico City Spanish), a nonstandardized dialect of a world language (e.g., a nonstandard lower class dialect of Mexican Spanish), a standardized dialect of a regional written language (e.g., Standard Vietnamese), a nonstandard dialect of a regional language with a long written tradition (e.g., certain dialects of Chinese), a regional language without a long written tradition (e.g., Hopi or Haitian Creole). Furthermore, there are many possibilities for what varieties of English are used in the students' communities.

Teachers' Bilinguality and Biliteracy

Describing the bilinguality of teachers in a bilingual program may also be complicated. Teachers may have gone to school themselves and been educated as professionals in the students' home language and then received more professional education in the second language. Thus, they may be more literate in the home language than in English, as well as more familiar with oral school registers in the home language (e.g., Cuban teachers in Miami). Or teachers may share the students' home language but have no school experience with it, having been educated only in their second language. These teachers would be considerably more literate in their second language than in their first (e.g., some Chicano teachers in the Southwest, many Haitian teachers educated in French in Haiti). Or teachers may have attended lower grades in the students' home language and then received higher levels of schooling and all professional education in the second language (e.g., teachers who immigrated to the US in their teens).

Language Use in the Community

Moreover, outside the classroom, the bilingual program students' community is not one that simply 'uses language X plus English' or 'just' language Y. In each community, there will be differences in the settings and uses of English and the other language. In some locales, there may be clear boundaries for the use of one language or the other, with business and government requiring English and home and religion the other language. In other communities, each language might be able to be used in all settings but variation within the setting (who is speaking, who is listening, who is listening in, what purposes the language is being used for, how formal or informal the particular moment is) demands a shift from one language to the other (Grosjean, 1982).

Pressure from the 'Larger' Context

As noted in Chapter 2, other larger contexts — extending beyond but still impinging on and being impinged on in turn by the immediate neighborhood — contribute their own complicating factors to how writing occurs in particular classrooms. What complicates here is not the variety but the potential for tremendous and often deleterious impact. More global 'abstract' contexts (e.g., state and regional 'climates', national 'temper of the times', prevailing values), with their embedded discourses and ideologies, become concrete through school district policies, state legislative and state department policies and mandates, federal statutes, federal agency policies and recommendations, and state and federal court decisions.

Testing, for example, is a central influence in every public classroom in the US (and in almost all private school classrooms too). The power of a school's testing program to affect writing instruction comes from historical and political contexts outside the school itself. The general public's faith in tests and testing as valid indicators of learning, educational excellence, teaching, and so on (see Chapter 9 for a discussion of why the tests are not valid), the reliance on test data in recent national reports on education, the increased numbers of required tests for increased numbers of children, and the growing practice of publishing test scores in local newspapers put much pressure on the teacher and children in any particular classroom. Because of this wide acceptance of the supposed value and benefits of mass testing, the actual language of the tests (usually English) becomes the 'real' or important language of the classroom; the tasks demanded by the tests become the 'real' tasks, and the way test language is conceptualized (as consisting of small separable components with an emphasis on the most easily measured) becomes the 'real' way to think about language. In effect, a discourse of testing reconstitutes the 'realities' for teachers and students.

Mandated tests are tied to other moves in the larger contexts — moves for standardization and control over teachers. One example is pressure for a standard curriculum with a district-established scope and sequence for district-wide specified objectives. Like standardized tests, atomized objectives and scope and sequence charts emphasize low-level conventions. Such an emphasis stands in the way of learning to use written language effectively and appropriately for one's own purposes (R. Brown, 1987).

Still another factor pressing on bilingual programs and all that goes on within them, writing included, is the political climate for bilingual education. Relative to the later 1970s in the US at least, that climate has deteriorated. Federal guidelines for ensuring children's access to education through a language they can understand are being ignored; high ranking federal officials publicly state their opposition to bilingual education; support grows for proposals making English the 'official language' and for curbing any activity (including bilingual education) that would 'endanger' the position of English; bilingual education is being required to prove its effectiveness via test scores to an extent beyond that demanded of other educational 'treatments' (Crawford, 1987). (This last bit of evidence shows mass testing [and attendant standardization] being used *against* people — in this case, serving pervasive political imperatives against bilingual education and bilingualism.)

These are just a few of the factors that complicate decisions about written language instruction in bilingual programs. Some of these factors have similar effects, with minor local variation, across all bilingual programs (e.g., pressure from testing). Others vary widely from program to program (e.g., particular home language, extent and type of teachers' experiences with each of the school languages). This variation is behind our premise that highly specified blanket policies are bound to conflict with particular conditions at local sites.

 If we are urging policy makers to refrain from being bulls in the subtle china shops of individual community language situations, we are not asking them to be idle. Nor are we promoting extreme decentralization ('home rule', as it is known in the US). It is imperative to establish broad state and national policies regarding language rights and educational access for discriminated-against (not just numerical) minorities. Policy makers *must* make *general* policies. And they must make them according to a principle of equity. That means that even while they refrain from highly specifying the policies they make about bilingual programs (in order to allow for the diversity within many publics), they must see bilingual education in the light of equity issues. After all, the 'temper of the times' and 'current political climates' are never monoliths connected automatically to one line of action. They have minor keys and single clarion notes; they shift and change. While policy makers cannot ignore prevailing mentalities, they need not slavishly follow them either. They can listen to many voices and then *lead* in establishing *general* policy. They do not have to acquiesce to each aspect of the local situation, incorporating, for example, racist language attitudes into curriculum policies simply because such attitudes exist in the community. To prevent a potentially regressive 'tyranny of the local' (Wexler, 1987), they can create broad policies that promote equity while still taking care to permit local autonomy.

One way to accomplish such a feat is to establish broadly outlined goals (rather than highly specified policies) that respond to deep, consensual wishes. Now the various publics' wishes — consensual at some level though conflicting at others — will almost certainly show evidence of the hegemony of dominant class interests. But hegemony is full of contradictions (Williams, 1989). And so these common, probably 'colonized' social desires (Luke, 1990) also often contain widely shared progressive kernels (e.g., desires for peace, justice, satisfying work, and so on). It is those kernels that policy makers must use as the basis for enlightened policy. (And if policy makers themselves have oppressive agendas, then contesting parties will have to be the ones to appeal to those kernels in their struggles for change.)

One example of a kernel for which there is an overwhelming consensus in the

US concerns literacy; people want all children to be able to read and write. There is much less agreement on the importance of being able to read particular texts or write particular genres, on being able to write particular genres in particular languages, on such questions as *who* should read and write what. It is up to policy makers to take this kernel — at the level at which there is general agreement — and put it into a general goal (e.g., we aim to develop literate people) and then to *lead* by first refusing to derail that goal by subdividing it into subgoals and, further, by then interpreting that goal progressively. Progressive interpretation would extend literacy to mean the ability to read and write critically, to be able to evaluate texts for their support of democratice values. Of course a literacy goal interpreted thusly would have to be protected; it would have to remain general. It could not be operationalized with multiple trivial subgoals which can never add up to the ideal and which would take time away from — and prevent the achievement of — what was wanted in the first place.

Same w/ vision

Issues to Be Considered When Developing Local Policies

While decision makers at high governmental levels should be making general policies that seek to offset a history of discrimination, they should also permit those on the local scene to develop local policies that are congruent with the broad general policies and goals. Being closer to classroom scenes, those making the local decisions about writing curricula in bilingual programs would be more able to see details in local language situations. But they also must know what to look at.

What then must be considered in local policies regarding writing in a bilingual program? We see four general questions that must be asked, all of them implicating to some extent people's attitudes toward language in general and written language in particular.

1　What is the nature of written language acquisition?
2　What language resources are available?
3　How are written products treated in each language?
4　What is the value and what are the consequences of being able to write in each language?

Nature of Written Language Acquisition

This first area concerns general principles rather than local conditions. In formulating policies about written language education, the basic question is what is the best current understanding of how language is acquired. From there, policy makers must then come to grips with the details of the local language situation as these relate to the best available notions about written language acquisition.

Like oral language, written language is acquired through actual use. Some of that use occurs during interaction with others who demonstrate while they are using written language what written language is for and how it works (Smith, 1981; Harste, Woodward and Burke, 1984). In these interactions, making meaning is central — with the meanings being made for some purpose of the reader/writer (e.g., for killing time, for getting information, for reminding someone, for warning, for getting attention, for keeping track, etc.) On other occasions, the learner is alone but still using a *social* tool. That is, the written language being used and learned is shaped by a culture, governed by conventions shared by other members of the society, subject to social and historical constraints on how and for what it can be used. As with oral language, what is being learned in written language are the systems of rules/conventions/constraints for exercising freedom within cultural bounds, for making one's own meanings for culturally possible purposes in particular situations. That is, both conventionality and autonomy are critical aspects of oral and written language acquisition. The best 'teaching' in oral (Edelsky, 1978; Wells, 1981) and written (Calkins, 1986; Graves, 1983; Hudelson, 1986; Smith, 1973, 1981) language acquisition seems to require responding to what the reader/writer is trying to do. (This does not mean responding to the child's completion of a worksheet, but to a child's sincere effort to warn, wonder, inquire, scold, forgive, direct, and so on.) In order for a learner to have such purposes in school and in order for a teacher to be free to respond to them, both learner and teacher need autonomy to devise their own curricula, to become genuinely engaged. Local decision makers must work hard to encourage the existence of situations in which language can be acquired through real use and eliminate policies that prevent such situations from occurring.

Language Resources

Before making policy decisions about written language in bilingual programs, decision makers must examine the specific context of the local community, including the language resources available to the learners and to the school. Hymes (1980a) has written extensively about the need to consider local language resources, local attitudes toward those resources, and local ways of organizing those resources in language education policies. His work certainly applies to policies about writing in school programs for minority language children.

Many bilingual educators would argue that the children's primary available language resource is their already developed home language and that this language should be used for initial literacy development. From the perspective of writing and reading as activities in which learners actively compose texts and construct meaning (Lindfors, 1987; Tierney and Pearson, 1983), learners will come to the composing process with greater built-in language resources to create texts if they are creating them in a language that they control and see in use in meaningful texts and contexts around them rather than in a language that they are just learning.

Learning to write also involves language resources beyond the oral language itself. One of these resources is texts created by authors other than the learners. These texts will be more or less available depending upon the community language situation. One reality, common among Native American communities, may be that the native language has never been written down. This will mean that bilingual programs will not have available authentic native language texts that learners need, both to read from and to use to construct their own pieces. A variation of this situation occurs in communities where languages have only recently developed or are still developing and standardizing their written systems. In these cases relatively few printed materials will have been created. Frequently the creation of texts is slowed down by debates about which of several proposed orthographies should be used. For example, some Haitian Creole material in this country is not widely accepted because there is disagreement about which Haitian Creole orthography to accept as the definitive one.

Further, even though native language written texts may exist, the community may question the use of the home language and literature in the school. In some cases, the use of the language in the school domain is viewed as inappropriate because of the low social status accorded the language. For instance, in Haiti, French has a history of high status and prestige; Creole has been the lowly language of the poor and uneducated. To this day, many Haitians, having internalized the negative attitudes toward Creole, refuse to acknowledge that they speak Creole. These same individuals fight against the use of Creole in the school and against children learning to write and read in Creole.

In other cases, the question of utilizing language resources concerns not the status but the broader issue of the acceptability of vernacular literacy *per se*. In the Navajo nation, for example, Navajo traditionally has been the oral language of the home, community and tribal activities with English the written language for almost all situations. Although Navajo literacy was introduced in the early 1900s, it has been slow to take hold. Many Navajos have associated vernacular literacy with governmental, religious and educational efforts to assimilate the Navajos into mainstream American culture. Therefore teaching children to write and read in Navajo has been viewed by many as the first step toward cultural assimilation, a situation that has led to conflict over whether to make use of readily available written Navajo texts in bilingual classrooms (Spolsky and Irvine, 1982).

In other Native American communities in the southwestern US, community members disagree as to whether native stories should be written down and included in the curriculum. Like the Navajos, some elders believe such a move would contribute to assimilation; others believe the stories would enhance their children's chances of school success. The latter position seems to hinge on the following set of assumptions: school failure limits one's options; in a contact situation, a subordinate group's repeated failure in one of the dominant culture's institutions (e.g., education) also causes culture loss or at least distortion. So while written language resources in the native language may be available, and while native literature could be made available, it is not clear whether either would be well received in particular schools.

Even where the languages in bilingual programs are languages with written traditions, it is often difficult to get the quantity and variety of reading materials that are available in English (Goodman, Goodman and Flores, 1979). Few other countries in the world have a children's literature/tradebook industry that rivals that of the US. There are problems in importing books from other countries, and the books tend to be expensive in comparison to books purchased in the US. Teachers in Spanish-English bilingual programs often express concern about the relative lack of high quality children's books originally written in Spanish, even though some literature has been identified (Schon, 1978). The lack of authentic texts is even more pronounced in less common languages such as Vietnamese and

Lao. The question of quantity of materials is also affected by the issue of which dialect certain materials have been written in. This creates real problems in bilingual education programs, as Chicano Spanish speakers complain that they want material written in Chicano or at least Mexican Spanish rather than Cuban, Puerto Rican or Castilian Spanish.

Another complicating factor is the quality of material available in home languages. Learners need real texts (not books written merely to give reading/writing lessons) that will demonstrate varieties of 'book talk' (e.g., the style of written narrative, written exposition, written directions, etc.) and also help them learn to write like readers (i.e., to make use of 'book talk' as they write, as well as to anticipate other readers' responses to their writing) (Goodman, 1986). Many of the non-English language texts do not meet the criteria of variety, natural language and authenticity. Rather, they resemble American basal reading texts in their approach to literacy (see Goodman, Freeman, Murphy and Shannon 1988, for an extensive critique of basal readers). In some cases, local bilingual programs have even created the 'readers' themselves, translating or adapting the more mechanistic approaches used in English. In Dade County, Florida, for example, *The Miami Linguistic Readers*, a series of phonics materials written originally for learners of English as a second language, was adapted into Spanish as part of the Spanish Curriculum Development Component. Later, the same principles of teaching reading through sound-letter correspondences and syllable patterns were used in the creation of beginning reading materials in Haitian Creole.[2]

A human language resource of critical importance for teaching and learning writing is the teacher. We know that in many 'regular' classrooms, English speaking teachers do not view themselves as writers and do almost no writing either for themselves or with their students. One of the assumptions of such in-service education efforts as the National Writing Project is that, in order to become effective writing teachers, teachers must themselves become writers. In other words, to develop literacy in others, teachers must be highly literate themselves. In many bilingual programs, as we have mentioned earlier, teachers have been educated in their second language, and most of the reading and writing that they do occurs in that language. There is a strong possibility, therefore, that bilingual education teachers do not view themselves as writers in the home language. In fact, many bilingual teachers rather consistently denigrate the variety of home language they speak and lament their lack of ability in that language. If teachers do not view themselves as writers in the home language (indeed, if they do not view themselves even as good speakers), this may affect their support of their students' writing in the home language. And if teachers do not view themselves as writers at all — either in the home language or in English — how will they nurture children in their development as writers?

Children learning to write need access to others who write. Teachers may serve this role if they write themselves. Additionally, one might assume that another source of access to writers would be the local community. But the case of Navajo, described earlier, shows that any such assumption needs to be investigated. Where one might assume that Navajo speaking adults would write in Navajo, in fact that often is not the case. English is the language most often used for writing by Navajos. If children do not see adults using written Navajo for specific individual or social purposes, they are likely to regard writing in Navajo as an exercise — not as written language for life. If children see adults using writing in any language for only a very limited number of purposes, they are unlikely to see a wide range of needs for writing or to incorporate 'writer' into their identities. As we look at various communities as possible sources for demonstrations of written language, we must ask questions such as these: Who in the community knows how to write? In what languages do people write? What kinds of writing do people do? For what purposes do people write? How can schools both use and extend community resources so that children will become writers?

Treatment of Written Products

As will be argued throughout Part II, considerable research and theory take the position that writers learn to write by seeing demonstrations of authentic written language, by writing for real and varied purposes, by sharing what they have written with varied audiences, by utilizing the reactions of others to revisit and revise some of what they create, by working through changes in order to express their intentions in written form. As writers construct meaning, they experiment with forms, generating and testing hypotheses about how written language works and using what they know at that time about written language. Any product a writer produces, therefore, is really a reflection of the ongoing process and context of creating text. Further, the written products provide evidence of children making use of what they know about written language to work out their ideas, of children solving their problems of expression by using resources available to them, of children controlling the processes of composing and responding to the contexts of composition.

But not all teachers agree with this. Many teachers believe that children learn to write by practicing a set of discrete and isolated skills until these have been 'mastered'. Only then do teachers consider learners able to create text in the sense of working out ideas using written language. Our experience has been that many bilingual teachers share the latter view of written language acquisition, regardless of whether children are writing in their home or second language (Edelsky, 1986b; Hudelson, 1985). This view may reflect conventional wisdom or professional education (for example, many Spanish speaking teachers educated in Cuba or Mexico have been taught to teach writing by teaching letter sounds and syllables; many Haitian teachers have learned to direct children to memorize words and take dictation; the writing approach in many US bilingual programs emphasizes exercises with small segments of language). In any case, evidence mounts that teachers' beliefs about how writing and reading are learned have a direct effect on how they teach (DeFord, 1985; DeFord and Harste, 1982), including how they react to student products and student errors.

As one example, here is a short piece written by a first-grade Spanish speaking child enrolled in a bilingual program that emphasized children's written expression:

Cuando llo se lla grande boyaser una maestra y boya garar mucho dinero para comprarles as misinos ninos les boya comprar ropa y jugetes.

53

Standard Adult Spanish: Cuando yo sea grande voy a ser una maestra. Y voy a ganar mucho dinero para comprarles a mis niños. Les voy a comprar ropa y juguetes.

English translation: When I am grown up I am going to be a teacher. And I am going to earn a lot of money to buy [things] for my children. I am going to buy them clothes and toys.

From one perspective, this piece could be viewed as a demonstration of creative problem solving, risk taking and using what one knows about the written system of Spanish to express an idea. The child's invented spellings, unconventional segmentation, cross outs and lack of punctuation might be analyzed in terms of working hypotheses about how written Spanish is organized (Edelsky, 1986b; Hudelson, 1981–82). The piece may be used to analyze what the child knows and thinks about written Spanish. But from a different perspective, the piece could be viewed as riddled with mistakes — as a demonstration of the writer's lack of knowledge of sound-letter correspondences, inability to spell words correctly, laziness about punctuation, and forgetfulness about leaving spaces between words. The piece may be used to judge what the child does not know about standard adult forms of the language, instead of what the child knows. Teachers who believe that products such as the one above show children's inability to write may discourage further experimentation, may fail to promote early and sustained writing experiences and may, in spite of good intentions, actually prevent a child from learning to write effectively.

Teachers' and parents' views of how people acquire written language will affect how they treat children's written products. These views may also have an effect on the kinds of writing that go on in bilingual classrooms and on the display of this writing. If educators and/or community members believe that writing stories is 'a waste of time', this kind of writing will probably not happen much in classrooms. If educators and/or community members believe that to display less than letter perfect writing (in terms of standard forms) is to 'encourage sloppy work' or 'provide a bad model for the others', little work may be displayed around classrooms and schools and the same children's work will always (not) be displayed. These may or may not be realities in any given local setting. Questions need to be asked in order to find out what the local beliefs and actions are; efforts must be made to educate teachers and community members about beliefs that interfere with children's development as written language users.

Value and Consequences of Writing Ability

Both transitional bilingual programs (where bilingual education is offered only until the child can make the transition into an entirely English curriculum) and maintenance bilingual programs (where bilingual education is maintained throughout school, with shifting allocation of curriculum between the two languages) claim that first language writing is important. No matter how it is seen — as an entry to the world of literacy, as a bridge to writing in a new language, as a lifelong ability to be nurtured throughout school, as the ability to perform spelling and punctuation exercises or as the working out of ideas — first language writing has a place in US bilingual programs. However, having a place does not mean having a place that really counts. Does the first language appear in writing on signs? tests? forms? bulletin boards? Or is it relegated to use on notes to parents who would not otherwise understand? All the various ways print is used in the school affect what is learned about print, including which language has what importance.

The same questions must be asked regarding first language writing outside of school. Being able to write/read in English clearly matters (note the recent mass media campaigns regarding illiteracy). But what about being able to write in Spanish or Hopi or Chinese? How does first language writing function in the students' community? It is necessary to find out who writes in the first language (their social status, age, gender, societal roles) and for what purposes (whether these are private or public) in order to understand, even in part, how students and their families and their communities will view the inclusion of first language writing in the curriculum.

To educators, being able to write is presumed to be empowering. It is necessary (though not sufficient) for access to certain societal resources (e.g., jobs requiring writing) and services initiated or legalized through writing. As a tool for thinking, it offers additional, perhaps unique, opportunities for reasoning, reflecting, interacting with oneself. It expands ways of interacting with others, including increasing the possibility of having a public voice. In a society where tested 'literacy levels' help uphold a myth of meritocracy, we learn to consider an inability to read and write as shameful — disempowering in the extreme.

But whether writing has such benefits or not, learning to write can change the *status quo* for the community as well as the child. In opening up new social roles for the writer (and possibilities for new relationships), learning to write in either language brings social change in its wake (Hymes, 1972a). Understanding and predicting a community's reaction to students as writers depends on gathering information under the guidance of an ethnography-of-writing perspective (Swzed, 1981; Woods-Elliott and Hymes, n.d.). For example, communities of newly arrived immigrants may not yet have established any stable pattern to their written language use in the new community. English — oral or written — is only one of the many new features these immigrants have to work into their social and intellectual lives. If the native language of the immigrants has included writing, that too has been disrupted through immigration since print resources (newspapers, signs, books, etc.) and written language networks have changed (Weinstein-Shr, in press). As their children learn to write English, what impact does that have? Does it change their relation to family members or community elders and to family members in interaction with the larger mainstream society? If they learn to write in the home language but first language writing in the native country was limited by gender or social class, what happens to social roles as writing ability 'spreads'? Or do the children refuse to learn to write in the first language rather than violate native norms?

In contrast with communities of new arrivals, communities made up of either indigenous people or longstanding immigrants are more likely to have stable existent patterns of written language use. The question then is whether learning to write in both the first and second language would produce a challenge to the community's language situation. If it does, it is important to identify who wants the change and who does not. In anticipating whether there will be arguments over first language writing in school in indigenous and established immigrant communities, it is equally important to learn whether first language writing will be a red herring. That is, what other community battles (e.g., over traditional versus 'modern' ways, over separation and nationhood versus annexation) may underlie disagreements over whether, which, how much, and who learns to write in the first language?

Conclusion

The picture for writing in bilingual programs is indeed complicated. What happens in any given classroom will be influenced by a host of locally varying factors arising from many larger contexts. This means that there can be no uniform, highly specified written language policies or programs that will be effective everywhere. On the other hand, given a combination of local language situation details, neither is there one automatic local policy response. In fact, there are so many possibilities, each with so many possible attendant pitfalls that a reasonable question to ask is this: Why would anyone even try to develop a local policy or program that would require accommodating to so many contingencies and that would be fraught with so many opportunities for creating havoc in the speech community? The answer is vision. To engage in such a precarious endeavor, local planners would have to be able to see beauty in the idea that goals can remain general and that plans can be built on equity. To weave their way through such a complex contextual tapestry they would have to be able to envision a chance to create a plan that would challenge the usual relations of domination and subordination — relations that not only affect education and writing and bilingual programs but, as Williams (1989) says, that saturate the whole process of living.

Notes

1 On occasion, we have been asked to specify what we think would be appropriate policies or programs for some of the situational characteristics we describe. To be true to our call for autonomy for local administrators, teachers, and students, we believe we must refrain from specifying policies or programs. To do so would reify our suggestions while implying that one could optimally and mechanically relate condition A, condition C, and condition F to Policy no. 1, conditions B, D, and E to policy no. 2, etc. Even worse, it would contradict our major point. That is, the complexity of each situation, which can only be known by insiders and sensitive, longtime outside observers, requires tailor-made locally specified policies about written language education, not policies generated in the abstract by outsiders to fit generic combinations of features.

2 Whether or not published materials written in languages other than English can make their way to bilingual programs in the English speaking world, and whether other-than-English texts will follow the format and content of highly profitable English language materials like

basal readers is not simply a coincidental given in a particular educational setting. Decisions made by former salesmen turned editors and corporate managers in an industry organized for profit figure heavily in producing these conditions (Apple, 1989). So do the politics of establishing selective literary 'traditions' that privilege certain genres and voices and exclude others (Kimberley, 1989; Wald, 1989).

reachmany view of publishing

The Effect of 'Theory' on Several Versions of a Popular THEORY: Plus Ça Change, Plus C'est La Même Chose

Both 'theory' and THEORY are systems of beliefs that organize expectations and perceptions and influence decisions and behavior. The difference is that people's 'theories' are usually tacit, unexamined taken-for-granted foundations for more explicit beliefs, while THEORY is a system of explicit coherent beliefs formalized according to the conventions of some scientific community. Recently, as part of a general trend to attend to people's meanings and not just their behaviors, researchers have become increasingly interested in teachers' 'theories'. The assumption, of course, is that teachers' 'theories' have some relationship (e.g., causative or legitimizing or dialectic) to what they do in classrooms. (For a beginning look at the interesting array of research conceptions and aims in studies of teachers' beliefs, see Clandinin and Connelly, 1987; Clark and Peterson, 1986; Hatton, 1989; Nespor, 1987; Shulman, 1987; Shavelson and Stern, 1981.)

Teachers, however, are not the only ones who have tacit beliefs that are implicated in their professional work. Researchers too have taken-for-granted beliefs that affect what they do professionally (e.g., how they see phenomena, what they identify as interesting problems, which methodologies they choose, what models they develop). Thus their 'theories' are infused into their research findings — and ultimately into their THEORIES — before their research is ever begun (Bogdan and Biklen, 1982). One such 'theory'-influenced THEORY is that developed by Jim Cummins to explain the relationships between first and second language proficiency and between second language proficiency and success in school. Like a match thrown on dry brush, this THEORY has caught on and swept across a discipline; and like that same match, it is both useful and dangerous. Because it has been adopted so quickly and so widely (i.e., its constructs seem to now be part of the conventional wisdom in bilingual education in North America; its arguments set the parameters for conversation about the education of children who do not speak the majority language), it is important to look closely at the 'theory' that pervades this THEORY.

Initially, Cummins' THEORY was proposed to account for various inconsistencies: 1) home-school language switches have been detrimental to 'submersion' but not 'immersion' students (Lambert and Tucker, 1972; US Commission on Civil Rights, 1975); 2) bilingualism has provided a cognitive advantage to some but not others (Peal and Lambert, 1962); and 3) older immigrant children have been more successful in school than younger ones (Toukomaa and Skutknabb-Kangas, 1977). Later versions aim, additionally, to elucidate the changing nature of language proficiency in relation to school achievement.

All versions of the THEORY are appealing, well-argued, unquestionably well-intentioned — and wrong. They are wrong in basic premises (i.e., in 'theory') about reading and writing, wrong about what should constitute education and therefore achievement, wrong in relying primarily on test data for support. Wrong or not, from its earlier presentations (Cummins, 1979) to now, Cummins' formal THEORY, with its intent of improving the educational fortunes of poor, minority language children,[1] continues to be a convenient and effective weapon in bilingual education's fight for survival. But in the long run, progressive intentions notwithstanding, the 'theory' underlying all versions of the THEORY as well as the central constructs in his earlier discussions are likely to be dangerous to the very children who are supposed to be the beneficiaries.

The THEORY in Brief

Hypotheses, Constructs, and Policies

At first, the THEORY proposed two new constructs (CALP, cognitive academic language proficiency, and BICS, basic interpersonal communicative skill) and borrowed one old one (semilingualism) in order to discuss two hypotheses (the developmental interdependence hypothesis and the threshold hypothesis). Later versions make less use of the three constructs (semilingualism is now called limited bilingualism), has added another pair of acronyms (CUP, common underlying proficiency; SUP, separate underlying proficiency), and now emphasizes two continua: context-reduced versus context-embedded situations for language use; and cognitively demanding versus cognitively undemanding language tasks.

The threshold hypothesis states that there is a threshold level of linguistic competence which must be attained in each language in order for bilinguals to avoid cognitive deficits and to benefit cognitively from their bilingualism (Cummins, 1979, p. 229). The developmental interdependence hypothesis says that 'the level of L2 competence which a bilingual child attains is partially a function of the type of competence the child has developed in L1 at the time when intensive exposure to L2 begins', Cummins, 1979, p. 233). The three constructs name kinds of language competence. CALP (cognitive academic language proficiency) is those aspects of language proficiency 'related to the development of literacy skills', namely 'vocabulary-concept knowledge, metalinguistic insights, and knowing how to process decontextualized language' (Cummins, 1979, p. 242). BICS (basic interpersonal communicative skill) includes oral fluency and sociolinguistic competence (Cummins, 1979). CALP, the more advanced proficiency, taking longer to develop, is what is needed for school success. Semilingualism refers to the language (dis)ability of a bilingual child who may have 'surface' fluency in each language (i.e., high BICS) but who knows neither well enough to handle 'abstract cognitive/language tasks' (Cummins, 1979, p. 231) (i.e., low CALP).

The additional acronyms in the newer versions, CUP (common underlying proficiency) and SUP (separate underlying proficiency) (Cummins, 1981, 1984) are competing notions. CUP is intimately related to the developmental inter-dependence hypothesis. Cummins maintains that people's belief in either CUP or SUP control various entrance and exit policies in bilingual education.

In place of the older two-pronged language proficiency (CALP and BICS), newer versions of the THEORY propose two intersecting continua. Context-embedded to context-reduced communication refers to the amount of contextual support available in different communicative situations. The other continuum, cognitively demanding to cognitively undemanding language tasks, addresses 'developmental aspects of communicative proficiency in terms of the degree of active cognitive involvement in the task' (Cummins, 1984, p. 13). Though extensive discussions of semilingualism no longer appear in later versions, the term limited bilingualism stands for the same idea.

Cummins uses these hypotheses and constructs to make various policy implications for both minority and majority language children. Language of instruction must account for: 1) how well a child can handle context-reduced, cognitively demanding language tasks in school; and 2) outside-of-school availability of the target language for promoting 'surface' fluency. The minority language child, with (assumed) limitations in cognitive academic language abilities but much opportunity for out-of-school interaction in the second language, should be given extensive opportunity to develop the first language and delay the use of the second language in school. Majority language children from a family or community that desires rather than requires bilinguality, will have less access to out-of-school interactions in the second language but greater academic language proficiency in the first language. That child can succeed in an immersion program and in fact needs more school exposure to the second language since both interpersonal and academic language proficiency will have to be acquired in school (Cummins, 1979; 1981; Swain, 1981).

Critique

I do not dispute the existence of the discrepancies in school success that Cummins' THEORY was originally developed to explain. My disagreement is over a basic premise or 'theory', some of his older constructs (though they no longer appear in his own recent work, they are catching on and being used by others), and his supporting data.

The Disputed 'Theory'

The fundamental problem with all versions of Cummins' THEORY is that it is premised on an erroneous, psychologically derived 'theory' of the nature of reading — a conception of reading as consisting of separate skills with discrete components of language. What counts as either reading-in-action or as evidence of reading ability is 'reading skills'. These are demonstrated by performance in miscontextualized tasks (performed for the sole purpose of either demonstrating proficiency or complying with the assignment) or on tests whose scores are presumed to represent some supposedly context-free reading ability. And what counts, in turn, as 'academic skills' is primarily 'reading skills'; thus what counts as school achievement is scores and performance that represent 'reading skills' (i.e., standardized [reading] test scores and performance in tuned-to-the-tests curricula).

Harste and Burke (1977) describe three theoretical orientations or 'theories' people might have about literacy: 1) the *decoding orientation* (reading is first of all a matter of turning symbol into sound and then capping the translation with meaning; pronunciation of print is the primary data for assessment); 2) the *skills orientation* (reading and writing are composed of individual 'skill slices' in decoding, vocabulary, grammar, and composition; the word is primary; tests of separate skills are the appropriate means of assessment); and 3) the *whole language orientation* (orthographic, syntactic, semantic, and pragmatic cueing systems of written language are interactive and interdependent; multiple cueing systems are used simultaneously during reading and writing to construct meaning; appropriate assessment requires observation of the entire [whole] language-using activity [constructing context-bound meaning within a particular situation]). A chasm — a different paradigmatic view of literacy and of linguistic and social competence — separates the last from the first two orientations.

Despite Cummins' occasional use of 'whole language' terminology (e.g., 'inferring', 'predicting' 'large chunks of discourse'), his underlying skills orientation shows through. He writes of reading as consisting of reasoning separated from decoding ('as development progresses, word meaning and reasoning-in-reading [e.g., inferring and predicting text meaning] rather than word decoding skills account for the variance between good and poor readers', Cummins, 1981, p. 15). The data on school achievement that Cummins relies on to suport his THEORY come almost entirely from studies using tests of separate so-called reading skills. (No wonder. His small-parts, psychometric orientation that views all human activity as first divisible into atomized skills and then measurable would certainly lead him to prefer such evidence.) It is that skills 'theory' of reading — derived from his psychometric stance — that prevents him from questioning all the phenomena in the relationships he has theorized about and that makes him just settle on one. That is, in investigating the relation between failure to attain high levels of second language proficiency and 'consequent' academic failure, he questions and theorizes about language proficiency. However, in no versions of the THEORY does he look closely at *what counts as* academic skills, academic tasks, or academic achievement. Instead, he explicitly accepts prevailing instructional and evaluational practice as a given (Cummins, 1984) and limits himself to relating students' language proficiency to such practice.

The goal for education, embedded in this THEORY, derives directly from this 'theory' (that literacy is a collection of skills which can be justifiably represented by and equated with scores on reading tests). Instead of promoting meaningful, irreducible activity like reading and writing in actual academic and life contexts, Cummins' THEORY encourages the reduction of reading and writing to their supposedly component parts — that is, academic skills as evidenced by test scores.

When Cummins simply refers to (rather than presents) his THEORY of language proficiency and instead devotes his attention to school and what should be happening there, he uses a discourse of empowerment and puts forward a set of suggestions that implicitly contradict his 'theory' of reading as consisting of separate skills (Cummins, 1986). Is it the case, then, that he really does not hold this 'theory'? After all, empowering minority students does in fact require a different conception of reading and therefore a different conception of academic tasks, academic skills, and academic success. And Cummins uses the right rhetoric. He talks of students setting their own goals and generating their own knowledge and he mentions congruent educational practice (e.g., he refers to reports by Graves and the Bullock Report). Even so, that separate skills 'theory' slips out and he contradicts his own message. For example, for empirical support, he relies heavily on test score data that can only provide evidence of how well students perform on skill exercises. He applauds and describes at length programs that operate according to a skills 'theory'. For instance, he talks of two programs that make language or cultural accommodations which benefit minority language children by helping them attain readiness or success. Readiness for what? For the academic tasks of the traditional kindergartens the children will enter in California. Success at what? Success in doing reading exercises in tests and basal reader lessons in Hawaii. It is hard to believe, then, that when he uses Graves', Lindfors' and Giaccobbe's terminology (e.g., 'generating one's own knowledge', 'setting one's own goals'), he means the same things they do. It is more likely that this is another case of something I will discuss shortly: Cummins' tendency to take trivial activity (e.g., a psychometrically defined skill) and cloak it in important sounding cognitive terminology.

Because of the contradictions he fails to see (e.g., juxtaposing Graves' pedagogy with test-score evidence), he is forced into another contradiction: his entire THEORY does not fit his proposals for an empowering kind of education. Therefore, he abandons key parts (the threshold hypothesis, increasing context-reduction as a critical characteristic of academic tasks). And instead of explaining failure or success with the psychological constructs he has been using, he turns (without acknowledging them) to what his critics have used all along — socio-political explanations invoking notions of context-dependence, dominance, intergroup relations, and interactional roles (Adelman, 1984; Edelsky, Hudelson, Flores, Barkin, Altwerger and Jilbert, 1983; Martin-Jones and Romaine, 1984). Decrying the transmission model of traditional disempowering pedagogy, he advocates a reciprocal interaction model of empowering pedagogy. But judging from the programs he cites and the criteria he uses for success, the point of it all still seems to be to increase children's ability to perform reading and writing exercises — perhaps more sophisticated and complex than the workbook exercise activity he mentions as examples in his earlier presentations of the THEORY, but exercises just the same.

In the various presentations of the THEORY itself, Cummins' 'theory' about literacy, and therefore his unquestioning acceptance of current school definitions (reading and achievement equal scores on reading and achievement tests), are the flaws which lead to all the rest of the errors. It accounts for his choice of data and for his indirect blaming of the learner for failure (deficient testing and deficient school language policies mask the deficiencies the child has in performing in what

Cummins accepts without question — an 'abstract' skills curriculum). And it explains why this THEORY gained popularity so fast and was so effective in influencing policy. That written language consists of separate skills, that curriculum should teach those skills, that tests can assess them — these are all ideas that undergird predominant thinking about education in North America. Cummins' contribution is to argue that the language of skills instruction need not be English. His THEORY changes nothing but the language of instruction. It does nothing to change the prevailing model of education which effectively disenfranchises minority students in the first place. It not only leaves intact beliefs in a skills 'theory' of reading and writing; it actually strengthens those beliefs and, along with them, promotes a congruent goal for education: the attainment of higher scores on artificial tests.

Disputed Data

Almost all the evidence Cummins uses comes from research that operationalizes, that lets one thing stand for another. Although the substitutions may be reasonable, they often turn out to distort the phenomenon of interest (see Mehan and Wood, 1975 and Blumer, 1969 for a discussion of problems in operationalizing). Once something (e.g., responses to test items) is operationalized as a measure of something else (e.g., reading), one is prevented from counting reading a book and talking about it, for instance, as reading even though such activity seems to represent the phenomenon of reading at least as well as test responses. Thus, children who were able to make inferences about test stimuli in interviews still scored low on 'inferencing skills' because their responses to a test of 'inferencing' were incorrect (MacKay, 1973). In addition, by attempting to separate and isolate variables, research that operationalizes misrepresents the interactive constitutive nature of human phenomena like achievement, reading, learning, proficient language use, and so on (Garfinkel, 1967; Mehan, 1978).

The second problem with the data concerns what Cummins means by the terms he uses. In general, he takes his sources' labels without making clear how the original research operationalized 'reading', 'English skill', 'French skill', 'academic skill', 'native-like levels in both languages', 'cognitive retardation', 'English achievement', 'French achievement', 'deeper levels of cognitive competence', 'higher levels of cognitive skills', etc. It is therefore very easy to believe that what was measured was some common-sense notion of reading, for example, or cognitive skills — something like being able to understand a printed story or being able to remember information important to the rememberer — and that some children were poorer readers or less cognitively skilled in this ordinary, non-trivial sense. But when Cummins does specify or when one goes back to the original research, the equivalences prove to be inadequate. 'Cognitive aspects of language' (Cummins, 1979, p. 231) meant the ability to match synonyms. 'Cognitive advantage in bilingualism' became the ability to find ambiguities in isolated printed sentences (Cummins, 1979, p. 232). 'Ability to extract meaning from written text' was actually a score on a standardized reading test (Cummins, 1979, pp. 233–4), and 'native-like competence' in a language was scores on vocabulary tests (Cummins,

1979, p. 231). Important notions were thus demeaned in the original research and that demeaning is passed on, unexplicated, in Cummins' formulations.

Third, most of the evidence used to support the older CALP/BICS and semilingualism notions come from tests such as the Peabody Picture Vocabulary Test, the Inter-American Test of Reading, Inter-American Prueba de Lectura, Metropolitan Achievement Test, Illinois Test of Psycholinguistic Ability, Wepman Auditory Discrimination Test, Canadian Test of Basic Skills, and so on. Even in the newer versions of the THEORY, though the model implies that what is cognitively demanding in a context-reduced setting (the more sophisticated conceptualization of the old CALP) could be any language task, the supporting research and at least some of the discussion appeals to 'reading skills', 'grade level in reading', 'finding ambiguities in sentences' — again, to language exercises in test settings.

One problem with making such substantial use of test data is that of construct validity — the tests do not measure what they purport to measure; i.e., the operationalizations fail, distorting the phenomena under investigation (see Chapter 9). Moreover, items on reading tests especially do not represent skills that are essential to the general activity supposedly being assessed. For example, if the tests actually tested reading, scores would not vary when such things as the color of the test booklet were changed (Orasanu *et al.*, 1977). What happens on a test of reading is that print is interacted with in replicable ways that correlate with other replicable events, none of which may be instances of reading (Harste, Burke and Woodward, 1982). The same can be said for tests of other processes that exist in everyday life. For instance, much of the evidence Cummins uses for 'cognitive functioning' (as opposed to 'school success') of bilinguals does not come from standardized tests but is the product of testing situations. Sometimes, as in dichotic listening tasks, most unlanguage-like stimuli are used in place of language (e.g., meaningless syllables, functionless isolated words).[2]

Compounding this is that test data assumes standardized settings and tasks, which further assumes that the nature of a task is *in* the task. But a task only takes shape as an interpreting social being interacts with a task-potential. Different people interpret the 'same' task differently (Labov, 1970; Wells, 1977), making it unlikely that all test-takers have actually worked at the *same* task. Yet another problem arises when norms for standardized tests are established because half the scores *must* fall below the norm. Programs that raise scores for large numbers of children may help those children in the short run but they merely up the ante for the younger siblings, since new norms then have to be established so that half are again below average. And with token exceptions, it is easy to predict in which half poor and minority language children will be overrepresented. In short, Cummins' supporting evidence is neither convincing nor socially progressive. A THEORY which is so closely tied to test data for support or for later verification will eventually undermine its intended lower class beneficiaries.

Constructs in Earlier and Later Versions

The earliest versions of the THEORY proposed a language proficiency distinction (CALP versus BICS) and borrowed one notion (semilingualism). Later versions elaborated some constructs and de-emphasized others. In disputing the validity of those constructs, old or new, I am not claiming that all children are equally competent. Nor do I believe that proficiency with *any* language variety, in either oral or written modes, enables one to do *everything* humanly possible with language. Though *potentially* equal, at any given historical moment different language repertoires (including literate repertoires) of particular speech communities are unequally efficient for all purposes and even then, unequally assigned to members (Hymes, 1980b; Graff, 1986). However, the nature of those repertoires, their functions, their meanings, and their inequalities must be determined by ethnographies of speaking and of literacy, not by differential performance in one (testing) context that is subject to extensive criticism on multiple grounds. The same is true of individual language repertoires in native and second languages. What Cummins has done is to develop a THEORY of language proficiency based not on any extensive participant observation of repertoires in use, but on children's responses to a skills-based curriculum and to tests of separate language skills. This THEORY restricts what will ultimately count as 'empowerment' to improved performance within instructionally bound speech and literacy events.

Older Versions

CALP and BICS

Though Cummins only uses these acronyms as points of reference in more recent versions, the terms and ideas are still in wide use. Thus, they still warrant comment.

Cognitive academic language proficiency (CALP) is presented as the highest level of cognitive functioning and language development. It is equated with Oller's (1978) global language proficiency which, in turn, is presumably related to general intelligence (Cummins, 1980). The message then (unintentional or not) is that since poor minority language groups consistently score lower on tests of 'academic language ability' (e.g., standardized reading, vocabulary, and verbal intelligence tests [Samuda, 1975]), general intelligence is distributed differentially according to social class or ethnicity.

I believe it is more accurate to call 'cognitive academic language proficiency' or 'global intelligence' by a different name: test-wiseness. It is then more understandable that middle class mainstream populations score higher; they are coached during early socialization (Heath, 1982). Test-wiseness also explains why older child immigrants would do better in school than younger ones. The older children have learned to cope in their first language with the 'highly abstract school curriculum' which Cummins respects but which could just as well be seen as out-of-context nonsense (Smith, 1986). Their greater success comes not from a more advanced first language proficiency but from having been 'schooled' (literally) in nonsense through something that makes sense, their first language. They do not have to learn about school nonsense through another type of nonsense, the strange sounds of a second language.

Central to the early THEORY was a distinction between basic interpersonal communicative skill (BICS) and cognitive academic language proficiency (CALP). Though there were occasional disclaimers (which few of his colleagues took seriously [see Rivera, 1984]), BICS and CALP were presented as being essentially separate and unequally valuable in school. BICS is supposedly social; CALP is cognitive. BICS, therefore, should not entail the proficiencies included in CALP — linguistic manipulation, cognitive strategies, logic, conceptual knowledge, metalinguistic awareness and so on. Even scant familiarity with the child language literature should reveal the absurdity here. BICS is also not supposed to lead to success in school. Wells' (1979) and Wells and Raban's (n.d.) work is cited as evidence. In that research, assessments of spontaneous language use (BICS) did not correlate highly with later reading test scores (CALP). What did show high correlations were test scores and conversations in which the child and an 'enabling adult' negotiated meaning. One can only wonder why such conversations were not considered evidence of BICS. Or why Cummins ignored the wealth of information on the social and interactive knowledge required for text competence (CALP) in order to maintain that CALP and BICS are separate.

Semilingualism

When bilingual or lower class children lack proficiency with meaningless, non-functional print on tests or in lessons, they are said to be semilingual, having less than native competence in each language (Cummins, 1979, p. 230). The label 'semilingualism' dates back at least to the early 1960s (Hansegard, 1962, cited in Skuttnab-Kangas and Toukomaa, 1976). Then and now, it is a confused grab-bag of prescriptive and descriptive components, including the size of vocabulary, correctness (based on rules from standard language using speech communities), ability to neologize, and mastery of cognitive, emotional, and volitional functions of language. Children who have limited academic language proficiency are semilingual (semilingualism and CALP are defined by the same features (Cummins, 1979, pp. 230–1). In other words, poor test performance means one has less than native-like competence in one's native language. The question, then is this: if an entire group is 'less than native-like', who are the natives whose language and cognitive abilities *are* native-like? How can whole speech communities be semilingual in anything more than the trivial sense of not being able to perform well on tests?

Unfortunately, regardless of its triviality, the term semilingualism fits all too well into popular stereotypes about children who 'don't know English and don't know Spanish either' and 'therefore' do poorly in school. That schools' (and researchers') tightly interwoven and faulty conceptions of literacy, curriculum and evaluation, and not children's language proficiency, might be the culprit is not considered.

Newer Versions of Cummins' THEORY

One general problem is that there are unaccounted-for waverings (with the exception of when he substitutes context-embedded/reduced and cognitive demanding/undemanding for the old CALP and BICS, Cummins does not acknowledge former positions and gives no reasons for changes in position). This permits much room for disputed interpretations, depending on which version someone has read, and for evasion (Cummins can always claim that readers have misinterpreted when in fact they correctly read only one version). For instance, the term semilingualism no longer appears in recent versions. Indeed, Cummins (1982) has indicated that he repudiated it several years ago. Still, the *idea* is present in the latest versions, only now it is called limited bilingualism (Cummins, 1981). Once Cummins (1980) accepted Oller's proposal of one underlying global language proficiency/global intelligence, at least as it concerns academic language and academic task perform-ance. Recently, however (Cummins, 1984, p. 16), he disputed Oller's claim but did not explicitly acknowledge the about-face. Such an omission increases possibilities for blaming readers rather than explicating changes in thinking. Nor does he admit that the rhetoric at least, if not the examples he uses, for suggested educational practices that would empower minority students (Cummins, 1986) are very different from the practices he alluded to (through his supporting data) in his earlier theoretical statements.

In shifting from use of the CALP/BICS distinction to use of two intersecting continua, the changes are explicitly acknowledged. But while substituting context-embeddedness and cognitive demandingness as continua increases the subtlety of the THEORY, it doesn't change its basic tie to a skills 'theory' of reading. For instance, how much reduction is legitimate in context-reduced comunication? From the research he uses, Cummins seems to be saying that context can be reduced (or rather, that the pragmatics can be *changed*) to the point where whole systems of written language (e.g., syntax or semantics) are eliminated, as they are in many tests, literacy workbook exercises and experiments. However, as I argue in Chapter 5, when that degree of context-reduction occurs along with the pragmatic circumstances that created such a reduction, then the original phenom-enon of interest (reading, discussing, arguing, etc.) is transformed into an exercise. In addition, Cummins gives the impression that better, more advanced readers or listeners do not rely on non-linguistic context. However, in other kinds of (*non-exercise*) reading, the more proficient the reader, the more nonlinguistic context (e.g., prior information, discourse expectations) and the less written information (Smith, 1982a) that person uses. Even young children's writing develops through becoming more rather than less context-embedded (Dyson, 1987). Pratt (1977) argues that contextual cues (type of paper, publishing company, illustrations on book jackets, publication itself, and so on) establish certain expectancies in mature readers so that they can interpret literary discourse. In other words, in naturally occurring context-reduced situations the proficient reader re-*embeds*. Moreover, those naturally occurring context-reduced situations out of school are actually more context-embedded than the context-reduced situations of 'highly abstract school curriculum'. (See Enright, 1986, pp. 151–5 for a critique of the idea of decon-textualized language use.)

The proposed common underlying proficiency (CUP) that accounts for transfer of reading ability across language is right BUT. The 'but' is that proficiency is always in relation to something. Based on the cited research, that 'something' in Cummins' THEORY is the ability to do artificial literacy exercises.

In discussing the threshold (level of second language proficiency needed for reaping cognitive advantage from bilingualism), Cummins (1984) admits that different thresholds might be required by the demands of different classrooms or grade levels. But given what counts in this THEORY as the mark of success (test scores or correct responses in literacy experiments), the threshold turns out to be nothing more than what is required to obtain a certain score. Thus 'cognitive advantage' must actually mean 'scoring advantage'.

Although in newer versions (Cummins, 1984) there is a concession that cognitive academic language is socially grounded (developing out of human interaction), nowhere is there an indication of the extent of the social grounding. In fact, from the use he makes of Wells' research, Cummins seems to interpret the social grounding of CALP to mean no more than a correlation between test scores and certain kinds of home interactions. However, doing reading lessons and taking tests are themselves social work that is interactionally accomplished (Baker and Freebody, 1989; Jennings and Jennings, 1974; Moll, 1981). Children's writing (including everything from the content of their stories to their spellings) is fine tuned to their social histories and current interactions with peers (Dyson, 1989). Therefore, to try to understand reading or writing or talking in school by looking at static, reduced products like test scores not only strips away the social connections; it also distorts what is being looked at and, thus, actually blocks understanding.

One sign of the inadequacy of the THEORY is that Cummins has to go almost entirely outside of it, appealing to reasons that sound remarkably like Ervin-Tripp's (1970) still pertinent analysis, to explain why immersion students succeed through schooling in their second language while submersion (poor minority language) students do not. He tacitly indicates (Cummins, 1981) that the relative political positions of the two languages ensures that immersion students' first language is not swamped (in school or out) by their second language. He also explains immersion (versus submersion) students' success by different levels of prestige for the respective first languages, differences in security of identity, and differences in level of support for first language development (This is not exactly the same class-based, power-based, status-based explanation I offer in Chapter 1, but it is certainly more socially and politically inclined than would be an appeal to his own hypotheses about thresholds, linguistic interdependence, semilingualism, or two different kinds of language proficiency.) Although CUP, the underlying proficiency connected to support for first language development, *is* part of the THEORY, the other factors are not. Context-reduction, cognitive demands, and thresholds (central concepts in the new version of the THEORY) are not used in explaining why majority language children should succeed in school in a second language or why their first language should be better developed at home. Nor are any ethnography of speaking data provided which might show that the activity of particular minority populations does not support extensive first language development.

A Different View

Premises

While merely translating a mainstream curriculum into different languages may provide minority language children with a spurt in cultural identity (it might even prompt short term improvement in test scores — after all, at least now the vehicle if not the task would make some sense), it will not contribute to certain substantive educational goals. Those goals are for children to learn to think critically about a range of subjects, to pose problems and envision and work toward solutions, to make decisions based on articulated, informed evidence, and to be able to use written language for these ends. Reading and writing in this view entail the creation of meaningful texts. And the preferred reading and writing — the kind that comprises both the goal and the substance of daily practice — is the creation of meaningful texts for some purpose beyond compliance and evaluation (e.g., for synthesizing, reorganizing, critically analyzing, and generating ideas through print in naturally occurring contexts.) In other words, the goal is for children to control print so that it can serve personal and group interests; i.e., so it empowers. In this conception, the units of written language that children read and write are not analytical parts stripped of pragmatic or other cues (parts like the paragraph, the sentence, the word, the letter); they are functional wholes (stories read for entertainment, recipes written for cooking, letters written for permission, editorials read for critique, investigative reports read for information, congressional records read for documentation, etc.).

I believe that what Cummins calls skill with academic language is really skill in instructional nonsense (SIN, if another acronym is needed). By contrast, I am arguing for proficiency in controlling authentic texts — for 'power literacy'.[3] Classrooms where this conception of literacy and congruent pedagogy prevails are in the minority.[4] Still, they exist (see Atwell, 1987; Calkins, 1986; Dyson, 1989; Edelsky, Draper and Smith, 1983 and Chapter 7, this volume; Kamler, 1980 for descriptions of their various inner workings). These are not just classrooms where creative teachers make instructional nonsense culturally congruent or where they spice up a traditional curriculum with rocks, leaves, live animals and assorted authentic props or integrated units of study.[5] Nor do these teachers confuse comprehension with commercial 'reading' program comprehension exercises (Harste, 1989).

What they do instead requires perceptiveness and courage but no unusual materials. They write letters to children; they discuss literature with them, listen to children's responses to the books they are reading and suggest others; they encourage children to focus on meaning as they read and to reflect on what they write; they support children as they investigate their own questions about and critique the world around them; they enrich the oral and written language environment by loading it with 'whole discourses' (whole stories, plays, reference books, and so on, not analytical parts like sentences, and paragraphs). And the children grow into reading and writing the way they did into talking — with the intense effort and great satisfaction that comes from doing worthwhile, honest socio-psycholinguistic work as members of a literate community.

Data

Instead of looking at performances that supposedly stand for reading and writing, students' actual reading and writing are evaluated — both the products and the processes. A body of naturalistic research (Calkins, 1983; Dyson, 1989; Goodman, and Goodman, 1978; Harste, Woodward and Burke, 1984) shows that this is desirable and productive. This research does not conceive of reading and writing as accumulations of skills superimposed over individual abilities to perform tasks that hypothetically represent reading/writing but actually represent requirements of a particular instructional tradition (e.g., phonics, word attack skills). Instead, it views reading and writing as simultaneously linguistic, cognitive, and social phenomena. It is a view grounded in rigorous observation of readers and writers reading and writing.

Hypotheses

To counter Cummins' hypotheses regarding the relationship of language and school achievement, I offer the following:

1 It is difficult to learn skill with instructional nonsense in any language but it is probably easier to learn it in the first language.
2 It is difficult to acquire skill with instructional nonsense through meaningless literacy exercises alone. That is, regardless of language of instruction, if children's experience with literacy is primarily through written-for-instruction stories, worksheets and other pseudo-texts, they will have difficulty in becoming skilled with such exercises.
3 It is hard to become literate through nonsensical exercises. The tortuous strategy of aiming for reading through a steady restricted diet of reading-exercises will result in some 'false positives' — children who manage to acquire some skill with the exercises but who have meager abilities to cope with genuine texts in the world.
4 Interpersonal oral communicative activity is a significant basis for learning to use written language. It is usually through the initial extension into print of language used interpersonally to convey intentions and mutually relevant meanings that one becomes able to transact meanings in solitary reading and to construct written texts.
5 It is easy to learn to read and write (as opposed to doing reading and writing exercises) when the school emphasizes reading and writing as *non*-exercises — an emphasis which entails a strong oral interactional component to the literacy instruction.
6 Once someone can *read* and *write*, it becomes easier to learn instructional nonsense if that is necessary for some narrow instrumental purpose. There are many children in school who are 'false negatives' (whose test performance underrepresents how well they can read and write for their own purposes).

Accounting for Group Differences

If the above hypotheses are correct, why is it that middle class mainstream children (who are also exposed to schooldays full of dittoed exercises *in* rather than the exercise *of* reading and writing) acquire skill with instructional nonsense (i.e., score higher on tests) while poor minority language children do not? And why do middle class children *seem* to become truly literate as a result of a diet of ditto sheets? Three possible explanations follow.

1   Mainstream middle class children are primed more appropriately for playing the prevailing reading-exercise game and for participating in the classroom discourse (the typical Initiation-Reply-Evaluation (IRE) sequence) that helps create that reading-exercise game (Heath, 1982; Morrison, 1982). In addition, they are more likely to be expected to derive entertainment from books. With better priming, they are more likely to be successful with early lessons on psuedo-reading. Feeling kindly, therefore, toward 'school reading' and feeling expected to amuse themselves with books, *they are more likely to pursue actual reading on their own. And it is this out-of-school reading, rather than in-school exercises, that promotes reading.* It is not that teachers are irrelevant; but when so much teaching is focused on meaningless practice, the main access to authentic literacy must come through out-of-school or self-directed efforts.

2   Middle class mainstream children and teachers do not have relational battles over which communicative system to use. All parties share norms for how to talk during reading time, sharing time, and so on (Collins and Michaels, 1986). Observational studies show, however, that when teachers and children come from different social class or cultural groups, there is often a struggle over which language norms to use (McDermott, 1977). One reason immersion program children succeed in school is that while they use linguistic features of a foreign variety to 'do lessons', they already know the interactional norms for 'doing school'. Relational battles over language may leave little strength for attention to less emotionally compelling schoolish tasks.

3   Middle class mainstream children and teachers are more likely to have 'trusting relations' with each other. This is McDermott's (1977) term for working agreements wherein each party can make sense of the other's interactional work and where the children can trust that the teacher's 'coercion' is in their best interests. When such a happy state of affairs exists, even nonsense can be seen as worthy of attention.

Conclusion

The argument here has been that a THEORY (one positing a dichotomous CALP and BICS and accompanied by semilingualism or revised versions with contextual and cognitive dimensions) tied to a 'theory' that substitutes 'reading skills' for reading and uses achievement tests (that only nominally test reading) for assessment and theory verification has great potential for being used against the very children it explicitly supports. Because it fits so well prevailing premises in education, it has had an easy time being accepted; because of its widespread acceptance and its advocacy of education in the native language it has produced short term benefits for bilingual education. That is certainly worthwhile. But in the long run, a THEORY based on inadequate 'theories' of language proficiency and literacy, a THEORY that locates failure in children's heads (in their IQ, their language deficits, their cognitive deficits, their learning styles, their underdeveloped CALP) will not help children learn to really read, write, or become well-educated. Moveover, labels like semilingualism or limited bilingualism provide a ready means for blaming the child both for not learning to really read and write and also for not learning how to do ersatz literacy tasks.

Instead of notions of language proficiency that support harmful conceptions of children and of academic activity, what is needed in bilingual education is a vision of education that would empower minority language students and a THEORY of the relation of language and an empowering education that would explain success in schools that empower. This vision as well as this THEORY must not have the internal contradictions that appear in Cummins (1986). Therefore, it must begin with a 'theory' that rejects separate skills notions of oral and written language and honors what people actually do as they talk, read, and write.

Notes

1   Clearly, cultural differences within the group called 'poor minority language children' make the category a questionable one. Heath (1982) shows how two groups, each non-mainstream and non-middle class, organize literacy events in different ways and how these go with or against the school's organization of literacy events. However, since Cummins used this designation in the early major presentation of his THEORY (1979), I use it here.

2   I am claiming that isolated pronunciation of phonemes or syllables (frequently used stimuli for dichotic listening tasks) is unlanguage-like on both theoretical and empirical grounds. Halliday's (1978) discussion of language as, at base, a *conflux* of ideational, interpersonal, and textual meanings realized through syntactic and phonological choices is at the root of the theoretical arguments. Empirically, neonates have been found to synchronize their movements with adult speech. While the synchrony occurred in relation to normal speech, it did not occur in response to disconnected vowel sounds or tapping noises (Condon and Sander, 1974); i.e., babies did not 'consider' isolated phonemes as sufficiently language-like to respond to them.

3   I am using 'power literacy' to mean Western mainstream norms for written language *use* (versus instruction). Those who are literate in that 'community' focus on meaning and use print for a great variety of intra- and interpersonal functions. There are other populations, however, which are also literate according to the norms of their speech communities, yet these people focus on something other than text meaning during literacy events (Bennett, 1983). Just as questions of proficiency always have to consider 'proficiency for what', so the idea of 'literate' has to consider speech community norms regarding written language.

4   The scarcity is more a function of enormous direct and indirect pressures from corporate, private, and public bureaucratic sources to operate from a skills 'theory' than it is an intrinsic lack of attractiveness of the approach.

5   Some examples that I have seen recently of 'creative' assignments for teaching instructional nonsense in a curricular unit on early settlers are: find the ambiguities in sentences about pioneers, circle short vowels in 'pioneer words', write pretend-functional letters to an imaginary pioneer for the purpose of learning letter format, take part in a simulation of a drought and argue for your position on whether to stay put or to migrate in order to practice making main points and to complete the exercise using supporting details.

Introductory Note to Part II

Part I urges the consideration of what is often not considered in language and education work meant to benefit minority language children. One of these frequently omitted considerations is a set of underlying assumptions about reading which are embedded in curricula, instruction, materials, and evaluation. Ignoring those assumptions is not peculiar to educational work with minority language children. The education of mainstream language children too suffers from that void. The essays in Part II provide counter-constructions of reading that contradict the usual, taken for granted view. However, most of the essays in this part of the book highlight not just reading but a theory-in-practice known as whole language.

Chapter 5 presents a theoretical discussion of some important distinctions in thinking about print literacy: distinctions between using print for making a text meaning or not, between engaging in a mere exercise or not, between being positioned as a Subject with power in the event or as an Object dominated within the event. These distinctions are based on a view of reading both as a socially shaped psychological and linguistic process and as a set of social relationships and culture-bound activities.

The view of literacy presented in Chapter 5 figures heavily in the remaining essays in this part. The whole language perspective discussed at length in Chapter 6 incorporates much of the foregoing view of literacy. Chapter 6 sets out to clarify whole language by comparing it to what it is not (whole word or look-say, kits and methods, teaching skills in context, the language experience approach, and open education) and what it is closely aligned with but still distinct from (writing process approaches).

Whole language teachers' views of what reading is differ fundamentally from prevailing views. That difference leads to or co-occurs with (the direction of influence is not at all clear) important differences in other areas; e.g., what school is about, important goals, optimal roles for teachers and students, and so on. Children who have attended school for several years in a culture that makes the main educational question be 'what works' have usually learned the prevailing views on reading, curriculum, roles, interaction — how to 'do school'; they have not encountered a whole language perspective. How do whole language teachers get children to buy into or even to 'see' a new view well enough so they can operate according to it? Chapter 7 reports how one whole language teacher 'hooked 'em in'.

Chapter 8 reports some re-thinking about whole language, specifically about the conflicts some children face when learning to read, when learning to read critically, and when learning to read in a setting that attempts to encourage relationships of collaboration and equality rather than deference and hierarchy.

Testing figures prominently in education for a stratified society. Chapter 9 presents a critical whole language analysis of what is wrong with testing programs. The critique, based on both social/functional grounds and also on view-of-literacy grounds, is augmented by suggestions for an alternative perspective on evaluation.

An intriguingly hopeful phenomenon on the educational scene is a grass roots teachers' movement that has sprung up all over North America. Though I am imputing movement status to it, I am not sure the teachers involved would see their efforts that way. Nevertheless, they *do* see themselves as belonging to small, local groups they have formed themselves for studying and supporting their own professional efforts. Chapter 10 describes this remarkable move to reclaim professional autonomy and dignity, all the more remarkable because it occurs in the midst of intensified political steps to deprofessionalize teachers.

Most of the local groups described in Chapter 10 form around a desire to develop whole language-informed practice. Growing numbers of teachers, teacher educators, and researchers see whole language as 'best practice', as optimal education for both minority and majority language children. I am among them. But I also see limitations and voids — which are fixable and fill-able. In Chapter 11, I discuss those limitations. As far as I can see, they stem from one major omission: the absence in whole language statements of a clear explication of a political stance and, therefore, the absence of political rationales for theoretical positions and pedagogical practices. Thus, this volume ends by re-thinking the educational alternative offered in response to previous re-thinkings — a fitting finish for a collection of essays emphasizing recursiveness and questioning within a deliberately political framework.

Chapter 5

Literacy: Some Purposeful Distinctions

> * Language Arts, Room 201: Read 'And Off They Flew'. Answer questions 1–5, p. 60.
> * History, Room 167: Pretend you are Abraham Lincoln. Write a speech on slavery which you will give before Congress.

Typical school reading and writing assignments. Though the second is more 'creative' than the first, both ask students to do exercises.

> * This study compares the quality of children's writing as dependent upon genre. Children will be shown landscape photos and asked to write (1) a story set in that locale; and (2) a persuasive essay on the need to preserve that locale.

A typical example of research on writing. The data gathered will consist of exercises.

> * Read the paragraphs on the next pages. Then answer the following questions. Do not turn the page until the examiner tells you to begin.
> * If you could have any pet in the world, what would it be? In the space below, write a paragraph stating your choice and giving reasons for your choice. You will have 15 minutes to write, including whatever time you take to plan your response.

Typical means of evaluating reading and writing. Again, both will evaluate how well students do exercises.

What does it matter if we intend to teach, research, and evaluate reading and writing but, instead, we teach, research, and evaluate reading and writing *exercises*?

Can't we learn about how people read the advice column in the newspaper at home from how they read test passages in a classroom or a research laboratory? After all, presumably reading and writing exercises (teaching them, researching them, evaluating them) are somehow connected (revealing, predicting or transferring) to 'regular' reading and writing. The problem is that this connection remains more presumed than proven. What is more, the presumption may be just wrong enough that it contributes heavily to educational failure and to general misinformation about reading and writing — and even about reading and writing exercises.

Background for a Proposal

The proposal[1] set forth here is that *literacy*, *reading* and *writing* are not interchangeable terms. Literacy is the superordinate category. It includes every use of print as print (but not as material for wrapping fish or washing windows).[2] Some uses of print as print do not result in the creation of a text meaning for the user. Naming the letters on a chart during an eye examination is an instance of literacy but not reading. (From here on, for stylistic ease, I will let the single term *reading* stand for both reading and writing, except where writing is highlighted.) Some literacy activity (both NOT-reading and reading[3] is undertaken by a person positioned as a Subject, in Freire's (1970) sense, in relation to others and to the text; some is performed by a person positioned as an Object. Some reading and also some NOT-reading, done by a Subject, amounts to an exercise; all other print use constitutes a non-exercise.

The difference between literacy as reading and literacy as NOT-reading refers to whether or not the reader aims to make a text meaning for herself. Someone might pronounce print in a foreign language 'without understanding a word' to someone else who does understand the language and therefore interprets a meaning for the text. The pronouncer, however, is not reading even though she may be taking part in creating a meaning for the event. The difference between the literate person as Object and the literate-as-Subject is social and political, not individual. It requires a look at who else is involved and how, and at the role and power of the literate in relation to the role and power of the other(s). Ultimately, it refers to the amount of control a person has over the print-use and the conduct of the literacy event. The difference between literacy as an exercise and all other literacy reflects a difference in the purpose of the literacy event. Exercises are primarily for instructional or evaluational purposes. Non-exercises are initiated for something beyond instruction or evaluation of the literacy itself.

If the literate-person-as-Subject is not distinguished from the literate-person-as-Object, if literacy events as exercises are not separated from literacy events as non-exercises, if literacy is not understood as covering both reading and NOT-reading, some major risks occur. It becomes all too easy to think one is researching reading but to actually be researching NOT-reading, to promise reading but deliver exercises, to promote literacy as a tool for empowerment but offer school literacy practices that disempower.

Figure 5.1   Some Distinctions within Print-use

		Literacy	
		NOT-Reading	Reading
Exercise	O B J		
Not an Exercise	E C T		
Exercise	S U B J		
Not an Exercise	E C T		

Others have begun to separate exercises from something that seems more authentic, to note what position the reader is put in by various reading practices, and to distinguish activity not by its outward appearance but by the goals and motives of participants. Atwell (1987), deCastell and Luke critiquing so-called stories in basal readers (1986), Edelsky and Smith (1984), Gee (1989c), Goodman (1986) and Gladwin writing about arithmetic problem-solving (1985), Graves (1979), Krashen (1988) and Raimes in relation to the talk in ESL classrooms (1983), Smith (1986), Torbe (1988), and Wilde (1988) have all contrasted exercises or school contrivances with 'the real thing'.

The difference between reading and *exercises* in reading might be inferred from Harste, Burke and Woodward's (1982) comment about responses to unpredictable, nonfunctional graphic displays being something other than reading. Harste *et al.* (1982) explain the difference by referring to Goodman's (1969) and their own work on the reading process. Others explain it socially, by associating it with different domains. Black and Martin (1982) and Moss and Stansell (1983) distinguish 'school reading' and 'home reading'. Florio and Clark (1982) contrast 'authorized' versus 'unauthorized' writing. Those making such comparisons usually note that children too distinguish these categories. In a sad turn of affairs, many of the children Hudson (1988) studied refrained from calling the unauthorized, furtive notes they passed to each other *writing*, reserving that designation for something connected to achievement.

Erickson (1984) distinguishes school reading from other reading on the basis of a more extensive analysis of the social relations involved. Luke, Freebody, and Gilbert (in press) discuss social practices too, but not as a way to distinguish exercises from non-exercises. Their interest is in practices that position the literate person in various ways and in a pedagogy that would help students come to understand how they are positioned as readers by both texts and talk. Supplying an overarching theoretical rationale for the distinctions I want to draw is Soviet activity theory (e.g., Leont'ev, 1978) which argues against the idea of the individual-as-*such* (with particular abilities and traits) and argues for looking at the individual-in-*action* in society and history.[4] Soviet activity theorists thus explain that since no activity exists unless there is an individual-in-action, any change in goals or motives or conditions of the action is a change in the total activity itself (Minick, 1985).

Clearly, then, the distinctions I am making are not unique. They owe much to the works cited here. But this proposal differs from the others in focus, detail, and comprehensiveness. Additionally, it unifies and reorders what is discussed separately by the various authors. The proposal is also a drastic revision of an earlier attempt at distinguishing reading from what merely looks like reading (Edelsky, 1986b; Edelsky and Draper, 1989; Edelsky, Altwerger and Flores, 1991. See also the original versions of Chapters 6 and 9). I now believe that that earlier theoretical formulation is wrong in important ways and that Erickson's (1984) focus on the social relationships is the right direction to take, though, as will be apparent, I find Erickson's analysis incomplete. This chapter attempts to provide a corrective by first explaining what is wrong with my own earlier formulation and then discussing details of examples associated with the new proposal.

My purpose in this whole enterprise has been and continues to be admittedly normative and frankly political. That is, fiddling with these distinctions (between literacy and reading, between reading and reading exercises, and between literate Subjects and literate Objects) — indeed making the distinctions in the first place — follows from a 'metanarrative' about what I think literacy *should* be used for (Luke, in press) and what education *should* be about. These are not just general 'shoulds', but as demonstrated in many of the chapters in this volume, specific, detailed visions of educational practice. The metanarrative is ultimately about improving children's educational chances by improving literacy instruction and research. It advocates the literate Subject who reads, at times at least, for critical citizenship (Edelsky, 1989). Thus, it constitutes a political agenda, aiming to undermine hierarchies and to enhance political and economic equity. That is, I am not trying to simply understand or describe literacy practices in and out of school and their relations with the social order; I am trying to do what I can to transform them. As Erickson (1979) said, I am trying to 'make this canoe better'.

And the canoe certainly needs improvement. Curriculum content is fragmented (Smith, 1986); little time is spent reading and writing (Anderson, Heibert, Scott and Wilkinson, 1985); decisions affecting a student's entire educational career are based on responses to tests of questionable validity (see Chapter 9). Underlying this state of affairs is a 'theory' about literacy prevalent in both folk wisdom and professional knowledge. This conception of literacy has at its center the idea that reading is a complex mechanical process consisting of separable skills (e.g., decoding, word attack, comprehending) internal to the reader and that teaching, testing, or researching even one of these separable skills is part of or sometimes the equivalent of teaching, testing, or researching reading. Closely related is a belief in transfer — that practicing separable skills of reading transfers to (because it is already a subset of) reading. Moreover, enveloping this entire conception is an aura of naturalness: what is typical of practice in teaching, testing, and researching reading is seen as intrinsic. Therefore, except for minor details, it is seen as justifiably unchangeable.

One of the major recent efforts to change conceptions of literacy does not rebut particulars of this theory; instead, it changes the terms altogether, switching the focus from psychological goings-on to social ones. This social theory conceives of literacy as literacies, and argues that rather than being one abstract psychological process, literacies are historically defined social practices. According to social practice scholars (e.g., Bloome, 1987; deCastell and Luke, 1986; Graff, 1987; Scribner and Cole, 1981; Street, 1984; Szwed, 1981), literacy is what it is by virtue of how it is used in social life.

Like all scientific endeavor, these theoretical propositions too seem 'purposeful', either motivated by or serving a political agenda. Graff's (1987) research on the context-dependent consequences of literacy throughout history delegitimizes both the myth that literacy always brings with it social and individual gains and the myth that illiteracy causes ills as varied as poverty and alcoholism. Street (1984) exposes racist undersides to popular theories based on a notion of The Great Divide (the presumed gap between literate and pre-literate societies and between oral and written traditions). Several pieces of work in this literacy-as-social-practice tradition aim to improve literacy education by broadening existing school definitions of literacy (Heath, 1983; Szwed, 1981). All use the term literacy and reading (or writing) interchangeably. In fact, Graff (1987, p. 3) made the equation explicit by defining literacy as 'basic or primary levels of reading and writing'.

With a view that literacy is *any* social practice involving print and with rich descriptions or fresh historical analyses of particular social practices, these researchers provide legitimacy for a general shift toward more inclusiveness in educational practice. But their equations alone could just as well provide a new theoretical rationale for the *status quo* in literacy education. That is, if reading is literacy and literacy (and therefore reading) is anything one does with print, then why not continue to see any use of print in school or in research as a legitimate instance of reading? Why do any more than add to existing school literacy practices? Why eliminate any?

Now the work of some literacy-as-social-practice scholars does not lead to such a conclusion. Luke *et al.* (in press) and Lankshire with Lawler (1987) — to take just two examples — are adamant about looking at literate practices that encourage critical awareness and transformative action as contrasted with those that do not. Not surprisingly, with the exception of case studies in already revolutionary contexts like Nicaragua, their analyses are much more detailed in regard to practices that are mystifying and domesticating. Thus, the proposals for curriculum that grow out of their analyses (e.g., curricula based on discourse critique or 'proper literacy') are intriguing but underdeveloped.

It is a short step from seeing literacy as a social practice to seeing it as *only* a social practice. And, in fact, because interior processes have been 'discredited' as 'psychological' within the literacy-as-social-practice view, this work discourages a serious consideration of the profoundly social nature of interior processes, and, reciprocally, the extent to which underlying processes are implicated in social prac-

interior processes as social in nature.

79

tice. The proposal presented in this chapter about literacy, reading, NOT-reading, exercises, and the position of the reader attempts to account for both process and practice.

The Proposal Elaborated: How It Began

The basic theoretical premise that initially prompted my thinking about literacy as distinct from reading as distinct from reading exercises is that *written language is language*. Taking that premise seriously suggests two major implications. First, if written language is language, then it has the characteristics of language; and second, if written language is language it is learned like language. Thus, like oral language, written language is a system of abstract conventions for making meanings in a context (Halliday, 1985). Like oral language, the 'default' function of written language is informational (Gee, 1989b). Written language, like oral, is socially shared and socially organized. Neither can exist without context (language always occurs someplace at *some* time among *some* ones for *some* reason, Hymes, 1970). Both are reflexive, being created through contexts and themselves creating the contexts in which they are used. Each is necessarily ambiguous (always requiring interpretation, always open to multiple uses and multiple meanings). Each is also predictable (offering cues for meaning) and redundant (offering more than one set of cues).

Like oral language, written language is learned through actual use, not through exercises for later use. An important question, then, is: What is 'use'? Drawing on the research and theories of Goodman (1969), Harste *et al.* (1982), Halliday (1978), Hymes (1972b), Rosenblatt (1985) and Smith (1982b), I believe language use is a sense-making transaction in a context in which particular relationships obtain to people and to text (spoken or written). During the course of a transaction, the language user predicts from systems of cues and with the knowledge she has of those conventionalized cueing systems (phonological — or graphic and orthographic, in the case of written language — syntactic, semantic, and pragmatic) in order to construct meaning (Goodman, 1984; Harste *et al.*, 1982). Because each of these language cueing systems (e.g., the syntactic system) is conventionalized and interacts with other systems which are also conventionalized (e.g., the semantic system), and since conventions necessarily means social conventions, the meaning constructed through these cues — no matter what else it is — is always a *social* construction.

The social conventions are conventions, not guarantees. They entail choice, interpretation, combination. They anticipate violation; there are norms for repairing and norms for violating the norms for repair and so on. This implies that language use also includes a huge potential for individual — but still interpretable, and therefore socially derived — variation (Becker, 1988). Most often, when people use language, they have considerable (if shared) control over how they use it, what they use it for, if they use it, when they stop using it, and so on. In other words, while all language use is socially constrained, it is usually not coerced.

Whenever language is used, it is used in events — events that capture and create relationships among people and between people and objects (material and otherwise) in the culture. What is learned when people learn language includes all those relationships that were part of the events carried out through language use. The language used within those events is usually used for some purpose other than instruction in or evaluation of the language use itself — for informing, persuading, joking, warning, teasing, explaining, cajoling, and so forth. Though language is learned *through* using it, it is not usually used consciously and deliberately *for* learning it. And though language is often used to create impressions and thus enters into evaluations, appraisals, and categorizations people are constantly making as they conduct their daily lives, it is evaluation of the person (her ideas, her status, her origins) that occurs through evaluation of her language use, not evaluation of her language solely for the sake of evaluating the language. What 'use' offers is demonstrations and engagement — demonstrations of how language works and an opportunity to participate with others. What learning through use requires is sensitivity to the demonstrations one is privy to through engagement in the interaction. That sensitivity comes from the taken-for-granted expectations on everyone's part that since the learner belongs to the community of language users, she will *of course* learn the language the other users use (Smith, 1981). No need, then, to elicit language just to see how well she is doing.

I still think such a view of oral language, written language, language learning, and language use is justified, as is my sense (shared with others who talk and write of genuine reading, real writing, real stories, real conversation, and so on) that exercises are very different from use. What has changed is my understanding of the nature of that difference.

My original analysis of that difference was based on examples of print use that seemed obviously artificial and examples that did not, collected from classroom observations, teachers' manuals, research reports, my own experience as a reader, and conversations with colleagues. At first, I tried to find what distinguished these two big categories by using such contrasts as in-school/out-of-school, assigned/ unassigned, official/not official, purposeful/not purposeful. Some of these contrasts were poorly conceived (e.g., nothing has *no* purpose; what matters is *whose* purpose and *what* purpose). Eventually, what I took as central differentiating factors between the two categories of clear examples as well as fuzzier ones were certain features of the reading process.

The Original Proposal — And Why That Was Wrong

As Goodman (1984), Harste, Woodward and Burke (1984), and Smith (1982b) describe it, when people read they predict with interdependent cueing systems in order to create a text meaning for some purpose. It was these features of the reading process — predictability and predicting, cues from interacting cueing systems, meaning construction, and purpose — that I came to believe were the dividing line. The earlier version of this proposal, then, can be summarized as follows: *literacy* was any use of print as print; *reading* was a particular kind of literacy in which a person predicted with cues offered by simultaneously present, interactive, interdependent cueing systems (graphic, orthographic, syntactic, semantic, pragmatic) to construct a text meaning. Reading, in other words, was defined in terms of *process*. By implication, if a person was not engaged in 'the process', if she was not constructing

former definitions for literacy + reading

a text meaning, or if she was not using cues from all systems (because she did not know how or because the graphic display did not offer them), or if the interactivity among systems was severed, what was happening was an act of literacy but not reading. It was something that only looked like reading — a simulation, a masquerade, an exercise, 'reading'. The reason researchers should not be studying and teachers should not be teaching responses to print that did not invoke the reading process (sense-making through the use of cues from all cueing systems interacting appropriately) was that such responses were acts of 'reading' but not reading.

Real reading, reading with no quotes around it, could be mundane (reading one's grocery list) or special (reading a telegram announcing one has won the lottery). It could involve short texts or long; socially acceptable or unacceptable ones (e.g., hold-up notes); it could have single or multiple purposes, be direct or full of innuendos, be well or poorly crafted. What mattered was the creation of meaning through the use of cues from all written language cueing systems interacting 'normally' with each other. Reading one-word texts (like single word bumper stickers or signs on doors) was reading because pragmatic cues would help one predict syntax (e.g., location on a car would signal 'this genre is bumper sticker' which in turn would allow one to rule out that the word on the bumper sticker would be an article or preposition); genre would also help predict semantic cues so that, with graphic and orthographic cues, a reader could guess the bumper sticker presented *Fore* but not *For*, *Tea* but not *The*. A single word flashcard in a lesson, however, could be any part of speech, any meaning that wasn't obscene, blasphemous, or unpatriotic. Decreased predictability due to missing systems (no syntactic cues) was what made a response to a flashcard a reading–exercise and not *reading*. Decoding the graphics of a language one did not understand was not really reading because one was creating no text meaning for oneself (e.g., my oral decoding of the transliterated Hebrew in a prayer book was culturally meaningful and constituted an interpretable text for a Hebrew speaker but was a simulation of reading for me since I knew no Hebrew).

But even when all systems were being used and a text meaning was being created, something could still be only a simulation of reading if the systems were not interacting. The reader's purpose is what could prevent them from interacting. Two purposes had that potential. Either using print just to comply or using it simply to prove proficiency would create distortions or would outright sever the connections among pragmatics and syntax or between pragmatics and semantics. For example, when letters were produced only to be graded but not mailed, normative expectations about genre and audience were violated and *expected* connections (e.g., between one's purpose, the genre, semantic and syntactic choices) were not made.

This earlier proposal distinguishing varieties of activity with print according to whether they constituted reading or merely something that looked like reading was a helpful one. It offered a principled guide for changing classroom literacy instruction. It helped explain why children who spent a school year writing for publication would revert to resistance and finally shoddy production when confronted with a school district-wide writing test at the end of the year (Edelsky and Smith, 1984). It made sense out of the fact that many people who can read adequately for their own purposes do poorly on reading tests. What it said was this:

These are different tasks, different phenemona — reading on the one hand, 'reading' on the other.

I still believe there is a difference between reading exercises and reading, but I no longer believe all exercises can be considered NOT-reading. I also still believe the process of reading can be described and that Goodman, Harste and his colleagues, and Smith have described it best so far. To be reading, a reader must be creating a text meaning for herself (not just for someone else, as in the case of pronouncing print in a foreign language). Thus, though it is rare, there *is* literacy (use of print) without reading (naming letters on an eye chart, pronouncing foreign language print without understanding any of it) and literacy without writing (copying an address in a foreign alphabet without even knowing which marks signal the street and which the city, producing a line of capital S's for handwriting practice in school). But my other defining criteria (lessened predictability, missing systems, lack of connections among systems — leading to all-around phoniness) simply do not hold up.

Using those criteria, too many examples that are clearly exercises or clearly not exercises can not be sorted as exercises versus non-exercises, let alone as instances of reading versus NOT-reading. For example, take all-around phoniness. The sense that something is a 'pragmatic set up' comes from a violation of normative expectations, often regarding genre. The writer of a report is expected to have more information (and report it) than the audience, and the norm is that reported information is to be used for something outside the report. In school reports, however, the norm is violated. The teacher audience is more expert than the writer and reported information is used only as 'data' to be graded. Similarly, the person named in the salutation of the letter is the expected reader of the letter, but in school letters the expected reader is the teacher, not the named addressee. Writing a report or letter for school is thus more often an exercise in writing a report or letter. It is true that these are exercises but not because of their falsity. It is a frequent occurrence in language that events, acts, and texts are not what they seem. Requests can be complaints, questions can be directives. 'Is that a threat or a promise' is a comeback that highlights language's pragmatic ambiguity. In other words, 'phoniness' does not make something an exercise. And straightforwardness (e.g., self-proclaimed workbook exercises) obviously does not prevent something from being an exercise.

The original proposal credited predictability with making the literate act an instance of authentic reading, but there are cases where print is being used with utter predictability yet the activities are clear exercises. It is highly predictable, based on pragmatics and graphics, that the mark to be made after the seventeenth capital T in a handwriting exercise will be another capital T. A youngster who has gone through the set of flashcards often enough can predict the next flashcard in the sequence without any cues from syntax or semantics (Gelb, 1990).

In the earlier proposal, predicting (and predictability) from all interactive cueing systems was necessary for real reading. Reduced predictability resulting from missing cueing systems or disconnections between what should have been interactive cueing systems made that instance of print-use an exercise. In making this claim, the earlier proposal took note of the fact that systems that seemed to be missing actually could be deleted. For instance, lists and other texts of single words were not necessarily texts with missing systems. They were more like performatives with the performative verb deleted; e.g., *I state* is deleted from *it is raining* (Fromkin and Rodman, 1983). Thus, grocery lists managed to offer syntactic cues because the genre signalled but then deleted *buy the following items*. Pragmatic conventions led people to expect only nouns or adjectives on doors of public restrooms — on airplanes, the frame *this facility is* sometimes appeared before the adjective in the slot: *vacant* or *occupied*.

Unlike these cases of deleted systems, there *are* examples in which whole cueing systems are missing, not merely deleted. According to the first proposal, these should be exercises. But they do not always seem to be. For instance, when the 4-year-old holds up a scrap of paper with one word on it (*building*) and says, 'Mom, what's this say?', Mom has no syntactic cues to help her predict. Now it is true that word identification in such a context entails attention to different language phenomena than does word identification in connected prose; and it is true that the meaning the reader creates with that single word (*building*) must remain less narrowed down without confirmation from other systems (is it 'building a house' or 'the building'? what kind of building is it? why was the source of the copied word written in the first place?). Nevertheless, the mother who responds 'It says "building"' is not just *simulating* reading. And when people look at Frank Smith's examples (1982b) of ambiguous print or when they work puzzles for fun or when they read personalized licence plates — all of which deliberately eliminate cueing systems to require 'tricks with print', doing those tricks constitutes a special (tricky) kind of *reading*, not something that isn't reading at all.

The original proposal also classified print use as non-reading if cueing systems were present but did not interact (if purpose did not help someone predict syntax, if genre did not predict semantics, and so on). The original proposal recognized that people could use genres non-normatively. For example, someone could write a thank you note, not to thank, but to make the addressee feel guilty. The writer's syntactic and semantic choices would then be fitted to this purpose as well as to the genre demands. Sincerity — being 'true' to the genre — was, thus, not a requisite for 'really' reading or writing because cueing systems would still be interacting, but in ways that would fit the atypical purpose. It was only when someone had compliance or proving proficiency as her sole purpose that cueing systems failed to interact, according to the original proposal. It is hard to admit it now but the only reason that can account for why I proposed this exception must be that I held a double standard about interactivity. It must have been that I was demanding more obvious interactions between syntax, semantics and a purpose of compliance or evaluation than for syntax, semantics and other purposes. It is apparent to me now, however, that the high school student reading a chapter in the biology textbook only to answer the questions at the end is making her own connections, selectively using graphic, orthographic, syntactic, semantic and pragmatic cues to fit her purpose — spend as little time as possible in order to be finished with the biology reading exercise. If someone can be using all cueing systems interactively when reading a mystery novel from an efferent stance (Rosenblatt, 1978) to learn about a character so she can dress 'accurately' for a costume party, then so can a student who is reading a mystery novel to learn about a character to score well on a test. Just as the cotume party goer's purpose is linked to her use of syntactic and semantic cues, so the student's purpose of proving she is competent to discuss that character is linked to how and what she samples from the cues offered. Rather than cutting off the interactivity among systems, purposes of compliance or proving proficiency (purposes that do not usually go with certain genres or semantic or syntactic choices) do not sever connections among systems; they simply create *non*-normative interactivity. And non-normativity of interactions does not ensure that a literacy activity will be experienced as an exercise.

Nor do apparent distortions in cueing systems. Reading an auto licence plate BRD4GZS (Be ready for Jesus) requires one to allow graphics to contradict semantics in order to overemphasize graphophonics while eliminating orthography — a seeming case of distortion and disconnection. However, all of those overrides and contradictions stem from, serve, and are intensely tied to pragmatic conventions about this particular kind of print and what one does with it. Moreover, after the reader gets the trick, she confirms using the systems interactively that were seemingly eliminated or disconnected. In other words, not only is the reader reading; but the systems are connected after all.

The major reason, then, that the original proposal for what distinguishes reading from reading exercises does not hold up is that in emphasizing one key feature of language (predictability arising from cueing systems), I had forgotten two others: arbitrariness and ambiguity. That is, while 'means condition what can be done with them' (Hymes, 1980b) and while usual questions about language are not about would it *ever* but would it *usually* (be used that way), the fact remains that *given the right circumstances*, any text (and perhaps any language resource) can be used for just about anything. And, of course, if the defining criteria in the original proposal did not stand the test of particular examples, then neither did the single two-part division: authentic reading versus simulations of reading. I had to admit that most exercises (e.g., reading a novel for an exam, writing an essay as part of a college entrance application) could not be dismissed as non-reading or non-writing (Gelb, 1990). What remained, though, was the sense that there were important differences between reading that novel to be entertained and reading it to be examined, between sounding out passages of a foreign language in a ceremony and sounding out nonsense syllables, and that those differences were implicated in whether a person learned to read and, therefore, in whether they would ever be able to use reading as a tool for societal change. `big leap!`

The Current Proposal

The current proposal relies on a conception of reading as both an underlying process and part of a variety of social practices. Process and practice alike have social and psychological dimensions. Neither process nor practice are strictly within or strictly between people. Social practices include beliefs; underlying processes rely on social norms. While that inseparability was noted in the earlier proposal, and while a reliance on normative expectations regarding genres, audiences, purposes, use of particular graphic displays and so on reflected an implicit accounting for social practices, those practices still took a decided back seat. The essence of the earlier proposal, in fact, was that what distinguished reading from all the look-alikes was a difference in underlying process. In general, this new proposal foregrounds social relations and meanings, though underlying processes are salient in one main division and in a part of another.

Three divisions are now necessary: reading/NOT-reading, exercises/non-exercises, and literates-as-Subjects/literates-as-Objects (See Figure 5.1). The earlier process-based distinction between meaning construction and no meaning construction is still useful, even though there are few examples outside of school (more, unfortunately, in school), where *no* text meaning is being constructed. An absence of text meaning is what characterizes NOT-reading. As in the earlier version, purpose is still crucial, but purpose is now seen as an outgrowth of a broader meaning pertaining to events, not just texts: What is this *event* about? And meanings (and therefore purposes) of events are shaped by social relations. These two dimensions working together — event meaning and social relations — distinguish exercises from non-exercises and literate Subjects from literate Objects. If the event is about instruction or evaluation of reading (so that the reader's purpose is to comply with an assignment or to prove competence), those are sufficient grounds to experience that event as an exercise (i.e., it is not necessary to make a further appeal to what is happening to cueing systems). If the event is instigated, ended, shaped, paced, 'topic-alized', assessed, and so on by someone other than the reader — if the relative control is in the hands of another — the event positions the reader as an Object.

This proposal assumes that people are either aware of these dimensions or that they at least orient to them. People using print know whether they are creating meaning for themselves with the print, know what the event is about from their perspective (even if they dispute or dislike what it is about), and know (or are made to know) when they are not in control of certain aspects of the event. If they are 'wrong' (e.g., if students believe they are writing to the President but the teacher has no intention of mailing the letters and will, instead, be evaluating them) it is their perspective that stands during the activity itself, though duplicity in one event will most likely affect how other events are perceived.

Like the earlier version, the present proposal says nothing about length, prestige, involvement with or import of the print use. A person can write a note of a dozen lines or do a writing exercise of dozens of pages, read a poem in the position of either Object or Subject, and write a phone message with no involvement or a classroom essay with intense involvement. Nor does quality of the reading or writing enter into the difference between reading and NOT-reading, exercises and non-exercises, or Subject or Object positions. A person who does not see how the clues led to the villain in the murder mystery is still reading, still reading as a Subject and still doing a non-exercise. A young child stumbling over words or an even younger one using at least some features of the print to reconstruct the story in a well-loved book is reading. Using print cues to make any text meaning is reading (though it may not necessarily be 'good', 'deep', 'sophisticated' reading, according to her community's standards). Nor are the divisions confined to Western technological society. The Hanunoo whittling courtship messages on bamboo

(McDermott, 1977) were writing, not doing a writing exercise; the literate Vai, pronouncing Qu'ranic verses during a religious ceremony in a language they did not understand (Scribner and Cole, 1981), were most likely not engaged in an exercise with no purpose other than instruction or evaluation, but they were not reading either. And doing reading exercises should not be associated only with school just as non-exercises should not be associated only with the out-of-school world. In classrooms where teachers are trying to buck institutional pressures and create whole language environments (see especially Chapters 6, 7, and 8), children read and write with considerable control over their non-exercise activity. But writing a sample movie review, solely to be evaluated on one's ability to write movie reviews as part of applying for a job as movie critic, is an exercise.

Figure 5.2 fills out the schematic of Figure 5.1. Some of the examples in Figure 5.2 and their placement will be referred to in the discussion of social relations, meaning of the event, and fuzzy examples.

Social Relations

The social relations among participants in an event may not highlight control (e.g., empathy, affection, or reciprocity may be more salient). And in terms of the meanings constructed (the semantic and syntactic interpretations about what these words mean in this combination, the pragmatic interpretations about what this text is doing here), control is not the only consideration. As Gilbert (in press) has argued, readers are positioned historically to construct gendered, raced, classed, ethnicitied, cultured, aged, able-bodied meanings, not just meanings reflecting their relational position in the literacy event itself. Still, control does matter (and, indeed, it is implicated in those dominance related constructions of meaning). If the print user is being controlled in her print use — if someone else decides what literacy event will occur, how it will begin, what it will be about, when it will end, and so on, then the print user is positioned as an Object. Being a literate Subject or Object is part of different literate discourses entailing attitudes, values, beliefs, and activities (Gee, 1989c).

It is not control over any single aspect of an event, such as who initiates the reading or writing, that renders someone a Subject or an Object. In Hudson's (1988) study, for instance, teacher initiation of writing resulted in children feeling powerless in some assignments but in charge in others. More likely, it is control over some combination of aspects of the event. Moreover, control over literacy is a peculiar continuum; i.e., both ends (total control and total freedom) are impossible. While there are social conventions — and therefore constraints — for every minute aspect of language, the conventions are not handcuffs. People are agents in their own language use, giving their languaging a hugely personal character (Becker, 1988, p. 31). Yet neither can people have total freedom in print use since, through following, violating, or modifying conventions that are social, the social is always a part. In other words, people's experiences, including their language experiences, 'can never be entirely their own' (Barone, 1990).

Nor does an overall hierarchical relationship between the parties guarantee

Figure 5.2   Some Examples of Distinctions within Print-use

		Literacy	
		NOT-Reading	Reading
Exercise	O B J E	Letter-naming, flashcard lesson; nonsense syllables, experiment; ?self-initiated calligraphy practice	take reading test; read essay to answer questions; fill in worksheet to be checked off; write essay for application; read word on flashcard; do puzzles/tricks with print on worksheets as a lesson; ?tricks with print for prizes; ?Freire's pedagogy
Not an Exercise	C T	eye chart; ?pronouncing foreign language print in rituals; ?copying address in foreign alphabet	parent orders child to write thank-you note; ?tricks with print for prizes; ?Freire's pedagogy
Exercise	S U B	?self-initiated calligraphy practice	worksheets in 'open classroom'; writing trial movie review to try out for job as movie critic; practicing writing 'purpose' statements in grant-writing seminar; ?Freire's pedagogy
Not an Exercise	J E C T	doodling decorative letters ?pronouncing foreign language print in rituals; ?copying address in foreign alphabet	reading essay to be entertained; writing movie review for publication *and* to try out for job; reading word in response to 'Mom, what's that say?'; drafting purpose statement for grant proposal; reading known language in rituals; ?Freire's pedagogy

that the subordinate person will read or write in Object position in a particular literacy event. (Of course, following from the impossibility of being totally constrained or totally free, there can be neither 'a compleat Object' nor a total Subject. While overall differentials in power will not mechanically determine which gross position a reader or writer is in during a specific event, they will impinge on the Subject-ness or Object-ness that is created.) Thus, a mid-level manager can write a

Subject / object example

report for a Chief Executive Officer and have considerable control over the writing. So can a writer writing a letter of apology, feeling decidedly one-down in the relationship and wanting desperately to appease by meeting the expectations of a perhaps controlling significant Other. Whether the other participants are physically present is not what determines who controls the event. Test takers can be in a room all by themselves, but an absent test writer and absent policy makers have great control over the reading that takes place during that test-taking. 'Social relations', then, means the particular relations among participants as they are played out concerning the reading or writing in a literacy event. While the broad outline of what those particulars might be can be sketched out, the specifics probably can only be identified after the fact.

Social relations that position the print user as Object may also mean the relationship between the reader and the print — the way in which the print itself and its use controls the reader. Certain genres like transliterations of foreign alphabets, charts of randomized letters, and tricks with print (puzzles, clever licence tags, nonsense syllables for experiments that announce 'let's see what you can do with *this*)', exert excessive control. To be used successfully, they must be used perfectly rather than plausibly. They have a combination of 'controlling devices'. If they elicit NOT-reading, they omit whole systems of cues and also do not permit the meaning-making that could help the print user confirm her response. With eye charts, handwriting practice, nonsense syllables in an experiment or on a worksheet, or transliterations of foreign language syllables, there is no way, using one's own knowledge of language conventions, to know if one 'got it right'. If the print *can* be read (i.e., given a text meaning), something about it controls how and when the reader confirms predictions. For example, instead of confirming periodically (constantly?), the licence tag reader suspends confirmation of all but the graphic system (and sometimes, when numbers are used for words — e.g., *2* for *to* — that too must wait) until she 'gets the trick' and the event is over. Not only does such print sometimes omit systems, but it is stingy with cues from the systems it does provide. Yet it allows the reader no leeway. The puzzle reader (Scrabble player, five-letter-word game player) and the reader of some worksheets and test items must supply more than her share of the orthographic or syntactic or semantic cues and then, to add insult to injury, must produce a perfect response. In other words, when the relations between print-user and print help create the literate as Object, those relations also distort the underlying process. *CBC exam*

Print use outside of school is usually like 'normal' language use in terms of control over the reading in the event; it positions people as Subjects. But not always. There are out-of-school examples in which the participants (or the print) make the reader an Object. Ordering a child to write a thank you letter to a grandparent, making sure she begins, overseeing her production, and telling her when she can be finished is a case of the writer-as-Object. Print use as part of the curriculum in school, creating literates-as-Objects, is often *not* like language use. But it could be. Literature study sessions (K. Smith, 1990; Edelsky *et al.*, 1991) in which children turn to the novel they have been reading as they initiate topics, ask questions of each other and the teacher, and establish the topic of next meetings, are events in which students are literate Subjects.

Meaning/Purpose of the Literacy Event

When print is used for the purpose of being instructed in or evaluated on print-using ability, it is an exercise. This includes print produced or responded to for scoring or categorizing by researchers. Since people not only give messages through language but also give off messages (Goffman, 1959), evaluation of language use is a ubiquitous feature of interaction. However, evaluating or being evaluated on language using ability is usually not a person's purpose for participating in an event in the first place. When it *is* the purpose, the meaning of the event is evaluation, and print-use by the one evaluated constitutes an exercise. Exercises may, ultimately, have very 'real-world' purposes. For example, many function as gatekeepers, giving or denying people access to jobs — a real-world purpose indeed! But though exercises may subsequently serve to gatekeep or to diagnose, their first purpose is to evaluate print-use *for the sake of evaluating the print-use*, or to provide instruction in print-use *for the sake of instructing in print-use*.

Bloome and Bailey (1990) maintain that all activity in school comes into being for the purpose of instruction, that nothing can be 'authentic', not even a vocational education project like building a house which someone will live in. However, I believe some projects (like building a house or publishing a newsletter or organizing a science fair or lobbying for better playground facilities) have the potential to override their instructional *raison d'être* so that other purposes can be foregrounded. If students take on any big project with multiple embedded tasks in such a way that learning is subordinated to production (which Minick, 1985, says is one characteristic of apprenticeships), then the embedded tasks at least, if not the big project, are no longer exercises. For instance, in the case of producing a newsletter, though the 'because motive' (what instigated the whole enterprise) might be instruction, the 'in order to motive' (the hoped-for outcome) of some of the embedded tasks (Schutz, 1962) can become more tied to producing the newsletter. Instruction in writing headlines, then, would not be instruction for the sake of instruction but instruction for the sake of the newsletter. The 'lesson' here is that school tasks do not *have* to be academic (i.e., instruction- or evaluation-focused exercises).

Two special conditions for some exercises should be mentioned. One set is that of a person voluntarily and deliberately seeking out instruction or practice in order to learn or to improve performance (e.g., self-initiating calligraphy practice or willingly practicing writing headlines for the class newsletter). Such practice, while an exercise, could be helpful if the reader or writer clearly sees herself using what is practiced in the near future. There is also a conflux of conditions that is especially detrimental. When exercises elicit NOT-reading or when they require someone to read by doing tricks with print and to be positioned as an Object, they deliver a triple whammy. They violate all the usual conditions of language and language learning through use (making meaning, having some purpose other than instruction or evaluation, having relative control). No wonder people *feel* the discrepancy between reading a tortured test item and reading a letter from a friend. No wonder children in remedial classes, deprived of chances to read as Subjects for some purpose other than getting a reading lesson, remain poor readers.

The exercise/non-exercise distinction may seem like it might duplicate the

Subject/Object distinction. But actually the two dimensions can be separated, if with some difficulty. It is possible to find examples where someone is doing an exercise but still has considerable control over the event and the activity, as Figure 5.2 shows. The reverse — not doing an exercise but still being positioned as an Object (i.e., having one's reading controlled by peculiar print or by another person) — is more difficult to find. Probably, this is because relations among participants and meaning/purpose of the event interact. That interaction can be seen most clearly when considering the role of the person who responds to the writing or to a sign of the reading. (In speech, the contrasting roles of the other party are seen in the difference between receiving 'thanks' after telling someone what time it is versus receiving 'good answer'.) The other person in a literacy event might accept the written apology, try out the written recipe, read the book a reader just praised, and so on. When the other participates in these ways as a co-literate, the reader or writer can become active in the post-event event (e.g., restating the written apology, asking for a recipe in return, checking the respondent's responses to the recommended novel). However, when the other's role is simply to evaluate the print use, the print user is out of the picture at the end. And, of course, when the other person's purpose is to evaluate the reading and the reader accepts that purpose because she only read in the first place in order to have the reading evaluated, the reading is an exercise.

Instruction for instruction's sake (the other meaning/purpose that defines exercises) also interacts with social relations. Instruction in language can be an 'exercise' in control in at least two ways. It can be an imposition. And it can be a cover for instruction in comportment — for exacting obedience (so that the writer's purpose is to comply — with being instructed).

Fuzzy Examples and What They Reveal

There are several examples preceded by a question mark that appear in more than one category in Figure 5.2. Categorizing something as reading or NOT-reading — as making a text meaning or not — was not a problem. Nor was deciding whether examples of NOT-reading were exercises (literates respond to eye charts for evaluation, but for evaluation of their ability to *see* the letters, not to name them). The double categorized items in the left-hand column, the NOT-reading category, are double categorized because I am unsure of the designation of Subject versus Object. And even here, there was little problem, typically, in deciding whether the task was being closely shaped by another participant. For example, one is an Object when responding to the eye chart when applying for a drivers licence.

The problem comes in considering events in which the literate person has reasonable control over the event in relation to other parties but is held on a short leash by the print. For example, the member of the congregation who joins with others to pronounce foreign language syllables in a prespecified ritual is collaborating with other participants in order to make the event 'go right', but is being tightly constrained by minimal cues from the print, absence of opportunities for any confirming triangulation from other cueing systems, and little latitude for interpretation. The 8-year-old self-initiating practice in cursive script has a similar problem. These conditions do constitute a short leash, but there are circumstances which could offset this bind. The examples with question marks all include voluntary participation, ignorance of the quality of one's own performance, and no evaluative consequences for poor performance, (though there may be penalties — e.g., a poor copying job in a foreign alphabet could well result in non-delivery of the letter). These conditions cast some doubt on whether these examples should be considered 'positioning the literate as an Object'. The questioned examples do not seem nearly as constraining for the print user as do tricks with print (scrambled letter games, puzzles, etc.).

One set of questionable examples in the right-hand column involves tricks with print. This time, the question is: Should these be considered exercises or not? When the trick reading is done for prizes or points (e.g., on quiz shows) and not just for 'fun', does the activity become an exercise? That is, is it right to extend the idea of gatekeeping to this case where a judge on a television show evaluates a contestant's response and grants or denies the prize? Is the quiz show event about proving proficiency?

The other set of repeated entries are the most interesting: peasants reading in Freire's circles of culture. In Freire's pedagogy, nonliterates voluntarily seek out instruction in learning to read. Their questions and comments shape the discussions in meetings (classes). But the larger topic is controlled by a sequence of pictures and a set of conclusions the coordinator (deliberately not called 'teacher') leads people to. (Two of these conclusions are: Some things are natural while others are cultural; people can make culture, but animals cannot). At the same time, the coordinator is trained to refrain from setting up hierarchical relationships that discourage dialogue among equals (C. Brown, 1987). Are the peasants positioned as Subjects or Objects or both? And are they doing exercises or not? They seek out activity for being instructed in literacy and so, even if the exercises are beneficial because the seekers see themselves as using the instruction immediately, they are exercises. But perhaps the instruction in print use is not for instruction's sake. That is, Freire's pedagogy is about conscientization, becoming conscious of constraints and taking action to transform situations. Do the learners know this purpose at the start? Does that purpose enter into the peasants' purposes in a given lesson? Moreover, while it is difficult to imagine Freirian coordinators saying 'good' in response to a correct decoding of a word, it is easy to imagine more subtle evaluation such as repeating the student's response immediately in the ongoing dialogue for liberation. Nevertheless, the evaluation (if it occurs) would not be for gatekeeping or diagnosing and would not, in any case, be the reason for eliciting the reading in the first place. Yet at least some of the reading in the culture circles certainly takes place for the purpose of instruction in reading. Are the peasants doing exercises in reading at that moment or are they reading for some communicative purpose?

The difficulty in categorizing some instances of print use according to these dimensions (meaning making — for reading versus NOT-reading; purpose — for exercise versus non-exercise; position — for Subject versus Object) reflects the nature of conceptual categories and conceptual dimensions generally. That is, categories in any scheme have prototypical and also fuzzy members; boundaries between categories are usually fuzzy (e.g., when is a chair a stool?); and the defining features of any conceptual scheme are not self-evident (e.g., just what counts as evaluation?). Difficulty in categorizing some instances also puts this entire proposal into perspective. Since it was formulated for politico-educational purposes, its three dimensions are more pertinent to literacy in educational practice (classroom life, educational policy, educational research, educational publishing, and so on) than to literacy in other domains. And while this proposal reveals some important features of these dimensions, the difficult-to-categorize examples show that it hides other features because it makes only one gross division within each dimension — that of yes or no.

Then What Good Is It?

Despite its limitations, this new proposal is an improvement and can also be a guide. The earlier version, while helpful because it too was an attempt to point out and then analyze a major distinction, was too easy to discount. After all, it is hard to tell a student she has not really *written* that friendly letter for her English class even though she recognizes that writing the letter to her friend who just moved felt very different.

More important than how this proposal compares to the first one, however, is how it can improve current educational practice. With its three dimensions, it cautions against two traps: the myth of total generalizability — that *any* use of print is reading; and the myth of total particularism — that *no* print use is comparable to any other. The former (that there are no important differences) leads to mistakes like believing an experiment on responding to nonsense syllables is an experiment about reading. The latter (there are no important similarities) provides no direction for anyone interested in connecting literacy education to projects of social transformation.

On *reading process grounds*, this current proposal steers one away from mistakenly substituting one phenomenon for another. That is, the reason some print use should not be taught, tested or researched if one is interested in teaching, testing, or researching reading is that, either the print user is not creating a text meaning at all or the print user is being positioned as an Object by the print (prevented from confirming predictions appropriately, forced to give too much to the transaction). In each case, basic characteristics of the reading process are either absent or distorted. *And on social relationship grounds*, this proposal also makes a case for not equating some phenomena but for at least considering the commonalities among others.

A good reason, according to this proposal, for avoiding reading exercises generally is this: since they are initiated for the purpose of instruction or evaluation of reading, exercises are unlike the purposes for which people generally use language. Two good reasons for avoiding the position of literate-person-as-Object are, first, that position is unlike the one learners are usually in as they learn language, a position in which, even in 'sit down and shut up' situations (Sulzby, 1990), learners control much of their own talking and even more of their listening. And, even more crucial, to use print for examining and critiquing taken-for-granted conditions in one's own life within one's own society requires the position of the literate-as-Subject. This proposal also highlights a major question for research: just how do the social relations of literacy events and the features of the reading process impinge on each other.

The major benefit of the proposal, however, is that it raises the most critical question of all — a question of value. Just what is it a student, a researcher, a literacy educator, a community wants? Print use with no meaning-making? Exercises in reading? Reading for submission? Because it assumes that the practices people participate in are the ones they acquire, the proposal promotes the question: what *should* those school and research practices be? And, therefore, what *should* be acquired? (Axiomatically, it discourages worrying about whether certain practices transfer to or predict others.) It is long past time for adopting a new metanarrative — one that says, among its major uses, literacy *should* be for learning how knowledge and interpretations are constructed, for challenging inequities, and for repairing a society that works only for the few. Recognizing the differences between reading and NOT-reading, exercises and non-exercises, and literate Subjects and literate Objects is central to this metanarrative.

Notes

1 I owe the shifts in my thinking about this topic to conversations with Steve Gelb, some nudges from Larry Friedman and Allan Luke, and the influence of writings by Dell Hymes. They may well contest what I've done with their views, but I remain grateful to them.

2 I am confining this discussion to print literacy and not extending it to familiarity with all codes for cultural information (e.g., musical literacy, computer literacy, etc.) for two reasons. First, print literacy is what people mean when they refer to literacy problems (*Why Johnny Can't Read* is not a treatise on computer use); and second, as Halliday (1990) says, if literacy is extended to all interpretions of any codes, we would have to come up with another term for what we do with print.

3 A pervasive problem in writing this chapter is the absence of an easy-to-understand, short label for what I am calling NOT-reading (repeating 'use of print with no aim of creating a meaningful text' is clear but cumbersome). The absence of such a label is part of a more general phenomenon: there are few folk terms for different reading activities; far more for different speaking activities. Ask people what they are doing when talking and they might say: talking, just talking, conversing, gossiping, joking, lecturing, debating, arguing, holding forth, chatting, shooting the breeze, interviewing, confessing, conferring, consulting, rapping, reporting, etc., etc. Ask them the same question regarding writing and the possible list grows shorter: writing, just writing, jotting, scribbling, doodling, transcribing, (in school, I've heard journalling and composing; among researchers, I've heard memoing), filling out a form, taking notes ('dashing off' is about manner rather than type of activity). When it comes to reading, the choices are also few: reading, just reading, studying, scanning, skimming, perusing, speed reading. The list can be lengthened with objects: telling a story, telling a joke, giving a sermon (which is different from sermonizing, a comment on manner); writing a letter, book, note, message; reading a letter, book, note, message. The shorter lists for reading and writing probably reflect a folk theory: reading and writing are relatively undifferentiated, though the objects connected with the activity are varied. It is precisely this folk theory I counter with the present proposal.

4 Minick (1985) identifies three kinds of theories about human functioning. Isolating theories assume an individual whose 'psychological characteristics can be defined in isolation from the

concrete characteristics of the external world' (p. 18). Contextual theories attribute psychological characteristics to the individual but maintain that these characteristics cannot be understood in isolation from the tasks or contexts in which they are manifested. Activity theories, on the other hand, presume that the individual has *no* psychological characteristics in isolation from actions which are themselves part of larger action systems constituting the social system in which the individual finds herself.

Chapter 6

Whole Language: What's New?

with Bess Altwerger and Barbara Flores

More and more educators are warming to a new idea in education — Whole Language. Those of us who want to see fundamental change in schools — the kind of change that improves all children's educational chances, the kind that does more than simply offer a traditional curriculum in two languages rather than one, the kind that resists centralized control over teachers, that resists practices that perpetuate societal inequities, that democratizes classrooms and encourages pluralism — are, in turn, gratified by this increased popularity for a pedagogy with just those intents. But the gratification is tinged with worry, because, as often as not, the same statements and activities that support Whole Language reveal outright confusions about it. So while we are delighted with the increasing popularity, we wonder what it is that is popular: The idea of Whole Language? The label? Innovation *per se*?

Educational innovations have not fared well in the United States. Open Education was a recent casualty. It was widely distorted so that open space was substituted for openness of ideas, learning centers for learning-centeredness. The final irony is that it was judged a failure even though (because of the distortions) it was never implemented on any broad scale (a few exceptions still exist — e.g., Prospect School in Vermont, Central Park East in New York City, and scattered classrooms elsewhere).

Whole Language is too good an idea to suffer such a fate. It has the potential not only to change educational histories of a token few who might otherwise have failed in school, but to change the terms of educational discourse itself — to change what is meant by 'literacy', 'achievement', 'educated', 'evaluation', and so on. That potential cannot be realized, however, if the complex meanings of Whole Language are reduced to nothing more than teacher behaviors or sets of materials or classroom activities. Widespread understanding of the substance of Whole Language, rather than widespread adoption of the label, might be one way to prevent this possibility. Some recent writings have responded to both the popularity of the label and the need for describing the substance. In addition to earlier writings by Newman (1985) and Goodman (1986), at least one major journal has devoted an entire issue to Whole Language (*Elementary School Journal*, 1990, **90**, 2). And professional organizations such as The International Reading Association and The National Council of Teachers of English have plans for publishing collections devoted to Whole Language. Still, the same misunderstandings are displayed again and again. This chapter addresses some of the phenomena that are most frequently confused with Whole Language. But first a brief description.

Whole Language: What Is It?

First and foremost, Whole Language is *not* merely practice. It is a set of beliefs, a perspective, a *theory*-in-practice. It must become practice (i.e., it must turn into ways of handling error, interactional choices, instructional behavior, materials, curricula, schedules, etc.), but it is not the instructional behavior, the materials, the curricular choices themselves. Because Whole Language depends on a perspective held by the teacher, it cannot be mandated by an administrator or a school district. Districts can insist teachers have children write in journals or that they publish books written by children or conduct literature studies or thematic science units and so forth but these are not what makes a classroom 'whole language'. Rather, these practices become Whole Language-like because the teacher has particular beliefs.

What are those beliefs? A critical one is that systemic social inequality is undesirable and that education must work to end rather than to perpetuate a stratified society. Much educational activity (e.g., that which goes into testing and tracking) contributes to stratification, as discussed in Chapter 11. Whole Language opposes that activity as well as the language and language learning 'theory' and THEORY that support it (see Chapter 4).

A Whole Language view of language includes the following ideas: (a) language is for making meanings, for accomplishing purposes; (b) written language is language — thus what is true for language in general is true for written language; (c) the cueing systems of language (phonology in oral, orthography in written language, morphology, syntax, semantics, pragmatics) are interactive and interdependent; (d) language has the potential for multiple interpretations because language use always occurs in a situation; (e) situations (both small, local face-to-face situations and larger ones that concern what is happening culturally and historically) are critical for making sense of and with language (that includes the language of face-to-face interactions, the language of informal texts like jotted down phone messages, the language of large official texts like district curricula, the language of aesthetic forms like poems, and so on). Since language in use has at least these features, anyone using language (a baby, an adult, a second language learner) is demonstrating all these features (i.e., they are using the embedded situations as well as cues from language subsystems in order to make meaning to accomplish one or more purposes).

Whole Language beliefs about language acquisition center on a key theoretical premise: the world over, babies acquire a language through actually using it, not through practicing its separate parts or practicing with only one or two systems until some later date when the parts are assembled or the system is reintegrated and the totality is finally used. Whole Language also views language acquisition (both oral and written) as natural — not in the sense of innate or inevitably unfolding, but natural in the sense that when language (oral or written) is an integral part of the functioning of a community and is used around and with neophytes, it is learned 'incidentally' to what else is learned (Ferreiro and Teberosky, 1982; Lindfors, 1987).

These two sets of beliefs have two major implications for thinking about instruction in literacy as well as other school 'subjects'. First, if language is acquired through use, and if written language is language, then written language too is learned through use, not through practice exercises. And second, if language is a tool for making sense of something else, then the 'something elses' must have prominence in the curriculum.

These implications in turn lead to certain likely practices. For example, an overriding consideration regarding classroom reading and writing is that these not be *exercises* in reading and writing (see Chapter 5, for the distinction between reading and reading exercises). Thus teachers with a Whole Language perspective take great care to provide both print and assignments that at least have the potential to elicit actual reading and writing. They create a print-rich environment that demands use of that print for something beyond instruction and evaluation. They eschew materials written specifically to teach reading or writing. Instead, Whole Language teachers rely heavily on literature, on other print used for appropriate purposes (e.g., cake mix directions used for actually making a cake rather than for finding short vowels), and on writing for varied purposes. Social studies and science topics receive a big chunk of the school day, providing contexts for much of the reading and writing. Assessment is focused on constant kidwatching (Y. Goodman, 1985) and on documenting growth in children's actual work rather than on comparing scores on work-substitutes.

Whole Language is thus a perspective on language and language acquisition with classroom implications extending far beyond literacy. Many descriptions of Whole Language appear in the literature (e.g., Edelsky, 1986b; Edelsky, Altwerger and Flores, 1991; Edelsky, Draper and Smith, 1983; Goodman, 1986; Goodman and Goodman, 1981; Harste, 1989; Newman, 1985). Nevertheless, as we have indicated, Whole Language is frequently misunderstood.

Common Misunderstandings About Whole Language

The following are some frequent confusions about Whole Language:

1   Whole Language is thought to be another term for the whole word approach;
2   Whole Language is seen as another way of 'teaching skills in context' or of 'integrating skills' with an emphasis on comprehension skills;
3   Whole Language is presumed to be a method or set of methods;
4   Whole Language is heard as a new term for the Language Experience Approach;
5   Whole Language is considered to be an updated term for the Open Classroom of two decades ago;
6   Whole Language is thought to be interchangeable with Writing Process.

Sometimes, these confusions appear as genuine questions ('isn't Whole Language just a new way of describing "skills in context"?'). Often they are offered as fact ('Whole Language and Language Experience Approach are the same thing'). These typical confusions will be presented below as questions, but whether question or statement, they are all reasonable. That is, the misunderstandings have a foundation in current practice, recent history, or prevailing beliefs. Therefore, we will first present what is sensible about the faulty equation before presenting the Whole Language position.

Is Whole Language a New Term for the Whole Word Approach?

It Could Be ...

Equating Whole Language with whole word may stem from a conception of reading as a matter of 'getting the words'. *The Great Debate* (Chall, 1967) was presented and continues to be thought of as a debate between two distinctly different conceptions of reading — look/say and phonics. Actually, the two are simply variations on a single theme — a phonics approach to 'getting the words' and a look-say or whole word approach to 'getting the words'. Each has strong roots in behaviorism (i.e., getting the words means *saying* the words, making a verbal response to visual stimuli).

Conventional wisdom and school paraphernalia, as well as a long history of viewing reading as word-getting (Monaghan and Saul, 1987), support the notion that reading is 'getting the words', indeed that language development amounts to knowing words. Vocabulary exercises and vocabulary tests are an important part of many language arts series and of reading instruction and assessment programs. Moreover, vocabulary is one means of social class gatekeeping. Much, then, in the general and school culture supports the idea that reading amounts to 'getting the words' and that there are only two basic ways to 'get words'. It is reasonable to assume that Whole Language might be one of them.

But It Isn't

The Whole Language view of reading is not one of getting words but of constructing meaning for a text in a situation (see the development of this view in the writings of K. Goodman, Gollasch, 1982). Word boundaries and lexical features are indeed used as cues, but meaning is created with many other cues too — syntax, semantics, and pragmatics (including the reader's purpose, the setting, what the reader knows about the author's purpose). To believe that reading means getting words assumes that words have constant meanings; yet words like *Mary*, *lamb*, *had*, and *little* in the following examples derive meaning from the clauses which follow them.

1   Mary had a little lamb.
    Its fleece was white as snow.

2   Mary had a little lamb.
    She spilled mint jelly on her dress.
3   Mary had a little lamb.
    It was such a difficult delivery the vet needed a drink.
    (Example adapted from Trabasso, 1981; also in Edelsky *et al.*, 1991)

The varied meanings of *Mary*, *had*, *little*, and *lamb* provide evidence that as we read, we create tentative texts, assigning tentative within-text word meanings which must often be revised based on later cues.

A belief in reading as getting and *saying* the word implies that we have to know a word orally in order to read it (get its meaning). In fact, we learn words through reading just as we learn them through conversing. (How many of us learned words like *Penelope* and *orgy* through print and were later surprised to discover they did not rhyme with *antelope* and *morgue-y*?) A vocabulary item is not part of a list of words in one's brain but a set of potentials (e.g., meaning potentials, word class information, morphological possibilities, possible metaphorical usages) related to other sets of potentials, embedded in a variety of schemas for social life. It is the set, the range, and the schema-type storage that permit us to relate the two lines in examples 1, 2, and 3 so that we create different meanings with them.

A belief that reading means getting words also assumes that word meanings, once 'gotten', are added up to produce a text meaning. In fact, the whole far exceeds the sum of the parts. Print provides a text potential (Harste, Woodward and Burke, 1984; Rosenblatt, 1978; 1985). When we read, we turn that potential into an actual instance, creating details of meaning that must be inferred from but do not appear in the printed cues. The meaning, that is, can *never* be *in* the print — not *in* printed words, not *in* whole printed texts. Rather, we create meanings for texts-in-situations. Whole Language focuses on those texts-in-situations and on how people create meaningful texts by filling in. A whole word approach, by contrast, has a completely different focus, is based on a completely different conception of reading, and entertains faulty premises concerning words and word meanings.

Is Whole Language Another Term for Teaching Skills in Context?

It Could Be ...

A popular view of language use (oral and written) is that it consists of isolatable skills (e.g., decoding skills, pronunciation skills, comprehension skills of finding the main idea, using details), separately learnable and separately teachable (DeFord, 1985; Harste and Burke, 1977). This is part of a more general assumption: If it is possible to identify subskills or to name subactivities in the proficient performance of any complex activity, then those subactivities should be taught separately. And this assumption is, in turn, part of a widespread instrumental mindset that construes modern life in terms of skills (Gibson, 1986). Thus tests of separate skills and a fundamental skills outlook invade education to such an extent that the idea of separate skills remains a given for most people.

A similarly 'small parts' viewpoint is common regarding context. Context is often seen as a background 'part', rarely as the crucial medium for language use. Even less frequently is it seen as being inevitably and reflexively created by language use (see Chapter 2 for examples of how development occurs *through* rather than *in* contexts). Sometimes context is reduced to meaning merely the verbal setting (e.g., the story as background for the sentence, the sentence as background for the word). Such small parts conceptions of comprehension and context could be readily applied to a new idea like Whole Language. After all, Whole Language does emphasize comprehension (though not as one of many subskills), and it does emphasize context (though not as background). Moreover, sometimes Whole Language teachers *do* point out features of language as they are being used, which *could* look like 'teaching skills'.

Other sources add to the confusion. Beginning Whole Language educators, who do not yet know new ways of talking about their changing views, provide more grist for the skills-in-context mill. So do thoroughly Whole Language teachers who use the term 'skills in context' as a survival strategy. When they work in districts that permit only skills instruction, describing their practice to administrators in terms of skills may be the only way for them to be permitted to teach according to their Whole Language beliefs. Thus, people have much evidence from the talk of others as well as from their own viewpoints regarding what constitutes written language and what is meant by *context* for believing Whole Language is simply teaching skills in context with an emphasis on comprehension skills.

But It Isn't

Unlike the 'teaching skills in context' view that construes reading and writing as separable skills, the Whole Language view is that reading and writing are whole activities. According to a Whole Language perspective, any separate skill or subactivity performed outside the total act of reading functions differently from the way that subactivity works when it is part of the total activity. In other words, the 'skill' of decoding for decoding's sake (as on a worksheet or a test) is a different activity than decoding during the larger activity of reading for some other purpose. It is not only a different activity in Leont'ev's sense (Minnick, 1985); it is a different practice that 'positions the reader' (Baker and Luke 1989, in press) as active Subject in the one case, as passive Object in the other.

Moreover, the subactivity is not merely the behavior. It plays a role in the total activity; it interacts with other subactivities; it engenders consequences, and it does all this through a context. If the role, interactions, and consequences are taken away, what is left is only the behavior — meaningless in itself. It would be as if separate pedaling, handlebar holding, steering, and brake-applying did not need to be integrated, as if they could simply be added together to produce bike riding. The aim of a skills-in-context approach to bike riding would be to ensure pedalling skill or steering skill. In a Whole Language approach to bike riding, however, the aim would be bike riding. The emphasis would be on the entire activity — which could not occur in the first place without a context.

In written language use, cues from one system have an effect on cues from the other systems. Thus syntax influences phonology, permitting a reduced vowel when *can* is part of a verb (*the garbage /kən/ go over there*) but not when it is a noun (*the garbage /kæn/ is over there*). Syntax influences graphophonics so that the unit *initial th+vowel* is voiced for function words (*this, their*) but voiceless in content words (*thing, thistle*). Semantics controls syntactic parsing in such sentences as *flying planes can be dangerous*. Pragmatics is what permits variation in orthography (*lite/ light/; through/thru*).

It should be noted that the direction of influence is from high to low: information from the higher system is required in order to make a decision about the lower. This is just the opposite of the basic skills hierarchy which begins at the supposed beginning — the smaller units and lower levels.

Because language cueing systems influence each other, subactivities or skills employed during actual language use are interconnected. We cannot learn what readers do by looking at how they perform the 'skills' without those necessary interconnections. A major Whole Language goal is to help children use, not sever, these interrelationships among cueing systems. The means for achieving that goal is to engage children with authentic texts (versus textoids — material written solely for instruction or evaluation of reading [Hunt, 1989]) in the total activity of reading and writing. When Whole Language teachers point out and teach language skills as a child needs them during actual language use, the instruction is not for instruction's sake — not just so that the child will learn the skill — but for helping the child achieve whatever purpose the language is intended for (getting permission from the principal, entertaining her classmates, informing another class, persuading the City Council, etc.). A Whole Language framework insists that we become 'skilled language users', not that we 'learn language skills'. Altwerger and Resta (1986) have shown that many proficient readers cannot do skills exercises, while many poor readers can. That is, the activity of performing divisible subskills may have little or no relation to the indivisible activity we call reading. It is the latter activity that interests Whole Language educators.

Is Whole Language a Method? A Program? A 'Slant' for Basals or Other Packaged Programs?

It Could Be ...

To many people, method (and all the material accessories of method — textbooks, kits, boxed materials, 'consumables', and so forth) — and skills in using various methods are what constitutes professional expertise. In this view, the only thing interesting in education — indeed what teaching is all about — is method. Colleges of education in the US contribute to this idea. Separating theory from method and positioning the methods courses right before student teaching, much professional education gives the message that 'at last, with methods and the press of 'real classroom demands', we're finally getting down to business'. The business', of course, is the how-to-do-it, the surface behavior.

Erroneous information from authoritative sources further legitimizes the assumption that the essence of teaching is surface behaviors. Documents such as

State Reading Guides describe Whole Language as 'one of many methods'. Publishers of instructional materials advertise Whole Language basals and Whole Language phonics programs. To top it off, many educators claim to be and in fact want to be eclectic. Believing that all is method, they categorize Whole Language too as a method to add to all the other methods in their repertoire. Link a preference for eclecticism to errors in education documents, to advertising pitches from publishers, and to the general idea purveyed in professional training that teaching is a matter of skill with a grab bag of methods (instrumental rationality again), and it is easy to see how Whole Language comes to be (mis)understood as a method.

But It Isn't

Whole Language is first of all a lens for viewing, a framework that insists that belief shapes practice. Equating it with a method is an error in level of abstraction. Each of the following is an example of one of many methods: writing chart stories with children, conducting spelling drills, holding writers' workshops. None of these are underlying viewpoints. The following are theoretical viewpoints: Skills and Whole Language. Neither of these is a method.

Frameworks:	Whole Language	Skills
Methods:	journals literature study writers' workshop	journals basal reading groups phonics exercises

Moreover, there are no essential component practices for a Whole Language viewpoint. Some practices are easily made congruent and are therefore typical in Whole Language classrooms (e.g., journals, reading aloud to children, silent reading, literature study, publishing books, content logs, small group science projects). However, none of these is essential. It would be possible, though impoverishing, to emphasize science projects and exclude literature, yet still have a Whole Language classroom. One could focus entirely on art, music, and drama (writing to publishers to obtain releases for play readings, writing off for catalogues of art openings, staging the school's own gala arts fair), or on a political issue within the community and never write any personal narratives and still have a Whole Language classroom. What is essential are certain principles or beliefs, including those listed in the earlier section describing Whole Language. A teacher who uses the 'method' (practice is actually a more apt term) of literature study and who has an underlying theoretical framework that defines reading as a collection of separate skills will turn those literature study sessions into skills lessons. What makes literature study or journals or Big Books or classroom publishing centers or thematic inquiry a part of Whole Language theory-in-practice is not the literature, not the procedures, not the journal time or the writing conferences or the 'expert' projects. It is the underlying Whole Language theoretical framework. With a different framework, those practices cannot be called 'whole language'. Like a liquid, practice takes the shape of and represents whatever belief-container it is in (Browne, 1985).

If thinking of Whole Language as method or component parts is a problem in mixing levels of abstraction, wishing to offer a little of everything — to be eclectic — constitutes magical thinking. How idyllic, how 'nice' it would be to have no conflict in underlying positions, no basic contradictions. But there *are* basic contradictions (e.g., the idea that reading consists of separate skills contradicts the idea that reading does not consist of separate skills). There is no eclecticism at the level of underlying beliefs, whether those beliefs are acknowledged or not.

Even though materials or methods can not guarantee that the resulting practice is Whole Language, materials which are written for the instruction of separate reading or writing subskills conflict with Whole Language beliefs by definition. 'Holistic' or not, phonics materials and basal series all most typically elicit reading and writing exercises, ensuring that the learner's purpose must be complying with the assignment or proving proficiency in an evaluation by someone else. Thus the basic Whole Language belief — acquisition through use, not exercise — is violated. The only way basal readers or phonics programs could be congruent with Whole Language beliefs would be for children to use these materials as data (e.g., as documents in an historical study of changes in school culture [Edelsky *et al.*, 1991], or as instances of discourse to critique [Baker and Luke, 1989]). They could not be used for practicing or learning supposed subskills of written language — including the supposed subskill of comprehension — and be congruent with Whole Language beliefs. (In Whole Language, reading includes making sense. If no sense is being made — if there is no comprehension — there is no reading. Comprehension is not a subskill.)

Whole Language teachers *do* use methods. And they *are* eclectic in one sense. That is, they have a large repertoire of materials, modes of interacting, ways of organizing classrooms, and so on. Indeed, they are particularly sensitive to the need to vary their approaches with different children for different purposes. However, eclecticism usually means something else when used to explain why one has appropriated a few 'whole language methods' — something more like typical practices borrowed from conflicting paradigms, but unwittingly 'biased' by one unacknowledged, unexamined single underlying paradigm. In contrast, Whole Language teachers try to be conscious of and reflect on their own underlying beliefs; they deliberately tie practice and theory.

Is Whole Language a New Term for the Language Experience Approach?

It Could Be ...

The two certainly share some ties in practice. Written statements about Whole Language (Edelsky *et al.*, 1983 and Chapter 8, this volume; Goodman, 1986; Newman, 1985) and written statements about the Language Experience Approach (Allen, 1976; Ashton-Warner 1963; Lamoreaux and Lee, 1943; Peterson, 1981; Veatch, Sawicki, Elliott, Barnette and Blakey, 1973) advocate an abundance of books written by children about their own lives. Both Whole Language and Language Experience paint images of rich classroom environments; both emphasize the importance of literature. Both treat reading as (at least in part) a personal act, arguing for the need to accept and work with whatever language varieties a child brings to school. Visitors to Whole Language classrooms indeed see children writing books, working with literature, and using a variety of symbol systems. Moreover, with the recent popularity of the term Whole Language, many Language Experience Approach teachers using dictation during reading instruction now call this Whole Language, thereby confusing method with framework. Thus, there are similarities in statements, in practice, and a frequent mislabeling of practice that would give people a good reason for thinking Whole Language is a synonym for Language Experience Approach.

But It Isn't

One primary difference concerns premises about the relation of oral and written language. Language Experience presumes that written language is a secondary system derived from oral language. Whole Language sees oral and written language systems as structurally related without one being an alternate symbolic rendition of the other. Moreover, written language learning need not wait for oral language acquisition. People can learn vocabulary, syntax, and stylistic conventions directly through written language (Edelsky, 1986b; Harste *et al.*, 1984; Hudelson, 1984).

Dictation provides another symptomatic difference. Language Experience teachers plan frequently for taking dictation from students. Whole Language teachers may take dictation but less frequently and usually only when prompted by the child's request. The underlying reasons for this disparity are critical, revealing an example of evolution in, not merely competition between theories. At the time Language Experience Approach was being developed, an implicit theory that was embedded in that Approach was that writing amounted to taking dictation from oneself, that composing occurred prior to transcribing. By the time Whole Language theory was being developed, the conception of writing had evolved to viewing meaning-making as occuring during the act of writing (Smith, 1982b). Taking dictation deprives language learners of a key context for making meaning — the act of writing. It also deprives them of the opportunity to make a full range of hypotheses.

[margin annotation: the act of writing]

While Language Experience Approach statements and recommended practices do not state that reading consists of separate skills, they do assume that reading entails knowledge about reading and that this set of 'sub-knowledges' is derived from skills lessons and practice, from teaching about parts of language (Allen, 1976; Peterson, 1981; Veatch *et al.*, 1973). Thus, after a child's experience is put to use in dictation, the transcription is often used to teach word attack or phonics skills. In contrast, Whole Language acknowledges that metalinguistic knowledge is part of written language competence, but it disputes that such knowledge is best gained through fragmented exercises.

One unfortunate similarity is poor translation. The literature on both Language Experience and Whole Language (let alone actual classroom events) sometimes offers an inadequate vision of how some abstraction might look in real life. For example, in Language Experience statements, important abstractions like *reflection* and *dialogue* are trivialized by being put to service in the teaching of punctuation. The Whole Language literature has its own share of bad examples. Children are supposed to write for their own purposes; yet in recent issues of a Whole Language newletter there were suggested activities (that word is used advisedly) wherein children would end someone else's story. Whole Language considers literature a way of knowing and also a critical medium for participating in literate communities. Nevertheless, literature is sometimes presented in Whole Language articles as a 'strategy' for teaching reading.

The main distinction, however, between Whole Language and Language Experience concerns theory. The Language Experience Approach made major breaks with established reading pedagogy. It taught reading without basal readers — in fact, without any single prescribed text, relying primarily on children's literature. It gave up the assumed sequence of reading before writing. It contradicted the presumed need to group children for reading instruction. It recognized the importance of children's own purposes and childrens' own language patterns. But it appealed to no developed theory to support these breaks with conventional wisdom. The best it could do, given the limits of linguistic and psycholinguistic theory in the mid-twentieth century, was to make some use of structural linguistics. Its references to child language consisted primarily of naïve views of vocabulary acquisition (appealing to studies of size and type of vocabulary and of frequently used lexicon).

We must emphasize here that in the 1940s through the 1970s, the Language Experience Approach was the most progressive (i.e., undermining oppressive literacy practices in schools) and comprehensive (i.e., explicating assumptions and suggested practice) view of written language teaching and learning. Though in 1990 Language Experience appears to be theoretically inadequate, it must be remembered that it had its beginnings well before the advent of Goodman's (1969) revolutionary research on the reading process. That Language Experience Approach educators did not account for literacy events, speech events, speech acts, or a socio-psycholinguistic model of reading reflects historical limits on knowledge rather than failure of vision.

Even though Language Experience was not accompanied by a paradigm shift regarding written language (the required information was not available), it may have been a necessary precursor to Whole Language. In fact, in the professional history of individual teachers, Language Experience Approach is often a bridge to Whole Language. Because Language Experience teachers have already broken away from traditional reading pedagogy at so many points, they find it easy to become Whole Language teachers. They can retain many of their practices and, armed with a new theoretical framework, can give a new Whole-Language meaning to those practices.

Is Whole Language a New Term for the Open Classroom?

It Could Be ...

Whole Language and the Open Classroom of the 1960s and 1970s (also known as the British Infant School Model or the Integrated Day) certainly bear a family resemblance. Comprehensive, respected statements on Open Education (Gross and Gross, 1969; Lucas, 1976; Neill, 1960; Nyquist and Hawes, 1972; Silberman, 1970) advocated something like the Language Experience Approach for literacy instruction. Similarities between Language Experience and Whole Language have already been described in the preceding section. But these are not the only likenesses.

Both Open Education and Whole Language note the active character of learning; both consider the 'whole child', understanding (with early critical theorists [Gibson, 1986]) that emotions and bodies cannot be separated from learning and thinking. Both see learning as rooted in firsthand experience, genuine problem-posing and solving. Both see the need for a curricular focus on significant content. Both are concerned with more than language and literacy, more than thought or learning in the abstract but with thought-in-interaction, with learning-in-life. With so many resemblances, no wonder Whole Language is seen not as a cousin, but as an identical twin of Open Education.

But It Isn't

We are deliberately avoiding, for these comparisons, using poor examples of Open Education practice. For example, in the name of Open Education, some classrooms were organized so children rotated in rigid time blocks among so-called Learning Centers at which they worked on ditto sheets (round tables must have seemed more 'open' than rectangular desks). Whole Language practice has its own examples of 'whole-language-in-name-only' where teachers make up 'whole language' comprehension questions to go along with the 'whole language' basals. Instead, we want to compare only the prototypical statements and congruent practice in Open Education with the prototypical statements and congruent practice in Whole Language.

Some minor distinctions between Whole Language and Open Education concern the role of the teacher and the view of the learner. Bussis and Chittendon (1972) describe a highly active Open Classroom teacher rather than a passsive reactor. Many Open Education statements paint the teacher as an ingenious, spontaneous facilitator, provisioner of the environment, and resource person. So do Whole Language statements (e.g., Chapter 7, this volume; Newman, 1985). The distinction here is one of degree. Whole Language statements and workshops offer less on provisioning the environment, highlighting instead how teachers can intervene and fine tune interaction, keeping it theoretically 'honest' and congruent with beliefs about language acquisition. Whole Language teachers are more likely to actively participate as co-learners, to construct meaning together with students rather than simply facilitate.

Despite the stress placed by Dewey (and Neill, 1960) on communities, the emphasis in the Open Classroom has been the learner as an individual, individually choosing topics of study or, more likely, selecting from among the options the teacher offered at Learning Centers. Whole Language views the learner as profoundly social. Therefore practice congruent with Whole Language includes participating in a community of readers (and speakers) during small group literature study, a community of writers in peer writing workshops, a community of learners in group social studies projects with built-in plans for collaborative learning.

An appearance of similar behavior may mask underlying differences. For instance, both Open Classroom and Whole Language educators oppose standardized testing. Open Classroom proponents claim that standardized tests fail to test what teachers are teaching (e.g., self-directedness, problem solving). The tests, in other words, are *insufficient*. Whole Language educators, on the other hand argue that tests fail to test what the tests themselves claim to be testing (i.e., reading). That is, they are *invalid* (see Chapter 9). Even if the class, ethnic, and gender biases woven into the very fabric of such tests could be eliminated, the tests could *never* test anything but test-taking.

This discrepancy in rationale for opposing standardized reading tests stems from a distinction in origins of Open Education and Whole Language. Whole Language takes its direction from a particular view of language acquisition and a theoretical definition of reading and writing. That definition, undergirding Whole Language but absent from Open Education and its embedded Language Experience Approach to instruction in reading and writing, is the most important difference between these two innovations. It is that definition which allows Whole Language educators to argue that standardized tests are invalid. That argument and its implications for then invalidating a wide variety of school practices (e.g., test-based grouping for reading, tracking, admission criteria, etc.) that deny people access to cultural capital lends theoretical support to a political Whole Language aim — a more just, equitable society.

The last important distinction concerns historical context. The rebirth after several decades of Open Education in the United States in the 1960s came at a time of both relative prosperity and widespread criticism of endemic, structured social inequities, a time when the modernist faith in technology and progress still had a hold on the public consciousness. Whole Language, on the other hand, is gaining momentum at a time when the homeless are increasing, when government social programs have suffered many cuts, when freedom to criticize, even to create, is threatened by right wing groups, when a growing postmodernist mentality acknowledges the damage done by 'progress' harnessed to technology. These contrasting contexts infuse Open Education and Whole Language with distinctive meanings.

Is Whole Language a Synonym for Writing Process?

It Could Be …

Writing Process classrooms are largely workshops. Children choose their own topics for writing and for investigation; they choose their own books for pleasure reading and for study. People work as colleagues with each other, children responding to each other's work; teachers teaching through mini lessons and through participating — taking part in literature studies, bringing their own writing to conferences, and so on (Calkins, 1986; Graves, 1983). Whole Language classrooms often exhibit the same workshop atmosphere. Writing Process teachers see themselves as 'kidwatchers' (Y. Goodman, 1985), as informed responders to what the student is trying to do (Atwell, 1983; Graves, 1983; Smith, 1982b). So do Whole Language teachers. Many Writing Process and Whole Language teachers meet regularly with their colleagues in grass roots groups to promote each other's professional growth (see Chapter 10).

In practice and in print (Atwell, 1987; Edelsky *et al.*, 1983 and Chapter 7, this volume; Hansen, 1987), Whole Language and Writing Process distinguish between writing exercises and all other kinds of writing. In fact, a fundamental premise of both Whole Language and Writing Process is that children in school should be doing what real writers do — they should write, not do writing exercises. Rather than seeing unconventional spellings as mistakes or bad habits which will interfere with correct responses, Whole Language and Writing Process teachers know that errors are necessary to the learner and illuminating for the teacher.

Both Whole Language and Writing Process incorporate such Vygotskian notions as:

1 culture and history are transmitted in part through (written) language use and transformed through language (Laboratory for Comparative Human Cognition Editors, 1988). For instance, through learning which genres are favored for what purposes and who should write what, children appropriate important features of culture and can then use this learning to change culture;

2 writing is a cultural tool that shapes thinking and that, with its historical and cultural particularities, constitutes a social practice (Vygotsky, 1978; Street, 1984). That is, people learn to write in contexts where writing has particular meanings and where the writer has particular social relations with other people and with texts. What is learned is thus a huge bundle — how to write plus what writing means plus which social relations accompany writing;

Both Writing Process and Whole Language also share another similarity: each has become a movement. As such, their informing perspectives or frameworks are often either not understood, ignored, or 'adapted' (co-opted) so as not to disturb dominant assumptions about language and learning.

With such apparently identical beliefs, practices, and even undesirable reactions, it seems right to consider Whole Language not just an identical twin of Writing Process but another name for the same thing.

And It Is ... Almost

While Writing Process and Whole Language are each frameworks rather than methods, the frameworks are not identical. Whole Language includes both an explicit theoretical base (about language and language learning) and pedagogical implications. It takes key features of the way language is learned as a 'best model' for all learning in school, not just language learning. In other words, Whole Language is an umbrella *theory-in-practice* aimed at all content and processes that might be taught and learned in school.

Writing Process is a perspective on a written language pedagogy that includes some usually *implicit* theoretical antecedents about the nature of writing. It takes key characteristics of the contexts writers rely on for their own growth as a 'best model' for learning to write in school. It now offers those characteristics (time, ownership, and response in a workshop setting) as the best context for all learning, not just the learning of writing. In other words, Writing Process is an umbrella *pedagogy-with-implicit-theory*, aimed at all contexts for learning in school. Whole Language educators agree with and in fact use that pedagogy though they begin with theory.

This somewhat subtle distinction between a theory-in-practice on the one hand and a pedagogy-with-implicit-theory on the other is reflected in how Writing Process treats reading and how Whole Language treats writing. In the absence of an explicit theoretical tie between writing and reading, Writing Process either ignored reading at first or treated it as pedagogically separate from writing (see Calkins, 1983, for an example). When Writing Process educators began to make connections between writing and reading, they gave curricular rather than theoretical reasons and made instructional suggestions that relied on sophisticated gimmicks like posing secret questions (Calkins, 1986). At that time, Writing Process statements seemed to be saying that literature was a means for teaching reading, as opposed to the Whole Language idea that reading is a means for learning literature (Edelsky, 1988; Peterson and Eeds, 1990). In more current statements, however, Writing Process educators have forsaken gimmicky external motivators and are now consistent with their new (and Whole Language's old) intent to capture what readers (not just writers do when they read (not just write). Even so, current Writing Process reasons for rejecting basal readers remain empirical (e.g., basals are not what readers *read* [Hansen, 1987]); no theoretical explanation is provided for why readers fail to choose basals.

While in its early years Writing Process was only about writing, Whole Language was not only about reading. From the beginning, Whole Language educators have looked at children's writing as well as their reading because they put the two in the same *theoretical* category — language. Thus, young children's invented spellings (Read, 1975) and their writing (Harste, 1980) provided evidence for Whole Language beliefs about children's language strengths in constructing the system of written language. Additionally, from the start, Whole Language educators welcomed Writing Process as being essentially Whole Language in spirit; indeed, they learned from Writing Process a more profound pedagogical meaning for their own Whole Language theory of learning language through actual use.

Another difference concerns the political implications of becoming a Whole Language or a Writing Process teacher. At the beginning (and also currently), when Whole Language teachers took control of their teaching, they explicitly advocated and acted to overthrow the established reading technology (basals, workbooks, commitments to publishers, packaged programs tied to tests with stakes attached, etc.). Before the advent of the now popular term 'literature-based', such an action had immediate political consequences. For example, some teachers were threatened with dismissal for insubordination if they refused to use the basal reader. Such actions also gave long-term 'lessons' by the reactions they engendered, demystifying the relation of big business and class ideology to curriculum and to teacher autonomy. And because they concern people as group members in work roles (the group called teachers), these actions by Whole Language teachers on behalf of their own professionalism had and still have a group meaning.

Initially, when Writing Process only pertained to writing, Writing Process teachers had comparatively little to overthrow. Writing Process did not advocate doing away with spellers or language arts texts, though that was certainly an implication. At first, Writing Process was simply about 'adding' a writers' workshop. While there were required language arts texts and spelling series, there were (and still are) no counterparts in writing that carry the same weight as that entrenched basal technology does in reading. Deciding to take control of one's teaching of writing, therefore, carried less political or economic threat within the big business of education. Such actions lack the built-in potential for revealing teachers' roles in relation to the structure of the institution and the larger society. Reclaiming professional control by Writing Process teachers, then, is bound to have a more individual meaning.

We have discussed these differences not because they are disturbing or divisive but because they are so intriguing. In fact, further exploration could well be enlightening for everyone.

Conclusion

We have tried to show that Whole Language is not a phonics program or a whole word approach to teaching reading. Neither is it a revitalized Language Experience Approach or another round of Open Education. If its newness is not recognized, we fear it will suffer the fate of these two past innovations. Language Experience was vulgarized to become a collection of flash cards hung on a shower hook. The idea of Open Education was distorted to mean an open pod. Lately we have seen Writing Process reduced to scheduled steps: rehearse on Monday, draft on Tuesday, revise on Wednesday, edit on Thursday, publish on Friday. And Whole Language is increasingly misrepresented. It appears as the new label for the whole word perspective (at a recent conference, a publisher was selling Whole Language pocket charts for sight words). It is widely equated with a program of component parts explained in old terms that render it 'nothing new'.

But it *is* new — new in theory and, obviously, different in historical context. Those who have conscientiously examined old beliefs and broken loose from the constraints of prevailing practice know first hand just how different — even provocative and threatening to established practice — it is. And a subset of educators who have gained a clear vision of the liberatory potential in this theoretical framework know full well how different Whole Language *could* be. We urge educators interested in a more just society to do the difficult but exhilarating work of coming to know this potentially transformative theory-in-practice.

Chapter 7

Hookin' 'Em in at the Start of School in a Whole Language Classroom

with Kelly Draper and Karen Smith

It is the afternoon of the first day of school for sixth graders at Laurel School. Twenty-five children, many of whom have failed two different grades somewhere between kindergarten and today, several of whom have reputations as 'bad kids' in this inner city school, have an assignment. They are to take potting soil and plant a bean in each of two milk carton containers. They will use their plants to begin the first of many experiments. The teacher tells everyone where to find the soil, seeds, and scissors. Children are to pace themselves for coming to the sink for planting: 'If there are five people at the sink already, use your own judgment about what else to work on. Work in your journals or decorate your folders'.

Forty-five minutes from the presentation of the assignment, with no reprimanding, no step-by-step directions, no close teacher monitoring of the clean up, the children have filled fifty milk cartons with soil and seed, put them on trays near the window, cleaned the sink area, and put finished journal entries on the teacher's desk. By the end of the first school day, these children look like self-directed, conscientious 'good kids', able to perform an intricate, efficient dance choreographed (but seemingly not directed) by the teacher. How did they learn the steps so quickly?

This chapter summarizes a study of how the school year began for one teacher and twenty-five inner city students.[1] This classroom was unusual because of its effectiveness and because it reflected a whole language conception of literacy and language development (see Chapter 6 and Edelsky, Altwerger and Flores, 1991, for lengthy descriptions of that conception). Although there have been many observational studies of the beginning of the year in classrooms with a skills view of literacy (see, for example, Moskowitz and Hayman, 1976; Sanford and Evertson, 1980; Tikunoff, Ward and Dasho, 1978), there have been no examinations of 'the establishings' in a whole language classroom. We contend that literacy instruction has such an impact on elementary school curriculum, on daily time allocations, and on assessment of learning that the failure to account for views of literacy in studies of classroom phenomena (e.g., in studies of how interaction is structured, how key events are organized, how school begins, how effective teachers teach, and so on) is a systematic omission of prime significance.

Of course it is not only conceptions of language, literacy, learning, or other topics in the school domain that remain unarticulated in classroom research. Unless the phenomenon of investigation is clearly related to class, gender, race, authority, and so on, it would be unusual to find researchers identifying and describing a teacher's beliefs about these topics. Yet just because the research phenomenon does not seem to be immediately affected by gender, race, class, or ethnicity (e.g., research on teacher knowledge or on effective teaching) does not mean beliefs about such issues are irrelevant. The relevance of prevailing ideologies cannot be gauged, however, if they remain hidden. Yet they (and their classroom effects) most often remain hidden because no counter-ideology is even considered. This state of affairs permits the fiction that the prevailing ideology is not ideological — that it is simply the way things are. (See Chapter 4 for a similar point in regard to the relationship between language proficiency and a particular definition of academic achievement and Chapter 1 for a discussion of the depoliticizing of second language research when the political relationship between native and second languages is not considered.) What happens, then, is that classroom phenomena are portrayed as generic rather than political (e.g., effective teaching is portrayed as effective teaching in general rather than as effective teaching by a teacher who believes in gender hierarchies). We too do not identify Karen Smith's political beliefs about social structure (nor do we try, for comparison's sake, to infer these beliefs for teachers in other beginning-of-the-year and effective teaching studies), but that does not mean they would be out of order. What we do here, however, is to at least begin to decenter notions about starting the year and, by implication notions about effective teaching, by claiming that the teacher's ideology of literacy is an important research consideration.

A basic assumption of this study of a teacher getting children to adapt at the start of school, then, is that the children are adapting to *something*. One of the key 'somethings' is the teacher's theoretical orientation to what written language learning is and how it occurs. As mentioned in Chapter 4, Harste and Burke (1977) identified three such theoretical orientations: decoding, skills, and whole language. The present discussion requires some elaboration of these orientations as they pertain to what happens in classrooms.

The decoding orientation views the sound–symbol relationship as the key to reading. Meaning is something arrived at after sounds are translated into larger units such as words and sentences. Function and purpose are not important issues. A teacher operating from the decoding orientation typically introduces each letter and assists students in associating letters and sounds.

In the skills orientation, the word is the basic unit in reading and writing. Assorted separable skills (decoding, word attack, comprehension) are learned and used separately. A teacher with this view typically uses grade-levelled, vocabulary-controlled basal reading texts and workbooks. New words are introduced and drilled. Assignments use stories and workbook activities containing those words.

According to the whole language orientation, meaning-making is the central focus of reading and writing. The complex, context-bound skill of reading or writing cannot be broken into component subskills. Thus, the whole language classroom looks different; there are no spelling books, no sets of reading texts with controlled vocabulary. Whole, meaningful texts are the materials, not isolated words, sounds, or paragraphs. The reading program is more accurately a literature program. Children write for real-world (rather than instructional) purposes. Significant content and interaction about that content (talk between teacher and student and among students) are essential to the whole language orientation.

The skills theory is the prevailing orientation in the United States. The dominant pattern of reading instruction involves relatively homogenous groups working out of a basal reader and the accompanying workbooks. The time spent on skill and drill activities outweighs the time spent reading (DeFord, 1981). Writing instruction consists primarily of exercises on isolated aspects of penmanship, spelling, punctuation, capitalization, vocabulary, and grammar; little writing is required (Graves, 1978). Virtually all commercial programs for teaching reading, writing, or language arts assume the existence of separate skills. Even in classrooms where creative teachers try to 'integrate skills' (with each other and with subject matter) by instructing for comprehension or word identification in conjunction with literature instead of basal readers, the skills orientation is what is driving the curriculum. In fact, 'the culture's implicit task analysis' of reading (decode first, comprehend next, then read functionally) stems from a skills orientation (Laboratory for Comparative Human Cognition, 1982).

What confronted the sixth grade students in this study, however, were the expectations of one of a minority of teachers who work from a whole language view of literacy.[2] Karen Smith's (KS) assumptions about language, language learning, and learning played a significant role in her curricular plans and in her interactions with students at Laurel School. From interactions over the course of many years, it is clear that KS holds the same assumptions that are listed in Chapter 6 and in Edelsky *et al.* (1991) as basic to whole language.

Laurel School has a student population of approximately 75 per cent Latinos, 10 per cent African Americans, and 15 per cent Caucasians. Over 80 per cent of the children qualify for free breakfasts and lunches. Absentee rates are high; test scores are low. By sixth grade, approximately one-third have failed at least one grade in school.

Despite the students' prior histories, KS and the students succeeded together. Absentee rates were low in her room. Visitors frequently commented that students were almost always engaged in appropriate tasks. Parents reported a sudden and dramatic turn to book reading and story writing as at-home activities. Students whose September journals had entries such as 'I don't got nuthin' to write' were writing full pages by October. Previous 'non readers' read award-winning children's literature and revised and edited multiple drafts of long, involved stories. By spring, children spontaneously discussed the literary merits of their own writing and of books they read, commenting on style, point of view, plot structure, and other literary elements.

We knew about KS's beliefs about literacy and had seen similar activities in her room the preceding years so we were prepared for these successes. It was all new to the students, however. Most of these children began the year as 'low-achievers'. Under ordinary circumstances there would have been no reason to expect a dramatic change. But circumstances were not ordinary. Instruction did not incorporate prevailing assumptions of the need to present a hierarchy of increasingly decontextualized literacy skills (Heath, 1982; Shuy, 1981). With such a discrepancy between students' past experience and KS' approach, how was the gap ever bridged?

Observing Effective Teachers

The phenomenon we were attempting to explore was how, at the beginning of the year, teachers 'coerce' children (following McDermott, 1977)[3] so that classroom life becomes what they want it to be. However, we were interested in more than just how that happens in any classroom, but in how it happens in a classroom with an effective teacher who has a *whole language* view of literacy. whole person / whole language.

Studies of teacher effectiveness almost always investigate teaching from a *skills* orientation to literacy. These studies follow steps outlined by Rosenshine (1971) including: developing an instrument for systematically recording specified teaching behaviors, ranking classrooms according to measures of pupil achievement, and relating teaching behaviors to class achievement scores. Effective teaching is equated with high scores on standard measures of achievement — all of which are based on a skills theory of literacy. The focus of beginning-of-the-year studies is usually some variant of the question: How do effective teachers differ from ineffective ones during the first days of school? Since beginning-of-the-year studies define effective teaching in the same way teacher effectiveness studies do, these too can be considered *skills-orientation* studies.

Our study of how the year begins, however, was not focused on finding correlations between prespecified behaviors and ranked classrooms. Rather, our aim was to discover and describe factors integral to one classroom. We relied on numerous markers of effectiveness: KS's reputation, our prior knowledge of student performance in her room in other years, observations of interactions, observations of children's actual work (their writing, projects, improvised dramas, discussion of literature) and spontaneous reports from parents. None of our markers was linked with a view of literacy as a set of separable skills. Moreover, our question itself accounted for a contextual feature that is usually ignored: teachers' theoretical views. Our intent is to produce a description that can enlarge the view of (and how to view) effective teaching at the start of school.

Procedures

Our main data collection was through participant observation of teacher-student interaction all day every day for the first two weeks of school and then three days per week for the next three weeks. Video and audio tape recordings, made periodically, were used to confirm and modify the focus of further observations. We made field notes during classroom observations and videotape viewings. Students were interviewed during the first and third weeks. We also interviewed KS prior to the beginning of school and during the fourth week. We returned in December and again in January to verify if the kinds of interaction observed in September were still occurring.

No researcher looks at everything. Decisions about what to look at are based in part on the researchers' prior knowledge. Since we began with considerable prior knowledge of this teacher, both the data collection and analysis were informed by this prior knowledge; one cannot unknow what one knows. We began with the questions: How does this teacher get children to meet her unusual expectations? Our initial observations were guided by an assortment of questions: What are the norms here for reading and writing? How does the teacher get students to expect to write? How are certain procedures established (e.g., journal and book writing)? What student-teacher relationships are in evidence?

We expected to see gradual change occurring over the first few weeks of school, with some students wavering in accepting KS's uncommon demands, some adapting to the new concept of school and literacy almost immediately, and others taking considerable time to adjust. However, during the first day of school it was evident that the students already were becoming what the teacher wanted them to be. By that afternoon, they were cleaning up without being asked, helping one another, and taking responsibility for making decisions and completing assignments. Here were children in a relatively new environment almost immediately performing like 'natives'.[4]

Obviously, it had been an error to assume adaptation would be gradual. The original plan had called for student interviews the second week of school, but now that it was apparent that the object of interest was rushing by, we interviewed children on the second day. Yes, they recognized this class was different — no spelling books, no textbooks. Yes, they had 'known all along' it was going to be 'hard' but 'fun' (they eagerly anticipated constructing a haunted house and putting on plays for the entire school). No, they couldn't say what KS expected or how they knew what she wanted them to do. And no, despite conducting science experiments, participating in discussions, rehearsing reading performances they would later give for first graders, and so on, they thought that so far they had not done any 'work'.

Interpreting the Data

The question: How does this teacher coerce? (and the related question: Coerce to what?) led to using the teacher's stated goals as organizers of the data. Other studies have used daily or weekly goals or lesson objectives as organizers (e.g., Green and Wallat, 1981). KS's goals, however, were for the entire year and beyond, rather than for the week or the lesson. She described three goals that we used as organizing categories:

1 *To get students to see opportunities for learning everywhere.* 'To get them to see learning as more than just books and school, and that out-of-school and fun things have purpose and can provide learning.'
2 *To get students to think and take pleasure in using their intellects.* 'To get them to seek out learning, to pique their curiosity.'
3 *To help students learn to get along with and appreciate others.* 'That they'll see you can get along with all kinds, to accept people, to look at the good in everybody.'

With these goals in mind, we examined the teacher interviews for statements explaining what she does to try to accomplish these goals. To get students *to see that learning is everywhere*, the teacher stated she used what they know and their experiences, emphasized functional learning, used sources of information besides teachers and books, and related in-school learning to out-of-school learning. To get students *to enjoy using their intellect* KS included: setting up thought-demanding projects, providing minimal help until the student first did some thinking, reinforcing students for coming up with good ideas or questions, dealing with high level content, and modeling that work is serious, important, fun and exhilarating. To develop their *ability to get along with others*, KS said she emphasized grouping for interaction, encouraged them to help one another, tried to build group cohesiveness and a sense of room ownership, and demanded that they respect one another.

Based on other statements she made, we inferred three additional goals:

4 *To manage the day-to-day environment smoothly* so other goals could be accomplished.

   KS's statements relating to this inferred goal included ignoring inappropriate behavior, being prepared and organized, getting processes or routines established, checking up and reminding, giving directions, making reprimands in private, and stating official rules.

5 *To get students to relate to and identify with the teacher.*

   Through respect, trusting, and identification, KS believed that her sixth graders would take on her values. Her stated ways of achieving this goal included helping children be successful in developing their ideas and interests, modeling appropriate adult behaviors, letting them in on her thinking, talking to and treating them like adults, and being an 'authentic person' herself.

6 *To get them to be self-reliant and sure of themselves, and to trust their own judgments.*

   The means KS stated in interviews for accomplishing this goal included: using student work and behavior as examples of what to do, giving students responsibilities, assuming competence, giving encouragement, and suggesting alternative behaviors.

KS's stated means for accomplishing these six goals were reflected in her behavior in the classroom. Although her statements do not account for everything she did, they show that she was exquisitely aware of her goals and intentions and the means she employed toward these goals.

We added two other major organizing categories:

7 *Teacher's knowledge and understandings*. This category includes KS's assumptions, beliefs and understandings of children, curriculum, and human relationships. It was prompted by notes on observations and interviews and our prior knowledge of the teacher.

8 *Implementing a whole language writing program*. This category includes any entry in the field notes that concerned writing.

These eight categories provided a basis for addressing the questions: What are students being taught to adapt to? How were they being taught? What we saw in field notes, interview transcripts and videotapes were the embodiment of particular values, the imposition of a few rules, the enactment of various roles, and the provision of cues. We sorted these values, rules, roles, and cues according to the eight goals to see if certain roles, for instance, clustered with certain goals. Our primary interest, however, was in characterizing the values, rules, roles, and cues.

Values

Those values derived from interviews and found most frequently in the field notes were collapsed to make the following categories (the original glosses are in parentheses):

—Respect (respect others; consider needs of others; see the good in all; all are equal but special; children's ideas are important);
—People Are Good (people are well-intentioned; people are competent; people are sensible);
—Interdependence;
—Independence;
—Activity and Work (work is enjoyable; work is purposeful; work is real, serious, good; being busy is good);
—Originality.

It is important to note that <u>we did not find interview comments reflecting common classroom</u> values of obedience, correctness, or silence. Nor did we find assumptions about 'human nature' such as children will try to get away with what they can or that children have to be motivated to do schoolwork. Instead, the values and assumptions consistently and unambivalently played out directly contradicted those frequently held.

Rules

KS seemed to be using four implicit rules: 1) Do exactly as I say, 2) Use your head, 3) Do what's effective, and 4) No cop-outs. The 'do exactly' rule was employed frequently during the first days of school to give directions and to indicate what not to do. On the third day of school, when the teacher asked the students to come and sit on the floor, a couple of students attempted to bring their chairs. The teacher explained,

If I say 'Floor', I don't want chairs. If I say 'Chairs and floor and table',
I want chairs, floor, and table.

Often, 'do exactly' was noted in the breach, as the previous example shows. After the third week of school, 'do exactly' requirements seemed to disappear.

Along with these explicit commands there was a push from the very beginning for independence. This was reflected in the 'use your head' and 'do what's effective' rules. 'Use your head' commonly was related to responsibility for independent work — whether in or out of school ('You know what to do', 'You're on your own').

'Do what's effective' was a rule often revealed by what the teacher did *not* say. Students in this classroom did not have to line up and wait for the bell to ring before entering the room (even on the first day); they entered the classroom at will. The school day usually began with students sitting on the floor in the front of the room, some reclining under a desk, others leaning against the wall, others sitting with folded legs. For viewing films the criterion was 'as long as you can see'.

The last rule identified was 'no cop-outs'. Students were expected to use their heads and do what was effective, but that did not mean they could weasel out of responsibilities. We saw no examples of the teacher relaxing her requirements because a child had not performed; instead, she just kept demanding. If a child said 'I don't know', the response was 'No "I don't knows"!'

The rules were not in force evenly throughout all the events of the day. Children were required to 'do exactly' in events called total group and scheduling, while 'no cop-outs' operated during small group work. 'Do exactly' instances pertained largely to the goal of *managing the day to day environment*; 'no cop-outs' to the goals of *self-reliance* and *using the intellect*.

Roles

KS did play the stereotypical part of teacher as lesson leader but infrequently. More often (as well as more interesting) was the total range of her roles: Lesson Leader, Information Dispenser, Scout Leader, Consultant/Coach, Neutral Recorder, and Preacher. Of course KS's roles were enabled and supported by a reciprocity on the part of the children who themselves took appropriate roles. However, because our recording was inadequate for preserving subtle features of language interaction for both teacher and child, and because our focus was on the teacher, it is KS's roles we highlight.

Unlike Lesson Leader, a role marked by talk structured by initiation-response-evaluation (IRE) sequences (Mehan, 1979), the role of Information Dispenser seemed to emanate from an FYI (For Your Information) posture. Here, KS delivered long explanations, drew diagrams, or offered factual tidbits. Children could take the information or leave it; they would not be evaluated with it (no 'Now what did I just say?' check-ups). This role was associated only with the goal of *using the intellect*.

Contrasting with Lesson Leader on several dimensions was Scout Leader. This role occurred most often during transitions. When the children were moving from one event to another, KS looked at individuals rather than surveying and supervising the crowd, stayed put for awhile, and otherwise signalled accessibility. Children approached, usually individually, and they and she seemed like peers. Interaction could be initiated by either teacher or child and the talk was conversational. Scout Leader was an affectionate friend who teased (and was teased back) and who shared anecdotes with her students. A sense of comradeship ('We're in this together') pervaded these exchanges. Not surprisingly, Scout Leader occurred most frequently with the goal of getting children to identify with and relate to the teacher.

The Consultant/Coach offered advice on schoolwork or helped students out of an academic dilemma (even if it was KS who had made the assignment and had thus created the dilemma in the first place). Focusing on what the student was trying to do, the Consultant/Coach elicited the student's perceptions, then gave advice or tips. The message was 'I want you to do well'. Conveying this message sometimes took the form of a pep talk or an offering of expertise.

> If anyone wants to stay in and practice reading for the first graders, I'm available after lunch.

The Consultant/Coach role ran through every goal except *managing the day-to-day environment*. The management in this classroom was done with dispatch: the teacher was in charge — no coaching.

Both Scout Leader and Consultant/Coach roles dominated for KS's goals of *relating to the teacher* and *relating to others* and for the category of *implementing a whole language writing program*.

Neutral Recorder was distinguished by the absence of evaluation. The Neutral Recorder offered her abilities at organizing and recording, but did not make final decisions. When a student asked the Neutral Recorder what to do, she replied, 'You decide', or 'What do *you* think?' Given this characteristic, it was not surprising to find the Neutral Recorder only in segments of field notes we had sorted as being about the goal of *using the intellect*.

When interviewed before school started, KS explained that she used 'preachy talk' only at the start of the year to emphasize cooperation and mutual respect. And in fact, the only instances of Preacher occurred the first week of school and only in connection with goals concerning relationships. True to form, there was no preaching about schoolwork or study habits.

Cues

Cues from KS were certainly needed to help students follow rules they had to figure our by 'using Their heads'. We identified twelve different cueing devices KS used for showing children how they should behave in relation to peers, teacher, academic content, and materials. Although many of these exploited language, not all did. The cueing devices were: Using the Work of Others as examples, Giving Directions (which included directions about desirable behavior), telling what not to do (Don't Do X), Ignoring Inappropriate Behavior, Reminding, Behaving As If the desired were actual, Modeling how to be, Structuring the Environment and Curriculum to provide the cues, providing Minimal Guidance, Privatizing Reprimands, using Written Cues, and providing an Exaggerated Display of desired ways to be.

Ignoring Inappropriate Behavior may seem like the absence of a cue; however, by attending with studious concentration to what she desired (e.g., refusing to interrupt a writing conference to reprimand others, continuing a discussion with no attention to silliness or groaning), KS gave information about what she desired. Sometimes, she gave some form of Minimal Guidance such as a nod or the 'evil eye' to direct a student to stop misbehaving. This served to get the erring student back on track without disrupting the flow of classroom activity. Why something as objectively benign as a 'look' should have been an effective technique with low-achieving 'bad kids' is a key question. For the 'evil eye' to work requires that the student was already identifying with KS, already trying to live up to her rules. Thus, the minimally intrusive evil eye had a double function — it was both a cue to how to act and, when acknowledged, a display that children were already acting that way.

When students were reprimanded at length about their behavior, the reprimands were usually Privatized. The teacher took the offender out of the room or asked the child to remain while others left the room. Public reprimands during which all could hear everything were almost nonexistent.

An especially interesting cue was Behaving As If — as if the students were competent, sensible, and well-intentioned. KS did not call attention to new responsibilities; she simply behaved as if the children had shouldered these all their lives. She did not line children up and walk them to art, music, physical education, and lunch; they were trusted to go on their own. She did not instruct on how to order the movies from the district audio-visual department; she gave two children the district forms and the catalogue and told them to do it. Props were part of Behaving As If students were already capable. They were used deliberately and matter-of-factly as concrete symbols of KS's belief in children's competence and good intentions. Examples of using props were: giving two boys a camera to photograph classmates on the first day, providing a clipboard for a group leader, supplying folders so students in charge of collecting money for book orders could organize their orders, offering flowered pink stationery (instead of lined school paper) to a child for the final draft of her letter. Props also signalled that the responsibility was really theirs. This was not 'playing at it'; it was the real thing.

KS's preference for Minimal Guidance covered both academic areas as well as comportment. As she roved around the classroom, working with groups or individuals, she would offer support but would refuse to take over ('You decide'; 'Whatever you want to say'; 'Spell it the best you can'). Nonverbal examples include an outstretched hand or shifts in posture to signal 'handing over' or a shrug to signal 'don't ask me; use your head'.

Directions also provided cues. KS's directions were effective (i.e., they were usually followed) but unusual. They were often minimal and frequently not delivered until an activity was already underway. The effectiveness of minimal directions is understandable here; when students carried out their own rather than the teacher's tasks, they needed no more than a scheduling signal since they already knew what they would do.

KS Structured the Environment to show the children how to view learning and schoolwork in this classroom. As she explained,

I want them to feel like they have too much to do that they want to do. When I say they don't have time to do the experiments they're talking about, that's deliberate now. I'll give them more time later. But now they have to come in before school if they want to do things or stay later, so they see it's serious and I'm here to help. I want them to see that learning is urgent and that ideas are tension-producing; you can't wait to try them out!

Another cue was Routines, which were also deliberately included as part of the planned curriculum — routines for writing projects, literature studies, science experiments, and so on. However, the teacher did not break the routines into steps and make each an 'objective'. Use of Others (or students' own experiences) as Examples was yet another device for 'coercing' students so that KS could accomplish the goals she set. These were always affectionate references:

> The teacher reminds Gloria of the time when abstract notions of measurement seemed to click for Gloria in an 'aha' experience. 'I think it was the first time in your life you ever really knew what a ruler was for — when we did the pinhole camera!'

The tone, topic, and effect of such moments were like 'family stories' about learning — past incidents, fondly remembered, making connections.

Exaggerated Display was a feature of many of KS's responses. She took special delight in only the slightest hint of a well-turned phrase in a child's writing; she showed intense attention when helping a child with an idea and prolonged interest in items children showed her. KS's Exaggerated Display of concentration (i.e., the posture of Rodin's 'The Thinker') effectively fended off students who might have interrupted a writing conference. Her stern expression, giving full attention to the performer, effectively dispelled any giggling during creative dramatics.

Like exaggerated concentration, the teacher's Modeling served to show students how to behave in a particular context. She modeled expressive reading, how to confer about children's writing, and how to be a serious, interested student:

> The teacher and all the students are reading during sustained silent reading time (SSR). The teacher glances around just once, then goes back to her reading. The bell rings, signalling that SSR is over, but the teacher keeps on reading. Some students get out their folders; others, following the teacher's model, keep on reading.

When we examined how these twelve cues were sorted in relation to goal categories, we found that the goals for *managing the environment* and for *establishing a whole language writing program* seemed to be cued the same way; management and curriculum were a tight fit. There was also some similar cueing for *building a relationship with the teacher* and *establishing a whole language writing program*. This clustering of similar items in the goals of relating to the teacher and implementing an important part of the curriculum occurred for KS's roles as well as her cues. Climate (cues and roles) and curriculum indeed were interrelated.

Discussion

This effective teacher provides a clear contrast with the picture painted in the literature on effective teaching (both during and at the beginning of the year). The research literature presents the effective teacher as stating clear expectations for behavior (Evertson and Emmer, 1982; Moskowitz and Hayman, 1976; Tikunoff, Ward and Dasho, 1978), yet KS established ambiguous rules requiring judgment rather than mechanical application. KS largely ignored inappropriate behavior; effective teachers have been found to nip it in the bud (Evertson and Anderson, 1978; McCormick, 1979). KS often gave minimal directions after many children already were engaged in the activity. Effective teachers wait for everyone's attention and then give complete directions *before* students begin working (Denham and Lieberman, 1980; Tikunoff, 1982). Effective teachers maintain short smooth transitions because these are seen as 'down times' when nothing important happens (Brophy and Evertson, 1976; Denham and Lieberman, 1980). By contrast, transitions in KS's class were few but long, included considerable movement and conversation, and served as important contexts for achieving a major goal (building a close relationship with the teacher). Effective teachers are portrayed as ensuring students' success by making simple unambiguous demands (Emmer, Evertson and Anderson, 1980); KS set tasks that were long, complex, and potentially ambiguous.

These are not contrasts in isolated features; they are contrasting gestalts in which interacting features can be isolated, contrasting total discourses, according to Gee (1989a). Similar discrepancies can be seen in how KS and 'effective teachers' begin the year. Beyond showing children the idiosyncracies of life in this classroom (where the paper was, whether ink or pencil was allowed, etc.), KS also had to get them to go along with a whole new and generally unshared set of underlying themes derived from a whole language orientation to literacy. How did she do it?

Overall, what KS did was maintain particular values, impose particular rules, play particular roles, and provide particular cues — all very deliberately and self-consciously in the service of accomplishing a few goals. Three of the goals were associated with the same values, roles and cues. For the goals of *building a relationship with the teacher, getting along with others,* and *implementing a whole language curriculum,* KS played the roles of Scout Leader and Coach, foregrounded the values of 'respect', 'people are good', and 'interdependence', and tipped children off with cues including Behaving As If, Using Others as Examples, and providing Exaggerated Displays. Certain roles contributed greatly to the character of this classroom. KS did not depend on the power of the stereotypical Lesson Leader role to coerce students. Effective work depended on students having access to her through roles in which the balance of power was more equal. The Scout Leader role was especially significant during transition times, embodying the offer, 'I'm available', which seemed crucial to relationship-building.

And how did it all begin? The only certain answer is that it happened very fast. During the first three hours of school, children's timing seemed to be slightly 'out of synch' as they looked around the room and to each other for guidance. Few answered questions; none ventured opinions. Nevertheless, during the first hour, when KS (Behaving As If they could) gave them a copy of the same complicated schedule she gave us, with the time blocks filled in for each day of the week, and told them to change the Tuesday 10:45–11:30 block from 'reading' to 'literature study', they rose to the occasion. Some of these poor readers glanced around quickly but then 'got hold of themselves'; all made at least some kind of mark somewhere on their copy of the schedule. Three hours later, they were having conversations with the teacher, cleaning up materials unasked, wondering aloud about scientific principles, and generally making themselves 'at home' in the room.[5]

We can account for the speed with which these children picked up on KS's desires and demands by positing that they came to school the first day primed to look for signals about how to survive there. Perhaps that is how people enter any new situation, actively searching for signals. Moreover, teachers who have been at a school for more than one year have a 'book on them' (to borrow a term suggested by Ralph Peterson), a reputation. Entering students thus come prepared not just to figure out a way to survive but a way to interact from the first moment with the teacher's reputation as well as with the teacher. The phenomenon that intrigues us, however, is that, more than being ready to figure out just *any* way to survive, the children all came quickly to the same conclusion: do what KS wanted. If the answer to 'How did she do it?' is 'Quickly, because the children's antennae were out for cues about how to make sense', that still leaves unexplained the issue of why they did what KS wanted. Why didn't they just as quickly devise ways to beat rather than follow her system? Why did something like the 'evil eye' work with them? To answer this we have to return to the theory that undergirds KS's approach to literacy.

What KS offered these students on the first day was purposeful assignments and a chance to read and write in a setting that acknowledged all the participants' 'ownership' of tasks, texts, and contexts. Moreover, she proferred relationships based on respect and interdependence. It was an offer that fitted her goals. Perhaps on the first day of school, every teacher offers a 'deal'. If the offer seems reasonable, if it seems to be in the students' interests, if the teacher does not undermine her own offer through ambivalently giving contradictory messages but instead keeps demonstrating the sincerity of the offer, the children do not make a counter-offer. They accept the teacher's offer while still learning and negotiating the details.

These sixth graders entered expecting a difference and expecting the difference to be positive. Their initial stance, in addition to their supersensitivity to cues available in new situations, speeded their adaptation to strange expectations. What the children came with (favorable disposition to KS and openness to cues in the new situation) and what the teacher offered (her 'deal') are what allowed them to take the initial leap and accept KS's offer before the first day was over. Accepting the overall offer meant a willingness to enter into a particular relationship with the teacher and also to believe in the substance of her promise — in this case, that she would have them engaging in real-world reading and writing in projects largely under their control, often with consequences extending beyond the classroom. The substance (not merely the lack of ambivalence) in such an offer is what we think held children so powerfully to their part of the bargain. Thus the evil eye, a subtle reminder tied to a human relationship rather than to object-connected punishment, could work very early in the school year, even with 'tough cookies'. Once the abrupt leap was taken, KS continued slowly and profoundly, via rules, roles, and cues, helping the children make sense out of the particulars of the deal.

In describing how teachers let children know how to act in their classroom, how teachers attempt to get students to achieve teacher-established goals, and ultimately, how teachers and students make sense of school — during the first days or the last — we cannot ignore what they are making sense of. We have to take into account what kind of literacy, subject matter, and relationship 'deal' is being offered. We have to come to understand that the most ubiquitous deals — whether a skills deal for literacy, a patriarchal deal, an élite social class deal or any other — are not givens. There are (or could be) contrary deals in just those areas that pervade classroom life. Until we seek out those contrary deals, we can never understand to what extent such purportedly generic activity as beginning the year or effective teaching is actually contingent and ideological.

Notes

1 Karen Smith (KS) was the teacher. Draper and Edelsky were the participant observers. All three took part in video viewing and coding of Edelsky's and Draper's field notes. Edelsky and Draper put pen to paper and thus were the ones who assumed and proclaimed KS to be an effective teacher. Therefore, what might look like continuous bragging on KS' part was not.

2 KS is a strong advocate of the Whole Language view. She has conducted workshops and taught courses on that orientation. Her teaching has also been videotaped by Carole Edelsky and Jerome Harste to teach others about Whole Language.

3 We considered the term 'enculturate' but found it lacking. It implies a group with a culture to transmit, not just one individual with a viewpoint. Though new members are not passive recipients when becoming enculturated, they get information about how to be members from many sources. In this school, the only source of KS's expectations, demands, or goals was KS — and what she provided. Others, too, have noted that the metaphor of classroom as culture has its limits, a serious one being that the teacher is the only native (Cazden, 1979; Florio, 1980). We wanted a term that allows for flexibility and active response on the part of all participants such as 'negotiation' — but negotiation implies that the outcome is more up for grabs than it is in this classroom. We also wanted a term that means the learning of a general underlying structure that can guide choices from a repertoire, such as 'internalization of norms', since it wasn't any mere surface matching of behaviors that was going on. But internalization tends to focus on an interior process and to skim over what is happening that promotes that process. We settled on 'coercion' because it acknowledges that it is the teacher's view that will prevail, but we recognize its limitations (failure to incorporate notions of negotiation and internalization of norms).

4 Ease of adjustment to a new system has been observed with much younger children in a study at the beginning of the year in a reception class in England (Willes, 1981). That researcher too was surprised to find immediate rather than gradual adjustment, with children seeming to learn to meet new demands in the course of a single session.

5 We do not know to what extent children came to share KS's views on reading and writing, just that they acted increasingly in accord with them. Through the year, KS's demands (but not her theoretical conception) changed. For example, she raised her requirements for what qualities in writing she would applaud and she changed the focus and intensity of writing conferences. In addition, the character of some of the activities changed as children invested the tasks with intentions that went beyond complying with an assignment. Perfunctory journal entries available to any reader became private conversations with the teacher, hunched over and covered up if anyone glanced over the writer's shoulder. Children moved from supplying a response to the teacher's questions about pieces of literature to asking questions of

their own and discussing each other's questions. What started as mumbled, awash-in-giggles dramatic portrayals became serious attempts to make particular characterizations 'believable'. But regardless of the changes in demands and the changed stance with which the children came to meet the demands, the process of 'buying in' began on the first day.

Risks and Possibilities of Whole Language Literacy: Alienation and Connection[1]

with Susan Harman

Literacy as Liberation

There is a long, honorable, and articulate literary and political testimony to the mixed blessings of 'the immigrant experience'. Abandoning one's social class roots and moving 'up' into the American Dream — leaving home — has always been risky business. And whether the journey is from the old neighborhood to the suburbs or condo; from the father-son union to a desk and white collar; from *kinder*, *küche*, and *kirche* to the schoolroom or real estate office; or from church picnics to dinner parties, the distance is rarely covered without leaving someone or something behind.

The achievement of literacy, however, unlike changes in social class, has been viewed as politically neutral, a tool, unambiguously positive, and universally powerful. Just as language lifts one's dreams out of the inchoate and makes them articulate, so literacy can *possibly* multiply those dreams by the factor of each that has ever been written down; it *can* allow the reader to borrow, steal, and adapt as her own every dream ever inscribed. Literacy *potentially* provides the ability to enter others' worlds, whether through novels or through political analyses, and that entrance immediately presents contrasts, alternatives, and choices; and hence, the possibility of change. There is, of course, no guarantee that the mere presentation of choices will result in a reader choosing something new and better, but without the data — the images of possibility — which literacy gives a reader, there is less likelihood she will invent entire new worlds out of whole cloth.

One need only consider to whom schooling has traditionally been denied (blacks, women, the underclasses of every culture) to recognize the awe in which literacy has been held and the frugal and discriminatory way in which it has been allocated. The legends of stolen literacy speak for its magic: Lincoln studying law in the flickering kerosene light of his log cabin, Douglass teasing white boys into spelling words out for him, Hassidic girls shearing their hair and binding their breasts to sit as boys in yeshivas, George Eliot creeping out of bed before dawn to write and then hide away what she had written before she lit the kitchen stove for the day,

Hispanic cigar workers in New York at the beginning of this century listening rapt as the professional readers read aloud the news and the classics.

But literacy is not necessarily liberating. First, merely knowing how to read and write guarantees neither membership in the dominant culture nor the concomitant political, economic, cognitive, or social rewards of that membership (Graff, 1986; 1987; Street, 1984). The consequences of literacy have always been related to how it is used and what it is used for, what value is placed on it, and who is permitted to become literate. Although one of the powerful meanings surrounding literacy in the Western world today is a belief in its liberatory power, in fact literacy is a necessary but hardly sufficient passport to the mainstream. If other stigmata — such as color, sex, or class — betray one's membership in a subordinant culture, one may not be able to talk (or read or write) one's way across the frontier.

Second, traditional approaches to literacy instruction can fetter students, not liberate them. Mastery of traditional literacy instruction sometimes permits access to certain societal resources. But these traditional curricula depend on: one single interpretation of one prescribed text; the use of conventional Standard English as the only criterion for evaluation of writing; and the standardized, multiple choice reading tests, which have only one right answer per item, as the passport to the next grade. Therefore these literacy curricula inordinately favor speakers from middle and upper-middle classes; from those dominant groups who simply 'acquire' Standard English at home, as contrasted with those who have to 'learn' it deliberately in school (Gee, 1987). Prescribed texts and standard conventions tend to be seen as the only 'true' texts and conventions, as 'natural' rather than constructed or chosen.

No wonder these curricula tend to maintain, rather than improve, the status of subordinate groups. Members of such groups are held behind 'gates' in elementary grades, kept from graduating high school by 'competency' tests, and reminded one last time (if they didn't understand before) when they score poorly on the standardized tests in adult basic education (ABE) classes, that they do not belong in the mainstream. As Villanueva (1988) describes his experience:

> I do not believe I had a problem with English after kindergarten. I could switch from Spanglish to Street to Standard at will. I read. I didn't fear writing. I could mimic the prestige dialects — both the spoken and the written. I could even add 'however' to essays on the basis of sound, although not often on the basis of sense. I was, however, apparently unable to mimic the school's way of viewing the world, the ways reflected in rhetorical patterns. The literacy we [Puerto Ricans] acquire tends to be of the wrong sort, even when the dialect is right. Basic literacy wields little power.

Despite the currently widespread unreflective faith in the benefits of literacy, neither the ability *per se*, the method by which it is acquired, nor the materials used to teach it, are neutral. Both the methodology and the content of the traditional curricula center on obedience and acceptance; e.g., there is only one English that is Standard and only one right answer for worksheet blanks and on multiple choice tests. This kind of curriculum is therefore more likely to be stifling than liberating, although it paradoxically may have one ambiguous advantage over more creative curricula — it shows the enemy's face. That is, the traditional, fragmented, authoritarian, and narrow approach to reading and writing is so plainly nonsensical and unrelated to life outside school that it permits students to make a clear choice between conforming to its standards or rejecting them (going to special education, dropping out of school, or simply not allowing oneself to be recruited or coerced into joining ABE classes). Of course, this 'choice' is less likely to be empowering, resistant, and liberating for the individual making it (and for her community), and more likely to be defeating for them both (Aronowitz and Giroux, 1985).

At the moment, there is much talk, considerable money, and an indefensible pedagogy (the same traditional assumptions, sometimes even the same traditional materials) aimed at 'curing illiteracy' in both adults and children. Government leaders, social scientists, corporate executives, publishers, and educators are united in calling for universal literacy, although the instructional methods they support practically guarantee failures. Our purpose in this chapter, however, is not to explain why these traditional approaches to teaching reading and writing usually fail; there is a large and growing body of literature on that (Goodman, 1986; Goodman, Freeman, Murphy and Shannon, 1988; Harste, Woodward and Burke, 1984). Nor do we attack the eccentric and peculiar kinds of reading, writing, and talking that go on exclusively in school (Edelsky, 1986b; Langer, 1986; Lindfors, 1987). We do not chant a misty-eyed paean to the supposedly automatic, revolutionary political and personal potential of literacy; after all, George Babbitt could read and write. (As psychologist M.M. Lewis, quoted by Graff [1987, p. 4], succinctly puts it, 'The only literacy that matters is that literacy that is in use'.) Nor do we explicitly criticize the monomaniacal, Eurocentric, trivia curriculum proposed by Bloom and Hirsch — although our nontraditional view of literacy is a clear and implicit antidote to their attack on pluralism. Finally, we do not join the broader issue of whether the institution of school is either necessary to literacy or good for anything or anyone at all (see, e.g., Bowles and Gintis, 1977; Graff, 1986; Illich, 1970; Scribner and Cole, 1978). Instead, we will look unsentimentally at the third reason why literacy may not be liberating: the price demanded by so fundamental a personal change may be too high. Rather than poke at the straw man of traditional language arts, we will focus on the unintended, ironic underside of an optimal classroom theory-in-practice: Whole Language.

The Problem

Our contention is that the acquisition of the kind of *ideal* literacy promoted in educational rhetoric but rarely in actual practice may have unanticipated repercussions in the lives of some learners. It is the kind of literacy that emphasizes reading and writing for expanding personal horizons, for understanding how texts have the effects they have, for considering alternate ideas. In the more progressive rhetorical statements, it is the kind used for critically analyzing conditions in one's life and finding effective ways to work with others to change those conditions — the kind promoted in actuality in at least some classrooms through the theory-based pedagogy known as Whole Language. As students in these classrooms — whether adults enrolled in basic education programs or children in elementary school — become literate in these ways and begin to feel the liberating effects of their ability to use written language to wonder, analyze, argue, critique, escape, or envision, they may paradoxically begin to feel the constraints of estrangement from their roots.

Because the explicit purpose of education has been the assimilation of subordinate groups into dominant American life, much has been written about the implied demand on those groups to reject their home communities, and of their ways of responding to that demand. Labov (1970) and Ogbu (1987) have described black teenagers' refusal to succeed in school in order to avoid becoming 'white'; Fingeret (1987) has reported adult illiterates' fears of losing their common sense or 'mother wit' and becoming 'educated fools', of 'forgetting where I came from'; Kingston (1976) has written movingly about her difficulty in reconciling the myths of her Chinese culture with those of the American educational establishment; academics who grew up in the working class have testified to their marginality in both worlds (Ryan and Sackery, 1984); and most notoriously, Rodriguez (1981), a Chicano, has argued for actively rejecting one's cultural and linguistic past as the price of 'making it'. Less has been written from the community's point of view about how it feels to watch children or adult relatives grow distant, become 'familiars' in another worldview that operates in a 'foreign' school and that threatens to invade the home as well; but the anguish is still there. Well documented or not, these are examples of conflicts induced by the 'otherness' of the school as a mainstream institution. Our concern is that Whole Language, with its ability to get more students to achieve the ideal literacy of educational rhetoric and its commitment to do so through classrooms structured democratically, may have an even greater alienating potential.

Whole Language Principles: Promise and Predicament

The primary principles of whole language are that learners are actively constructing meaning all the time, not just passively absorbing information; and that this language learning takes place in a coherent, sensible, predictable, purposeful environment in which coherent, sensible, predictable, purposeful language is being *used* — not practiced — both with and in front of the learner (see Chapter 6, this volume; Edelsky, Altwerger and Flores, 1991; Goodman, 1986; Newman, 1985 and others for descriptions of the bases of Whole Language). That is, Whole Language intends reading and writing to be seen by students as useful and relevant — as both *possible* to acquire and *worth* acquiring.

The choice between accepting and rejecting assimilation into the dominant culture is muffled in a Whole Language classroom, since the home cultures of all students — what Gee (1989a) defines as their primary discourses, their 'ways of using language, of thinking, and of acting', their 'identity kits' — are welcomed there. Whole Language is geared to the creation of texts for *use*; it encourages multiple interpretations of existing texts-in-the-world; it honors and uses the language norms with which students arrive; it not only accepts 'alright' and 'ain't' as linguistically legitimate, but it also accepts differing discourses, identity kits, and worldviews; it focuses on the ideas students have rather than the ones they lack; it assumes the expansion of roles so that students teach and teachers learn; it sets high but flexible standards; it emphasizes language repertoires rather than right answers; and it fosters questioning, analyzing, speaking up, and writing down.

In addition to its philosophical and political stances, Whole Language is a set of theoretical beliefs and educational practice based on a socio-psycholinguistic model of reading and writing (Goodman and Goodman, 1981; Harste *et al.*, 1984) and an interactive model of language acquisition (Halliday, 1977; Teale, 1982). It tries to create the conditions for written language acquisition that pertain for oral language acquisition: little direct instruction, authentic use of language within specific contexts, no apparent suffering, and essentially universal success. Like talking, reading and writing must be seen by learners as having obvious functions in the lives of those around them and those they want to be identified with. That is, the attention of talkers (and readers and writers) must be on something else, on what the talk or print is *about*, on the social work it is doing.

With language taking a supporting — although still essential — role, the actual classroom practice emanating from this Whole Language set of beliefs avoids workbooks, basal readers, controlled vocabularies, and kits. Center stage is occupied by what the language is about and what the adults and children *do* with it and why: cook, plan, build, experiment, make contact, label, organize, analyze, remind, play, imagine, threaten, inform, persuade, insult, entertain, interrogate, soothe, and so forth. The school day is spent *using* language rather than doing exercises with its parts, working with texts that have some function other than evaluation; e.g., recipes, letters, directions, labels, notes, tickets, games, maps, memos, magazines, newspapers, lists, reports, songs, journals, order forms, poems, menus, and stories.

It is this set of beliefs about language acquisition and these and other implied classroom practices that is what we mean by whole language. And it is this set of beliefs and practices — this challenging yet responsive, accepting whole language atmosphere — that may lull the learner out of her habitual wariness of the dominant culture, setting her up for disaffection from her community.

Traditional skills-based curricula create a different context. Such curricula are central components of a mainstream institution that has had the historical function of teaching mainstream ways of being and doing and then sorting the assimilated successes from the unassimilated failures. Subordinant groups have rightly had an ambivalent relationship with meanstream education; deliberate success in school — learning the ways of The Man — is often perceived as both an opportunity and a betrayal. Since traditional curricula in mainstream education devote so much time and importance to literacy exercises, to be successful in school means to learn to perform those exercises. Performing them well not only generates fears that the ensuing school success will mean becoming alienated *from the home community*; such successful performance also requires that students lose touch with their own boredom and anger — that they become alienated *from themselves*. Between the smell of danger that emanates from mainstream school in the abstract to the mind-numbingness of the daily curriculum in the concrete, many students refuse to buy in. They reject the literacy exercises of the traditional curriculum, taking the ultimately self-defeating but common route of maintaining personal integrity and a connection to the community by becoming alienated *from school*. In fact, in New York City 40 to 60 per cent drop out of high school and drop back into their home communities, with little to contribute from their years in school.

Whole Language, with its attention to students' interests and its valuing of students' home cultures, is not so likely to alienate students either from themselves or from school. Because it *is* so attractive, it entices students to connect with and succeed, sometimes almost in spite of themselves, not as reading/writing exercise-doers, but as readers and writers. In providing more students with at least this part of the entry fee to greater efficacy in the world, Whole Language benefits students as well as their communities. An unwanted stowaway in students' success through Whole Language classrooms, however, may be the tension between school and community that creeps out unexpectedly after the successful literacy learning journey is well underway. When the curriculum is engaging and inclusive rather than dull and exclusionary, it is harder to reject school and its teachings outright, easier, then, to be caught in a situation where one might think one has to choose between school norms and community norms rather than find a way to manage both.

Now, it is not Whole Language's success in promoting literacy *per se* that is the problem; after all, most communities in the US, at least, make use of *some* kind of literacy for *some* purpose. Moreover, most likely, the traditional skills approach does help some people learn to read and write (though we believe learners' own reading — in rare opportunities to *read* in school and abundant opportunities to read outside — as well as interaction with others who read in front of and with learners is what 'teaches' most people to read). The problem arises when, on the one hand, people learn to read how they should *not* according to their communities (e.g., to read and question in some communities, to write and imagine in others), or, on the other, when the contexts for learning (and therefore the meaning of the literacy that is learned) conflict with community norms. Except for the case where a community's norms prohibit certain categories of people from attaining *any* kind of literacy (so that even the deciphering of a mark if one were a woman or the making of a mark if one were a man of a certain status would contradict those norms), instructional activity in workbook-dominated skills classrooms is unlikely to violate community literacy prohibitions. Not so with Whole Language. The very beliefs and daily practice that makes Whole Language so successful (not merely in getting people to learn to read and write but to become readers and writers) also make it revolutionary — at once a welcome threat to the stability of existing hierarchies but also a disturbing threat to the stability of individuals' relationships to their home communities.

Perhaps the most powerful of these beliefs and practices, and therefore both the most liberating and potentially the most alienating, is the whole language commitment to a collaborative, democratic relationship both between the student and the teacher, and between the student and the text. Unlike traditional skills approaches, Whole Language teachers strive to demystify written language, texts, and learning. In a Whole Language classroom, students choose curricular areas to explore, negotiate activities with the teacher, collaborate with other students, take risks and chances with the structure and the content of their projects, work with and create texts *they* control, and learn to value varied 'readings'.

It is, of course, tremendously rewarding for Whole Language teachers to see their students more excited about publishing a guide book to guinea pigs than bothering the child next to them, or more engrossed in writing their autobiographies than watching TV. It may not, however, be quite so rewarding for the parents of young children or the spouses of adult students to see those same students growing away from them, and practicing at home the democracy and daring they have learned in class. Children in some communities may begin to feel cramped (where before they didn't notice) when the space that exists in school for multiple interpretations of a story shrinks at home because the family holds to the idea that a text is decipherable but not interpretable. Parents may perceive their children's new self-confidence and intellectual curiosity as talking back and arguing too much with them ('She always has an opinion on everything', 'He thinks he's so smart'). Husbands may resent their wives correcting their grammar, no longer needing to have newspapers read to them, and even having their own opinions about the articles they've read on their own.

Clearly, life in many mainstream homes is not democratic; moreover, many mainstream homes do not promote analysis, lively discussions or respect for divergent opinions. Nor is life in non-mainstream families necessarily authoritarian and oppressive. But the *ideal* of the critical thinking, experimenting, aware and reflective, independent man (and woman — a late twentieth century amendment to the ideal), educated to participate literately in a democracy, has a hold in mainstream culture. It is an ideal found typically in the *rhetoric* of traditional mainstream schools. Where it is actively sought after *in practice*, however, is in Whole Language classrooms. On a daily basis, conditions are enacted that promote that ideal (as well as many others concerning social responsibility, feeling, aesthetic response, and so on). Even if its real-life enactment may be foreign to many mainstream students, its position as an *ideal*, at least, is not. Students from non-mainstream communities in which the critical thinker is part of community ideals will also find a significant point of contact in Whole Language classrooms. So will many non-mainstream students accustomed to a community of arguers, discussers, story tellers, interpreters, and interpreters of the interpreters.

But for others, the discrepancy between school and community ideals and discourse practices is great. Since the Whole Language classroom is welcoming and supportive, such a student begins to learn *through* and therefore learn *to* use language in these new ways. Learning to read as a reader, as a Subject, can then catapult that student out of her family, community, class, or ethnic group, because she has learned, not simply a new way of using language or of comprehending text, but a new way of viewing the world — a new discourse. And, like the student in the traditional classroom who sees a forced choice down the road, the student in the Whole Language classroom too may believe she must choose between the old and the new discourse. Only in this case, she has already begun to learn (and choose?) the new.

Learning a new discourse is not the only strain on a student's loyalties. Teachers may reinforce unwittingly the student's conflict by holding affectionately and unreflectively to a 'melting pot' mythology which romanticizes rejection of one's roots as a prerequisite to upward mobility, self-improvement, and financial success. And even in Whole Language classrooms, the teacher's warm acceptance of the learner's primary discourse is not unconditional; certain written language situations demand conformance to Standard English conventions. The continuity between home and school that welcomes and reassures young children and beginning ABE students, that frees them to take the risks necessary to learning, begins to vanish when demands for conventions increase. The invented spelling that was charming in first grade is worrisome in sixth. No fifth grade or ABE teacher wants her black students to write 'He been knowing that' in an article for the class newsletter without clear awareness of its sociolinguistic import. The prescribed text of the traditional classroom reappears as the text which prescribes success in the world.

At some point the road forks, and the same choice must be made by Whole Language students as is made by students in skills classrooms: whether to adopt mainstream ways or not. As Smith (1986) says, to become literate one must 'join the club' and decide that reading and writing are things that 'people like me' do. But what kind of literacy club do I join, and who am I like: my Chicano (or African-American or Navajo or Thai or Afghani or working class) parents or husband, or my mainstream teacher?

There is a major difference, however, between asking who I am in a traditional classroom and asking that same question in a Whole Language classroom. The Whole Language teacher values a variety of discourses and ways of knowing, and has therefore sought out materials which support the study of folk categories, histories, stories, and literature told and written by 'people like me'. Thus the student in a Whole Language classroom is more likely to see herself as like others already in the club, and more likely to decide to *add* standard written English conventions to an existing repertoire, rather than to *trade* old ways for new. Still, in both Whole Language and traditional classrooms, there are students who could well see literate discourse as a threat to who they are.

If a minority language group is not literate, the children's literacy in the second language may threaten existing relations between the generations. Or the child may come from a literate minority community with norms that limit, by gender or social class, who writes what. Or appropriate ways of relating to text may contradict what the child is learning. (See Chapter 3 for a discussion of some of the range of possibilities.) No matter how or whether the conflict is reconciled, there will be a challenge to the community language *status quo*. And the challenge will be played out within the student, as well as between student and school, and student and home.

So, despite the correct pedagogy, good intentions, and great success of Whole Language, its students might arrive at the same crossroads as students in traditional literacy programs, thinking they have to choose between the mainstream and home. In fact, *because* of the theory and practice unique to Whole Language, and the taste of democracy and power students have had in its classroom, the choice for these students may be even more painful.

For some students, then, their growth in competence as language users may bring to them and to their families a confused and confusing mix of pride, loss and pain. This pain has at least two sources: one coming from outside the student, and the other from within. The child or adult who has put one foot into the exciting new world where language is power may feel a strong tug on her other foot from those left behind. Family and friends may express resentment, jealousy, abandonment, or simply incomprehension at their loved one's movement away from them. And the student may ache with embarrassment at what she now sees as her family's inadequacies. Anna, a competent 10-year-old, watches her mother struggle with math problems for a high school equivalency diploma course, and brags that in her fifth grade she does *much* harder work (Wolfe, 1988). Although it may have been Anna's very success in a Whole Language classroom which inspired her mother to earn a high school diploma, there is now a gulf between them, across which the child mocks her mother's Puerto Rican-accented English and her efforts to educate herself.

And because adult's relationships with family and friends are probably less fluid than children's, the adult learner's world may be shaken more by the changing patterns resulting from acquiring a literacy explicitly intended for empowerment. Elsasser (1988) knows a woman whose husband kept her from attending her adult writing class at knifepoint. And Breslin (1987) writes the sad story of a young woman's need to educate herself (perhaps even become a doctor) and her hard-working, hard-drinking husband's baffled and limited response (that she should get pregnant).[2]

At the same time, the student may have internalized the mainstream culture's disdain for her old world (after all, the larger society as well as the classroom, communicates which discourse, which cultures, which people are legitimate); but she may not yet have mastered the new. She may not only suffer alienation from family and friends, but may also become suspended in self-doubt between the two discourses, especially as more competence — and more conformance to mainstream standards — is expected of her. Johnston (1985) describes his adult students as expressing 'concern over the increased responsibility that improved reading skill might engender. If they were to improve they might be *expected* to read, even by those who are close to them and know that they have difficulty' (p. 173).

Some Solutions

We are certainly not promoting illiteracy or failure in school as a solution to literacy-related alienation. Nor are we recommending a retreat to basal readers and worksheets, which produce exercise-doers rather than readers and writers and which, besides, can easily be dismissed as nonsense. Nor do we advocate abandoning such notions as multiple interpretations of texts, the reader as socially constructed author, or the writer as historically constrained Subject, because they may conflict with literacy norms of particular communities.

The solution to problems of literacy-related alienation cannot rely on any connection with traditional language arts instruction. Since traditional skills-based instruction makes no attempt to engage the child or adult in authentic language use or to begin that engagement with students' primary language; and since it is, therefore, less than spectacularly successful at promoting the acquisition of literate discourse, the skills approach may have less potential for alienating students from their communities. That 'virtue' is a direct result, however, of the severe damage traditional instruction does in the realm of alienation from *school* (students failing or dropping out) or alienation from *self* (students graduating bored, burned out, and cynical). The solution, therefore to the problem of alienation from *community* does not lie in trading the power and liberation of Whole Language for the relative safety, ineffectiveness of, and even harm from traditional instruction. Rather, we must begin by first *noticing* that all change has repercussions, at the same time that we take pride in those changes. And then, we must respect those repercussions and take seriously our obligation to find ways to use them.

We propose four ways of doing this. The first is to treat all discourses as if they were equally interesting and legitimate objects for scrutiny. The second is to act on the results of that scrutiny. The third is to stretch dominant discourses into accommodating more subordinate discourses. And the fourth is to reconnect literacy learners with their communities.

Objects for Scrutiny

In *Ways with Words*, Heath (1983) describes how three different discourses were collected like specimens and brought into the classroom, where they were examined as if in a laboratory. The fact that one of the discourses belonged to black working class farm children, another to white working class mill children, and the third to the black and white townspeople/teachers did not stand in the way of the children's evenhanded examination of them. Through their examination of the characteristics and complexities of the three discourses, the children's appreciation of, respect for, and fluency in their own — as well as the other two discourses — grew. They began to become bi- and some even tri- discursive.

One way to ease the pain of literacy-induced estrangement from one's roots would be to borrow from Heath. If teachers can persuade children and adults that it is safe to bring the discourse of their homes and families — their primary discourse — into classrooms with them, and if students and teachers can examine and explore that collection of subordinate and dominant discourses together, with the same objectivity and care they would give to a collection of seashells or snakeskins, then perhaps they too can create multi-discursive classrooms.

It is already integral to Whole Language classrooms that students' questions, perceptions, histories, background knowledge, and preferred ways of making and expressing sense (their primary discourses) are used and respected. But we are suggesting going beyond merely using these as vehicles for the study of something else, to making the study of the various discourses themselves into a 'science of language' curriculum. Jordan (1985) provides a moving example of this curricular shift which results, like Fiore and Elsassers' (1982), in a letter to the editor, in black English, occasioned by the death of a student's brother at the hands of the police.

We join Gee (1987) in proposing that school should enable children to investigate and critique their primary and secondary discourses, including dominant discourses. This extension of language-as-tool to language-as-topic would be an innovation and possibly an amelioration of the problem of alienation.

meta linguistic awareness.

Acting on the Results of Examining and Critiquing Discourse

An even bolder step, one more in keeping with the political progressivism embedded in Whole Language, is that being developed by Martin-Jones and her colleagues at the Center for Language in Social Life (CLSL) in Lancaster, England. The language scholar-activists there criticize liberal mainstream programs for treating discourses as neutral data or 'objects of nature' (as Heath did). Instead, concurring with Aronowitz and Giroux (1985), who make the same case for cultural knowledge in general, the CLSL group maintains that all discourses (subordinate and dominant) are social practices which must be subjected to close 'interrogation'. But interrogation leading only to a heightened awareness of, a 'critical relation' to, one's own knowledge, is insufficient if action does not follow from it. CLSL members and Aronowitz and Giroux insist that asking questions (such as who has access to what knowledge? to which ways of using language? why is access to certain discourses unequally distributed? who benefits or suffers from the unequal access?) without tying that investigation to action can be *dis*empowering. It can generate feelings of impotence, and even increase alienation.

On the other hand, the investigation can be made 'purposeful' (according to the CLSL), creating both a 'language of possibility' and a context for 'transformation' (according to Aronowitz and Giroux), by linking it 'to a vision of the future that not only explode[s] the myths of the existing society but also reach[es] into those pockets of desires and needs that harbor a longing for a new society and new forms of social relations' (Giroux, 1984, p. 38). These visions, desires, and needs could lead to: a) investigations of the possibilities for changing both the discourses and their social contexts; and b) investigations of the contexts and the particulars of other struggles for change (e.g., studying various literacy campaigns or campaigns for instituting anti-racist/anti-sexist language policies).

We believe the best place to begin such an enterprise is with the mainstream culture's discourse. We can explore, for example, how the asymmetries of doctor-patient or teacher-student talk or of boss-employee written exchanges 'contribute to [people's] understandings of what [they] are allowed to say and therefore allowed to be' (CLSL, 1987, p. 30). Such a critique, requiring as it does a stepping back and examining as if from the outside, is especially possible for students who have already come from outside. Their journey from home to the mainstream may have given them the tools for this interrogation: the knack of putting one world into perspective from the distance of another; and the customs of democracy brought from their Whole Language classrooms.

The dominant discourse should be the first to be interrogated because it is more impervious to criticism, and because critiqueing it will be less likely to separate students from the discourses in which they are rooted. However, all discourses, subordinate as well as dominant, offer comforts and constraints in unequal measure for different categories of people. Therefore, the ultimate aim is not only to legitimize primary discourses and the community's cultural knowledge, but to critically analyze these, too, for their strengths as well as their weaknesses (Aronowitz and Giroux, 1985).

Students who take part in such an education would certainly not be able to continue to participate unconsciously in either their old or their new discourses. This consciousness could itself lead to alienation — students could well be doubly alienated, from both their home discourse and that of the mainstream — or it could lead to examination and action. A scientist, after all, one who studies something consciously and objectively, doesn't love her subject less because she sees it clearly.

137

So by acting, by working with others from both dominant and subordinate groups to change what is oppressive in both discourses, these newly conscious learners would be *connected* to some of the 'old' and some of the 'new' critiquers, but in new ways. In that sense, a critical study of primary and secondary discourses would not be alienating; it would, instead, bring learners together into a new community, sharing a common responsibility for effecting change.

Stretching Dominant Discourses

Subordinate discourses could challenge dominant discourses to accommodate to their literacy — to their language, to their topics, to their worldviews. Zora Neale Hurston (1979) began publishing in the 1920s — too early for black English (and black lives) to dent the mainstream. It took *The Color Purple* (1982) to expand the boundaries of acceptability. Soto's *Spiks* (1973) is written in English, Spanish, and Spanglish, but it is not on many first-year English reading lists, even in colleges with substantial Hispanic enrollments. Gilman's *The Yellow Wallpaper* (1892/1973) was first published in 1892, after many rejections, despite her reputation as an accomplished economist; Chopin published *The Awakening* (1895/1972) three years later. Both of these profoundly feminist stories had to be rediscovered by the recent women's movement, since they had not been continuously read as part of mainstream discourses.

If Whole Language educators are serious about helping child and adult learners find their voices, then it seems to us, we have a concomitant obligation to provide forums for those voices in the mainstream. It is not enough to welcome subordinate discourses into our classrooms, as Whole Language teachers already do; we must also wrest space for them in the dominant literate world.

Reconnecting Learners with Their Communities

Although the Schoolboys of Barbiana (1970) held the naïve belief that literacy always meant power, they were quite sophisticated about the politics of the distribution and use of literacy. They carefully documented how few peasant children were allowed by the schools to graduate from the university, in comparison to children of the 'big shots'. Their solution to the dual problem of literacy distribution and use was to have two school systems: one, called the 'School of Social Service', for those who decided to dedicate themselves to serving 'the family of man'; and the other, called the 'School of Ego Service' (those we have now), which would perpetuate the *status quo*.

We can borrow one part of the Schoolboys' solution as a real option for some new graduates, but forego their innocent confidence in the power of literacy *per se*. Their recommendation that each new literate feed her knowledge back into the community (although rigidifying if all students were to follow it in that it does not allow for geographic or social mobility), may be a very good way for some students to avoid alienation. This solution would respond, for instance, to fears that learning school literacy *requires* leaving home. Just as they are better equipped for gaining entrance into the mainstream if that is what is desired (having acquired literate discourse), graduates of Whole Language environments are also well suited to this kind of investment in service, having already been members of democratic learning communities. Instead of feeling like graduation demands moving on and moving out, tearing up roots and leaving home communities ever more impoverished, some graduates might well prefer staying as important and connected members, creating new learning communities at home. (Horton [1990] gives many examples of community education projects stemming from a community leader's attendance at and then *return from* the Highlander Folk School, a school sharing many features with Whole Language classrooms.)

The Dual Potential of Whole Language

Learning to read and write can be both empowering and alienating, but learning to read and write in a Whole Language classroom carries with it special potential — for both more power and more alienation. This is because Whole Language is simply more successful than traditional approaches in developing thoughtful, confident readers and writers. It is because, being more successful, Whole Language is more likely to put some students into the position of experiencing discontinuities between the kind of literacy they learned in school and the sometimes covert, sometimes overt literacy expectations and desires of their communities. It is because democratic, critical, analytical work is intrinsic to the practice of Whole Language; and learners may turn these tools against their home discourse. It is because the collective dialogue and individual critique characteristic of Whole Language classrooms are likely to lead to personal and political change; and change can be exhilarating — but it can also be painful.

But it is exactly these aspects of Whole Language which also offer an antidote to the alienating effects of literacy acquisition. The Gee, Heath, CLSL, or Aronowitz and Giroux models of analysis of subordinant and dominant discourses are more likely to occur in Whole Language than in traditional classrooms. Those teachers who will help students solve the dilemma of the negative consequences of literacy success are more likely to be Whole Language teachers, with their commitment to respond to students' needs. And the liberation of learners from the confines of the either-home-or-mainstream-discourse dilemma into active struggle with the issues of literacy, community, identity, and social change is more likely to come from the power of the critical thinking and collaboration learned and practiced in Whole Language settings.

Notes

1   Many people commented on earlier versions of this chapter, especially Stanley Aronowitz, Nan Elsasser, Michelle Fine, Hannah Fingeret, Yetta Goodman, Gregory Tewksbuy, and John Wolfe, none of whom are responsible for how we finally worked out these ideas.
2   Kate Miller, the copy editor for this manuscript, cited other examples and a more general point. While we do not gloss education for empowerment as education for upward mobility,

and while we do not mean that becoming literate is the same as learning a standard dialect, Miller rightfully points out the double alienation women can suffer in acquiring a literate discourse or even a prestige dialect.

'... [this is] reminiscent of the situation in the film *Educating Rita*, in which the female protagonist's husband would rather have babies than a wife who is "educated out" of her class. The same author who wrote that screenplay, Willy Russell, also wrote two other plays/screenplays in which a woman liberates herself [but alienates] peers and/or family: *Shirley Valentine* and *Dancing Thru* (sic) *the Dark*. Melanie Griffiths' character in [the film] *Working Girl* manages to get promoted (in part by losing her thick New York accent and pretending she is upper middle class) and keep her best friend (female) but loses her partner (male). And of course the grand-daddy of the *literary* concept of education alienating peers is George Bernard Shaw, in whose *Pygmalion* Eliza Doolittle is tutored in the intonations of Standard English. As a result, she is fettered, unable either to return to her Cockney roots and sell flowers or to participate in the upper middle class ladies' past-time of selling themselves (society called it "marriage"). Finally, "blue-stocking" is a feminine pejorative term without a male parallel, and, if the term is not now widely used, the concept of educated women being "unwomen" remains. An educated woman thus not only loses her class discourse; she is traditionally held to lose her feminine discourse as well.

... [it seems that] in the media, a person (usually portrayed as a woman) who loses her class roots through education is offered a trade-off that more than outweighs what she left behind (i.e., upward mobility). However, the reality often seems to be that she loses her same-class peers and position without gaining anything but a posh accent and alienating ideas. No Cinderellas in real life!'

Chapter 9

One More Critique of Testing — with Two Differences

with Susan Harman

For years professional organizations have criticized the increasing emphasis on literacy tests in education. Unfortunately, recent reports sponsored by the United States government, the Center for the Study of Reading, and various governmental commissions (e.g., *Nation at Risk, Becoming a Nation of Readers, What Works*), as well as a popular perspective known as 'effective teaching' that relies almost exclusively on test-based research, support the proliferation of tests and enhance their legitimacy.[1] Outside the US too (e.g., in Mexico, Canada, Britain), use of more standardized literacy tests and tasks have increased. Notwithstanding these trends, many professionals and parents nevertheless maintain an aversion to testing and standardized assessment but lack rigorous arguments against it. This chapter attempts to provide that rigor.

Those of our arguments concerning various biases of tests (as to social class, culture, ethnicity, gender, region, and curriculum) have been presented by others (Adams, 1985; Deyle, 1986; Hale and Potok, 1981; Meier, 1981; Owen, 1985; Tittle, 1973; Troike, 1984; Webster, McInnis and Crover, 1986). Our claim about the pernicious consequences of testing for education and for a democratic society were made by Hoffman in 1962, long before the recent intensification of testing. Despite these earlier and frequent criticisms, testing's hold has tightened. Clearly, critical arguments are not sufficient, then, to reverse the intensification of testing. Action (demonstrations, lobbying, organizing) is needed. But arguments are a necessary part of that action. Therefore, we offer here not only a restatement of earlier scattered critiques, but also two unique contributions: the theoretical argument that tests can *never* test reading (or writing) not only because of various biases but because the conception of reading (and writing) inherent in tests is faulty; and suggestions for alternatives to testing that are congruent with a more adequate conception of reading (and writing).

For a variety of reasons, schools test — to check up on whether students have learned and teachers have taught, to admit students into (or bar them from) certain activities, to justify and fund certain programs, and to appear modern and scientific — not just a representative sample and not just occasionally. Tests — tests of reading, of reading readiness, of basic skills, of minimal competencies, of teacher competency, of academic achievement, of academic aptitude — dominate the education scene. It is no error, however, to think of all of them as types of reading tests. Regardless of whether the test is called a test of verbal intelligence, a test of reading achievement, a test of scholastic aptitude or a test of basic skills, the items are often indistinguishable in format, content, and task demanded (Johnston, 1984; Oller, 1980); the tests could all equally well be called vocabulary tests, tests of prior knowledge or reading tests.

The problem with the tests is not just that they are all the same. Ever since Ebbinghaus invented the nonsense syllable a century ago, testers have been trying to perfect a context-free test. The closer they purport to get to their goal (context-free texts/tasks are theoretical impossibilities), the further they take us from the context we want information about — the child in the classroom — and the more they contribute to maintaining social stratification and to deprofessionalizing teachers.

We want to make five general points about these tests:

1 Though tests claim to test reading, they actually test similarity to the test writer.
2 Test scores are not what they seem to be.
3 The task reading tests require is not actual reading but a simulation of reading.
4 Tests incorporate the wrong assumptions about education.
5 Testing, taken seriously, does long-term damage to education and to our society.

Reading Tests Do Not Test Reading: They Actually Test Similarity to the Test Writer

Reading tests tap a variety of kinds of background knowledge like factual information, familiarity with test formats, and similarity to the test writer's class-based, culture-based, and region-based assumptions. For instance, example (1) is a test item that tests quite specific factual information.[2]

(1)　The frequency of a sound determines its:
　　　treble　　pitch　　volume　　harmony

One could argue that in fact it is not possible to read this item if the meaning of *frequency* and *pitch* is not known; thus, not knowing the factual link is in fact the equivalent of not being able to read that item. But making poor sense is not the same as making no sense, as not being able to give this *any* reading. Unfortunately, the response to this item and to the totality of items on a test is interpreted as reflecting reading ability in general, not just an ability to read those particular items.

In (2), a wrong answer could have as much to do with one's experience with peach trees as it does with reading.

(2)　If you picked all the peaches off a peach tree, would the tree die?
　　　　YES　　NO

The tests also test one's experience with format — not only with shading in 'bubbles' and lining up answer sheets so as not to be off by a line, but also performing certain kinds of feats like those demanded in (3).

(3) Read each line. In some lines, three of the four syllables when put together, will make a word. The other syllable is extra. Find the *extra* syllable in each line where three syllables will make a word. Fill in the space that has the same number as the syllable you have chosen. If *no word* can be made, fill in the space marked N.

| 1 num | 2 tor | 3 cal | 4 i | (1) | (2) | (3) | (4) | (N) |
| 1 pha | 2 al | 3 tion | 4 bet | (1) | (2) | (3) | (4) | (N) |

Test-takers who do not answer these items quickly and correctly are supposedly deficient in study skills needed for reading. But the ability to re-sort syllables is *not* needed for reading or for studying. Though it might be needed for some commercial instructional program or for some activity a teacher devises, re-sorting syllables is not necessary for *reading*. This skill falls under the heading 'tricks with print' (see Chapter 5 for further discussion of tricks with print).

The tests also test age, social class, culture, and regional dialect. Example (4) asks young children to consider *teeter-totters*. In Arizona and perhaps other regions of the US, however, children play on *see-saws*. It also asks them to think of walking from one place *directly* to another.

(4) (shows map of playground)
In walking from the teeter-totter directly to the door, which of these would you pass first?
picnic table   door   bike   slide

Many Arizona second graders would walk *straight* to a gate, not directly. That might be a regional dialect preference; it might be an age preference. But in any case, the item is testing experience with particular terms, not reading.

Phonics items, especially those focusing on vowels, often merely test how close one's regional dialect is to that used by the test item writer.

(5) (Teacher reads aloud.) Mark the word with the same vowel sound as in *for*.
wart   drop   roll   farther

In parts of Texas and New Mexico, *for* is pronounced as /far/. How then does *farther* or *wart* sound in that dialect?

An item such as (5) highlights what is least important though what is most easily measured about language. And items like (6), which almost ensure that the teacher will give away at least one wrong answer through laughing or stumbling, are obviously biased against speakers of non-standard dialects.

(6) (Teacher reads aloud each of the following: children shade in an oval 'bubble' to correspond to the number of the 'best' sentence.)

1. Sue she have a pet fish.
2. He lives in a big bowl.
3. Him sometimes look at her.

But even if items like these were eliminated, others also test how well someone can think like the test writer, not how well he or she can read or reason.

(7)   An architect's most important tools are his
    (a) pencil and paper
    (b) buildings
    (c) ideas
    (d) bricks

Example (7) tests judgment, but not the child's straight-forward judgment of the item. A young child could make a good argument that an architect could not convey her ideas without 'pencil and paper' or a model of the 'buildings' she thought up. The judgment needed to get this item right is that of knowing that the test writer would pick the clever, unchildlike, almost jokey response, 'ideas'. One way to make the same judgments and have similar information as the test writer is to come from the same region. Another is to be from the same social class, the same ethnic and cultural group, and of the same gender and, therefore, be more able to take the test writer's perspective on the right answer.

Good test takers are not necessarily good readers. They do, however, know good test-taking strategies. One example of a test-taking strategy is knowing how to search for an answer. Right-answer-seeking strategies are especially important on a major section of most reading tests: the section on comprehension. As the preceding example shows, it is possible to comprehend without being able to choose the 'right' answer. But, as example (8) shows, it is also possible to choose the right answer without being able to understand anything more than the syntax or to do anything other than a sophisticated search and match exercise.

(8)   The three blugy chinzles slottled prusily on the flubbish werlies.
    1. How did the blugy chinzles slottle?
    2. What kind of werlies were they?
    3. What did the blugy chinzles do prusily?
    4. How many blugy chinzles were there?

Scores Are Not What They Seem to Be

If the tests are testing factual information, similarity to the test-writer, and test-wiseness, what then are the scores about? Clearly, they are about test taker's similarity to the test-writer, their test-wiseness, and the like. But besides the fact that they are not about the total act of reading, the scores are misleading on other counts as well. For one thing, they do not mean the same thing from one period of time to another. People taking a 1940 edition of a test in 1970 did much better on that test than people who took it in the 1940s (Harste, n.d., citing work by Roger Farr and

Leo Fay). Scores improve not because of any increase in reading ability, but because teachers teach to the tests and curricular materials are geared to the tests. That is, teachers, children, and the public in general become more familiar with the format and context of the test as teachers teach children quite specifically how to take them and as publishers quite deliberately produce textbooks and workbooks designed to match standardized tests. Such coaching does not, however, help children become better readers, just better test-takers. Over the years, hard items (more people get them wrong) become easier (more people get them right). Thus tests have to be revised to ensure a bell-shaped distribution of scores. Either items are made more difficult so the average test-taker gets the same number right or the norms are changed so that it takes more right answers to attain the same converted score (e.g., grade level equivalent). This is related to a feature of test standardization — the norming of scores.

Norming, with its requisite of bell-shaped curves, has other consequences. Besides upping the ante over time for what has to be done in order to simply maintain the same rating, norming makes it impossible to continue to raise the scores of the entire population for whom a test was normed. Over time, half the people have to be below the midline, and half above, no matter where the midline is, just as only half the baseball teams in a league can have won more games than they lost. The scores are simply a stand-in for rank ordering (Meier, 1981; Owen, 1985). They provide, in Owen's terms, a moveable gate for letting people in or keeping them out and for manipulating public concern ('something is wrong — SAT scores have fallen', or 'give credit to the new governor — SAT scores rose last year'). One example of the moveable gate occurred in Delaware. Teachers wanting jobs in that state were required to take the National Teacher Examination (NTE). The Educational Testing Service (ETS) recommended to Delaware that it review its passing score every year 'to take into account the supply and demand of teachers'. That is, ETS implicitly admitted that a passing score on the NTE is less related to qualifications of candidates and requirements of a job than it is to competition in the teaching job market (Owen, 1985).

If score equivalents shift (e.g., what counts as a passing score), so does the distance between raw scores. On standardized reading tests, the difference between raw scores of 34 and 35 and between raw scores of 42 and 43 is not one point in each case. In the middle of the bell curve, a one point difference — one more question answered right — does not matter very much. A raw score of 34 and a raw score of 35 are both converted to a grade equivalent of 2.8 in the test scores presented by Cook and Meier (n.d.). It takes many additional questions right to change a grade equivalent or percentile in the middle ranges. For high or low scoring students, however, only one question more right or wrong can entail a shift of several percentiles or months in grade equivalents. Cook and Meier (n.d.) documented for at least one test that a raw score of 42 counted as grade 4.4 while a raw score only one point higher translated to one entire year more in grade equivalence (5.4). It should be obvious then why both high and low scores are less reliable than middle scores and how test-based criteria for entrance to or exit from programs aimed at high or low scoring children (e.g., programs for the 'gifted' or the 'at risk') are suspect.

Because tests tap knowledge and language acquired through one's experiences

Table 9.1   *Relation of family income and Scholastic Aptitude Test (SAT) scores*

Family Income	Average SAT Scores	
(per annum)	Math	Verbal
under $6000	353	418
6,000 to 11,999	381	443
12,000 to 17,999	408	469
18,999 to 23,999	418	482
24,000 to 29,999	429	498
30,000 to 39,999	438	509
40,000 to 49,999	447	521
50,000 or over	464	538

(Ramist and Arbeiter, 1983, cited in Owen, 1985, p. 206)

as a member of a particular gender, class, culture, and region, scores reflect social categories like socioeconomic status at least as much as they predict future performance. Table 9.1 shows the relations of income to scores on a major standardized test.

The Task Reading Tests Require is Simply the Doing of Reading-Exercises

It is not only that tests are biased, scores misleading, and consequences pernicious; the very conception of reading underlying the tests is fundamentally flawed. The first misconception is that test writers and test buyers think reading consists of separate skills, so tests have sections on word attack skills as separate from vocabulary as separate from sentence comprehension as separate from passage comprehension. A related misconception provides a classic example of the conduit metaphor for language (Lakoff and Johnson, 1980); that is, meaning is presumed to reside in the print and to move from author's head via print to reader's head. Therefore, the tests assume that products — single right answers — are appropriate operationalizations of reading.

Contrary to the tester's conceptions, reading is a complex, simultaneously social and pyschological and linguistic activity (Edelsky, 1986b; Goodman, 1986; Harste, Burke, and Woodward, 1983; Smith, 1986). Tests wrongly assume that it is not, that it is instead a complex mechanical activity made up of separable components. Of course the activity *can* be analyzed after the fact into the ability to recognize words or identify main ideas. But just because the total activity can be analyzed into parts does not mean the separate parts add up to the total activity or that a part (like recognizing words) performed outside the total act of reading works the same way as it does during actual reading.

Reading is a *transaction* (Rosenblatt, 1978) between cultural/historical knowledge of written language cueing systems and the cues offered by the print and the context. What is transacted — what is created anew through predicting and confirming — is meaning-in-context. When we read we use cues from the higher level cueing systems (e.g., pragmatics — is the print on a wall in a public toilet? or is it on a satin banner?) — to predict possible general meanings. At the same time, we use the lowest level systems to start to specify that meaning (is it many words or a few? sentences or just a phrase?). We predict more particular meanings, using all the systems (pragmatics, semantics, syntax, orthography, graphics) simultaneously as we construct particular context-bound meanings (Harste *et al.*, 1983). Central to this process is pragmatics (which includes readers' purposes, norms regarding text genres, and the social relationships among reader, author, and any others on the scene; e.g., the teacher) and the interconnections between pragmatics and other cueing systems. When print is used (as it is in test-taking) as part of hierarchical interactions for evaluation only, sometimes without even any intent to create a textual meaning, the activity is merely an exercise. Even if every bias were eliminated, the tests would still be about a very peculiar version of reading.

[margin note: Not reading]

Of course, language tricks — reading exercises — are easier to control, measure, and test than more complex processes like written language-in-*use*. But the 'benefits' of ease and efficiency offer no surety of a relationship between reading exercises and reading. A study of 1000 children showed no particular relationship between their actual reading and their scores on the California Test of Basic Skills. Some children scored high but read poorly; others scored high and read well; some low scorers read well; others did not (Altwerger and Resta, 1986).

A person's score on a test does, however, predict how well that person does on test-like tasks in school. School tasks as well as test items consist largely of reading and writing exercises. However, there is no evidence whatsoever that the tasks on tests (like being able to identify short and long vowels) are used in reading. There are people who can read and even write novels who are poor short and long vowel labelers. The reason correlations are high between test scores and school achievement is because both the tests and the classwork require the same thing — reading and writing *exercises*. Tests and test-driven curricula either implicitly and falsely claim that reading exercises are the same as all other kinds of reading, or that the exercises transfer to or predict other reading and writing. Unfortunately, by taking up all the instructional and assessment time with exercises, tests and test-like curricula effectively prevent spending time on or assessing other reading and writing. In fact, Langer (1986) argues convincingly that school itself is rapidly becoming a test-like activity — to the exclusion of substantive instruction altogether.

Tests Incorporate the Wrong Assumptions About Assessment in General

First, they assume permanent traits rather than context-specific activity. For instance, in reading they assume that a person scoring 6.9 is some reified '6.9' regardless of purpose and across various reading materials and situations. Next, they trivialize the notion of situation, reducing it to such features as test directions and time allotments, thus assuming that standardized treatment of such superficial aspects provides every test taker with a standard situation. Situations, however, consist not only of what is outside the head, but also *how what is outside is interpreted*. Humans interpret constantly (see Mehan and Wood, 1975 for a discussion of the role of interpretation in human activity). Since no two people interpret identically, there is no such thing as a standard situation. For instance, when Jesse was 6, he told his mother he thought the way to take a test was to pick the answer he liked, so he read them all and then found the ones that sounded nicest. Mishi, a second grader, thought the idea was never to read the questions first because that would be cheating. Nicky, on the other hand, thought it would be cheating to look back at the passage because that would make answering the question too easy, so he covered it up. Alice could tell an experimenter the answer the test-writer wanted, but she disagreed with that answer and thought, if enough people picked *her* answer, the test-writer would see the light and change the answer key. Items cannot be made free from ambiguity so that all test takers will interpret the question the same way before they consider possible answers. Even attempts to acknowledge the importance of test-takers' prior knowledge and thus factor out this unstandardized 'variable' (as the new standardized Michigan and Illinois tests attempt to do in both test construction and scoring) can only account for that knowledge in the most superficial ways. The entire testing situation — from interpretation of item content to 'proper' attitudes toward answering to the impact of particular personal histories on any aspect of taking the test — can never be standardized.

Even more egregious, tests encourage a kind of magical thinking that the way to improve education or to increase any ability is to raise test scores. This would be like saying that the way to improve vision is to coach people on taking eye examinations (Meier, 1981).

Finally and desperately, tests entrench themselves. They are part of a climate in which we assume that because there are no well developed ways to assess reading-in-life, let alone genuine excellence in education, we have to use whatever tools and technology are available. Even if tests can only assess trivial, poor substitutes, the assumption is that tests *must* be used and developed even further because there is nothing else of consequence, that tests *must* be the major means of assessment, that test scores *must* be 'the bottom line', and that anything 'alternative' is simply a frill — nice if a school district can afford it or if the teacher wants to spend her time on it but not to be taken seriously.

In the Long Run an Emphasis on Testing Does Long-Term Damage to Education and Society

Tests now determine the curriculum. With so much pressure for higher test scores, teachers teach what is to be tested. Testing *reading tricks* means *reading tricks* are what is taught. From kindergarten on, in most classrooms teachers try to teach reading by teaching test-taking. In average classrooms, only about seven to eight minutes a day are spent actually reading (Anderson, Hiebert, Scott and Wilkinson, 1985). The rest of the time, test-driven curricula position both students and teachers as actors in someone else's play, performing exercises that lead only to more exercises.

In some districts, testing takes up a full month at the start of school and again at the end of school, decreasing by over 20 per cent the instructional time in a school year. Beyond that, there is the horrible tendency for minimums (as in minimum competency and basic minimum skills) to become maximums. Since people learn to read by reading, the less time they spend reading, the less proficient they are as readers-in-the-world. The loss is noted, anxiety mounts, pressure is applied to raise standards, schools test more in response, teachers teach more 'basic reading skills' (actually test-taking), cutting down even more on time for reading. The downward spiral is set. That anyone learns to read at all under such conditions is a testimony to two things: the extraordinary human push to make sense of the language around them; and the availability of real texts (texts for reading, *not* for reading instruction) and opportunities to engage with them *outside* of school.

But, of course, not all children can or do avail themselves of these opportunities and must rely on school to offer them the means to learn to read. For these children, tests are especially damaging. Along with promoting an impoverished curriculum for everyone, the increasing dependence on tests ensures that very low scoring children are placed in the lowest reading groups, where the differential between their scores as well as the quality of their experience and the scores and experience of the top readers will widen every year (Weinstein, 1976), or that low scoring children will be sent to low track classes or to special education and will stay there for their entire educational lives (Oakes, 1985).

As a society, the US is test-happy. In almost every family magazine and news-paper, there are tests to assess how happy the readers are, how assertive, how well-matched with partners, and so on. Perhaps this explains the widespread acceptance in the US at least of an emphasis on reading tests. That emphasis, how-ever, deepens those tendencies that permit acceptance of the tests in the first place — a reliance on numbers rather than judgment, an urge to oversimplify, and a transformation of complex socially shaped intra- and interpersonal activity into mechanical individual behavior.

The tests are often defended as being psychometrically well-constructed. But the key psychometric criterion is validity, and these tests are not remotely valid. The kind of data the tests generate (normed scores which simply tell us how many right answers a child gave compared to all other children) are not helpful in plan-ning instructional approaches for that child. In fact, the most use teachers make of these scores is in setting up their reading groups at the start of school. Others use scores even less defensibly. For example, real estate agents appeal to a neighborhood school's test scores in selling a house to newcomers (the test scores often become a euphemistic way to identify the social class and ethnic composition of the popu-lation of the school). Administrators use them to pressure teachers; school boards use them to pressure administrators; legislators use them to either 'sell' or refuse to 'buy' particular public programs. That is, the question of validity cannot be answered without also asking how the test results are used, and both research and informal observation indicate that their uses render them invalid (Johnston, 1984).

But even if we used reading test results validly, the 'reading' tasks demanded by the tests are ecologically invalid (Johnston, 1984). That is, they do not tell us anything about how children read in real life, but only how they 'read' in a test situation. In the tests' attempt to be objective, they distort both the motives and the strategies of the children taking the test and are an extreme in terms of intervention and lack of generalizability; i.e., they are *completely* invalid (Johnston, 1990).

Nor, despite their sacrifice of validity to claimed objectivity, are they even objective. The only thing objective about them is a mechanical grading process.

They are written by subjective human beings. Answering them correctly requires interpreting them (and the world) the way the test-writers do (Owen, 1985). The false claim that tests are objective produces their worst societal effect — masking societal inequalities with a supposedly 'neutral current of merit', thus 'enabling the fortunate to believe they have earned what they have merely been given' (Owen, 1985, p. 266) — a similarity in status to the test writer.

What Are the Alternatives?

Standardized tests have been (mis)used by a wide range of audiences — the public, the state, school administrators, parents, teachers, the children themselves, and researchers — to provide data to answer many questions. The one that is most crucial to many of these audiences is: Can we trust you with our children? It is undeniable that each of these audiences has a legitimate right to that answer. After all, it is as unrealistic for parents to turn their children over to schools without expecting safeguards and accountability as it is for them to leave those children with a strange babysitter. But, just as parents can not give a babysitter explicit instructions for every imaginable contingency but ultimately must trust her references and her good sense, so parents and the schools' other audiences can only impose so much oversight before they demoralize and immobilize the professionals responsible for their children.

Those of us who would like to see the tests abolished have mistakenly accepted the testers' premise that one instrument can satisfy all these audiences. Perhaps it would be more useful to develop a multi-tiered assessment process, each tier of which would satisfy a different range of audiences. This recognition that audiences at different distances from the reading performance need different kinds of information about that performance will radically change the kind of information sought, gathered, valued, and used. Moreover, the kinds of assessment we propose within each tier acknowledges the social, political, and contextually dependent nature of both assessment and literacy.

The audiences for the assessment tier furthest from the classroom are the public, the state administrators, and parents. These audiences need information about the school such as the condition of the physical plant, the teacher–child ratio, the overall size and population of the school, which schools the children go on to, the teachers' special interests and talents, children's attendance rates, staff turnover and absence rates, the racial balance, the enrichment programs available (such as violin-lessons or gymnastics), the content of the curriculum and the methods of teaching it, the orderliness in the halls, the observable engagement of the children in class. It may be argued that this information is too complicated to be easily gathered, to which it should be replied that the model for this tier of assessment is the routine site-visit evaluation of colleges and funded programs performed by independent reviewers at intervals for accreditation and refunding purposes. This assessment would provide the information necessary to hold the school to state standards, and to inform a public discussion of the results of the assessment and the steps to be taken next, if any.

The process of collecting and discussing the information will in itself be educational, and the breadth and depth of data collected will contribute to the political process in the community. This information, unlike test scores, is straightforward and accessible; test scores, on the other hand, are the disguised and deceptively simple results of the convoluted, sophisticated, and secret process of test construction.

Once the public, the state, administrators, and parents are satisfied as to the quality of the school, the next set of audiences, those close to the reading performance, can begin the second tier of assessment: that of the child. This assessment tier will tell these audiences — teachers, children, and parents again, in their peculiar dual role of concern for both the school as a whole and their individual children — about each child's literate activity *in that school*. This level of information will be instructionally valid because it will be both gathered from authentic classroom contexts and used to improve the child's reading/writing strategies.

At this tier, the objective will not be to identify what tasks students succeed or fail at but to investigate *how* students work on tasks that are 'worthwhile, significant and meaningful' (Archbald and Newmann, 1988, p. 1), tasks 'that have value beyond evaluation' (p. 6). For such investigations, product and process data will be collected through analysis of oral reading strategies, writing conferences and portfolios, observation, and reflective interviews. And the teacher will not be the only data collector and analyzer; parents and students will join in. Not multiple measures but multiple mirrors will be used to display many angles of a child's literacy and to reflect parents', teachers', and students' perspectives on the students' literacies while allowing each party to enlarge their perspective.

A simplified and abbreviated version of the Reading Miscue Inventory (Goodman, Watson, and Burke, 1987) is a clear and easy way of observing a child's reading strategies in process. We propose devoting a portion of the usual family-school conferences held at the beginning and the end of the school year to parents and teachers actually doing a miscue analysis with the child. We also propose collecting data on children's literacy through writing portfolios — collections developed by the child, chosen from pieces written for other purposes and other audiences, according to questions about range of repertoire, strength within the range, quality of and changes in the child's approach to revision, topic selection, involvement with a piece of writing, handling difficult ideas, and technical production (Sterling and Wolfe, 1990). Records of children's participation in literature discussion groups will focus on the child's aesthetic and critical responses to texts (Peterson and Eeds, 1990). Writing portfolios and literature discussion group records will also be evaluated by parents, teacher, and child together.

The purpose of the reading and writing data collection is as much to teach as to assess. In fact, the very act of assessing the processes of reading and writing, rather than just their products, makes those processes visible, and therefore subject to improvement. The goal of conducting reflective interviews (e.g., asking what the child thinks good readers do when they come to something they don't know (Goodman *et al.*, 1987) or asking what the child thinks she has learned about writing in the past few months and what her writing goals are for the near future (Atwell, 1987)) is to make written language processes and practices visible not only to the relevant adults, but to the child herself, possibly finessing adult interpretation. Helping the child become self-reflective and able to assess her own needs and progress is even more educative and liberating than opening those processes to adult observation.

The last audience whose needs must be taken into account are university researchers (teacher researchers have the same interests as teachers; school district evaluation researchers have the same interests as district administrators). University researchers differ from the other sets of audiences in that in their professional role, they are interested neither in funding, closing, or attending any particular school nor in improving instruction for any particular child. They might use any of the data generated for the other audiences, as well as assessment instruments of their own choice or invention, and perhaps even standardized tests given to samples of children for purposes unlike those for which they are currently used.

The appeal of this multi-tiered approach to assessment is that through it the pedagogical and political aspects of school inform and enrich each other. During the first tier of assessment, parents and state representatives can explain to each other what aspects of school are salient and important to them and why, and can negotiate funding and educational priorities. School representatives would observe the process, and likely be drawn into it as expert witnesses, to explain their practice and the theory behind it. The necessity to articulate and possibly defend their pedagogy would help them to become more self-reflective, and hence — like the children — more competent.

During the second assessment tier, teachers, parents, and children can review the children's progress by sharing their work, the social and psychological activity involved in producing it, and their respective perceptions of its quality. Teachers can explain to parents how curricular decisions are made for both individual children and the class as a whole. The result of this doubly open assessment procedure will be to optimize the possibility of mutual trust among the people who care about and are responsible for our children.

If we want a genuinely excellent educational system, the answer is not to try to raise reading test scores and to apply even more pressure to teachers, children, and administrators so that everyone is evaluated even more frequently on the basis of test scores that purport to be something they are not. The answer is to come to understand what reading actually is. We have to stop testing (and teaching) substitutes. Instead, we must engage in the kinds of assessment of our schools and our children that will promote, not test takers, but thinkers who can read and write.

Notes

1   'Effective teaching' names both a research paradigm and a pedagogical stance which emphasizes direct instruction of the entire class, breaking curriculum (seen as classroom routines) into small steps and teaching the steps, managing short smooth transitions from one subject to another, and assigning tasks with simple unambiguous demands. The measure of 'effectiveness' is standardized tests; thus, students who score well on the tests have been 'effectively taught'. See Brophy (1979) for a presentation of effective teaching research.

2   Due to increasing vigilance regarding copyright laws, lawyers have advised us not to use test items verbatim. Therefore, the examples here are either taken from a publication on testing or are items for which we have changed one or more key words. Examples (1), (3), and (7)

appear in Cook and Meier (n.d.). Example (2) is a modification of an item from the section called 'Sentences' in Hieronymus, Hoover, and Lindquist (1983). Examples (4), (5), and (6) are modified items whose originals appear in various sections of Hieronymus *et al.* (1983) (the section titled Visual Materials for (4), Words and Sounds for (5), and Usage for (6)). While Cook and Meier do not identify the source of their items, it is possible to find similar items on many tests. Example (1) resembles vocabulary items on the ITBS and elsewhere. Items like (3) frequently appear in sections called Study Skills; look-alikes for (7) appear in sections on Social Studies.

Chapter 10

Resisting (Professional) Arrest

Teaching is a profession and teachers are professionals — or so we are told. A variety of activity, however, increasingly puts teachers' status as professionals in question. Standardization of curricula and of criteria for assessing teachers as well as children, school policies that turn teachers into clerks, teacher preparation programs being reorganized to provide training in the narrowest sense rather than education — the moves to deprofessionalize abound. Nevertheless, there are some small but brilliant (not merely bright) lights in the darkness. Scattered around the North American continent are clusters of teachers who are part of what I call a grassroots teachers' movement, teachers actively resisting deprofessionalizing forces, teachers who are acting with determination to make a reality of the rhetoric about being professional. Before describing a bit of this activity, I want to elaborate on the context in which it is occurring.

In important ways, these are terrible times (despite recent astounding events in Eastern Europe). Global economic, political, and social problems seem to be worsening (ecological destruction — made even more visible to the West now that the Iron Curtain is down, enormous trade deficits for some nations, increasing monetary crises, increased proliferation of nuclear arms, unemployment, homelessness, drug traffic, etc., etc.). In recent history, education has been a convenient scapegoat during uncontained crises. The current time is no exception. (After all, if the United States imports more Toyotas than it exports Chevrolets, it *must* be the kindergarten teacher's fault, right?!) Anxious for quick, politically acceptable analyses of and solutions to horrendous (and horrendously intertwined) problems, federal and state governments identify education as the arena for attention. Governments appoint commissions which write reports that influence courts, legislatures, and state and local education agencies to take more control over what happens in schools. Most of this pressure for change and increased control is aimed at teachers (their skill, their training) and teachers' domains (curriculum, assessment). Few recent criticisms of education, for example, have critically spotlighted decisions by state agencies. No commissioned reports have faulted the ties between corporate sales practices and schools' reliance on textbooks and packaged curricula. None have complained about the role of media in misinformation about tests and test scores. Neither the cause of the previously mentioned problems of war, poverty, and environmental destruction nor the means for reversing them reside in classroom practices. But no matter — problems are redefined simplistically and the finger is pointed at schools.

Connecting trade deficits with kindergarten teachers could be a matter of deliberate obfuscation — an attempt to keep hidden the ways in which financial finaglings (junk bonds, leveraged buy-outs) and corporate decisions impinge on both national and personal life. Or the purported connection between international drug cartels and homework could be another instance of a dominant ideology at work — one that excludes any consideration of business interests and profit motives from an analysis of problems, one that defines the interests of business as 'national' or 'public' but the interests of women and minorities as 'special'. The most charitable explanation for such connections is that people feel impotent in the face of overwhelming problems. In what has the psychoanalytic look if not the psychodynamic origin of classic displacement, they substitute what is amenable to relatively immediate blame or control for what is not. And among all public domains, it is education that is imminently controllable.

Michael Apple's (1983) analysis of efforts to control education through controlling teachers is most helpful here. According to Apple, recent educational 'reforms' amount to deprofessionalizing — decreasing teachers' autonomy through the deskilling, reskilling, and proletarianization of teaching. *Deskilling* is a process in which occupational skills are redefined so that former skills entailing judgment and intuition and a sense of start-to-finish control over large work spheres become atomized, then behaviorally described, then appropriated by management. The purpose is to cut costs and increase efficiency as well as enhance management's ability to assess the execution of the now-atomized skills. The older more global skills atrophy since they are no longer needed. *Reskilling* refers to the substitution of a required new range of more mechanical, clerical, and management skills for the older, more global skills. Along with reskilling comes intellectual deskilling (e.g., relying on experts to create curricular and teaching goals) and intensification (e.g., increased demand for routine work such as grading more and more pre- and post-tests and worksheets, managing 'systems' of objectives and prematched packaged lessons, organizing and reorganizing multiple subgroups of students according to frequent mastery test results, etc.). Intensification frequently leads to 'burnout'. *Proletarianization* is a process of declining autonomy in an occupation. A key feature of declining autonomy is the separation of conception (e.g., development of instructional goals) from execution (e.g., instruction). What happens, Apple notes, when such a process is underway in education is that teachers' efficiency as managers increases while their control over curriculum decreases.

The irony is that such processes are now being called increased professionalism. I will not discount the possibility that deliberate misrepresentation of the notion of professionalism might be involved here. However, confusing decreased autonomy with professionalism actually has some basis in teachers' day-to-day experience. *Professional* includes the meaning of increased responsibility. With deskilling, reskilling, and intensification, teachers indeed have increased clerical responsibilities. In an extensive qualitative study, teachers felt so beleaguered by increased demands for testing, grading, and organizing lessons based on test results that their major goal had become 'getting done'. Nevertheless, they thought the longer hours spent on clerical and managerial tasks were evidence of their increased professionalism (Gitlin, 1980, cited in Apple, 1983). Accepting professionalism as a label for proletarianization comes from making incomplete or wrongheaded analyses, from asking the wrong questions. Enhanced professionalism is not an increase in just any responsibility. The question that has to be asked is: Increased responsibility for what? (This is reminiscent of Erickson's [1986] criticism of the time-on-task mystique. According to Erickson, from an anthropological perspective, everybody is on task 100 per cent of the time. The question is: What's the task?!)

If people are willing to equate professional with deskilled because they ask the wrong questions (or fail to ask any at all), they are aided in making that erroneous equation by the multiple, possibly contradictory meanings of the words *profession* and *professional*. *Profession* (from Latin *pro* [forward/before] + *fateri* [to confess/to own]) variously means a declaration, a vocation, an occupation that is not commercial, mechanical or agricultural, a calling (*Webster's New Collegiate Dictionary*, in fact, gives the example of 'the calling of teaching' which it distinguishes from 'the Learned Professions' of theology, law, and medicine). The *Oxford English Dictionary* adds that a profession is more than a noncommercial, nonagricultural, nonmechanical occupation; it is also one which has as a major activity the giving of advice or service (implying that a member of the profession professes). *Professional* not only means acting in accord with the norms and ethics of a profession. It also connotes being efficient, prompt, methodical and business-like on the one hand, remunerated (doing for pay what amateurs do for noncommerical satisfaction) on the other, and on yet another, having an insider's expertise (versus being a lay person). Thus, while teachers' experience of deskilling/reskilling/intensification is not related to the meaning of having autonomy over a large sphere of activity, it is certainly related to being methodical and efficient — another meaning of *professional*.

I have left an important factor out of this discussion of the definition of a professional — and so have the dictionaries. That factor is gender. In thinking of the meaning of *professional* and in discussing how deprofessionalization is now being called increased professionalism, it is critical to consider that teaching has its ranks composed mostly of women. Also, teaching — and women — are subject to frequent and successful attempts at external control. It is not coincidental, then, that the professional status of teachers, largely women, is ambiguous. Apple (1983) cites Hearn (1982) who notes that full (i.e., unambiguous) professional status is granted only to activities dominated by men — in both management and the ranks.

So far, the context presented for the current grassroots teachers' movement includes: severe, widespread noneducational problems, attempts at partial solutions to noneducational problems through 'improving' education, efforts to improve education by controlling teachers (who are largely women), control of teaching which entails proletarianization, 'selling' proletarianization as enhanced professionalism — that sale made easier in part by the existence of contradictory meanings for the term *professional*. In such a context, teachers' professional activities which run counter to proletarianization are acts of real resistance. And one of the most optimistic and optimism-generating examples of professional resistance is a networked (rather than an organized) grassroots teachers' movement.

Teachers in this movement know full well the oppositional nature of their activity; i.e., they are not unwitting resisters. They know they are reclaiming control over their teaching and, depending on the particular grassroots group, control over more or less of what goes with teaching (e.g., curricular decisions, assessment, choice of materials, placement of students, the right to hire their own administrators, as well as their new colleagues). They know they are joining with others so they can learn even more about their own professional field (teaching and learning) and its key topics, especially language in education and knowledge as social construction. Many in this movement focus more on their growth in understanding theoretically informed practice and less on the struggles which are bound to — and do — come when teachers confident in their own professional knowledge confront theoretically flawed and deprofessionalizing bureaucratic and legislative policies. Still, even those with this professional-growth-oriented focus on theory know that such a focus constitutes a profound opposition to institutional definitions of the 'professional' teacher as efficient clerk. If few teachers in this movement make any grand political analyses of *why* it is not they who are responsible for trade deficits, acid rain and the like, they are nevertheless aware that they are refusing to take the blame for these horrors. Thus, while teachers in these grassroots groups may not see themselves as 'political', their activity contradicts and resists prevailing currents.

Befitting its local, on-the-ground character, grass roots teacher groups are many and scattered. They can be found across North America, in small isolated school districts, in rural regions cutting across district and even state boundaries, and in huge unified districts in large industrial cities. They are composed of teachers with a particular perspective who have come together on their own initiative, to work as a group to improve education in their own communities. Some of the sites of such activity are: New York City, Philadelphia, Chicago, Detroit, Grand Forks ND, Prospect VT, Bloomington IN, Tucson and Phoenix AZ, Columbia MO, Redwood City, Fresno and Calexico CA, Albuquerque NM, Norman OK, Boone NC, Boothbay Harbor ME, and, in Canada, Winnipeg, Montreal, Edmonton and London, Ontario.

Some of the groups have names; some do not. Most are autonomous, although teachers in a grassroots group in one city often have connections with people in similar groups elsewhere. What are these grassroots groups like? They meet regularly — once a week for some, monthly for others. Meetings may include discussion of a prearranged topic or article or they may consist of participation in some theoretically grounded process such as 'reflective conversations' or 'staff review of a child' (see Carini, 1982 for a description of these processes). Meeting time may also be devoted to planning strategies (to help individual teachers or children, to try to change district policies) and to working on organizational activities. Organizational activities include such things as writing articles and books, selling books, publishing newsletters, offering workshops, and lobbying for changes in state laws.

The content of all of this activity incorporates particular assumptions about learning (e.g., people actively construct what they know; culture is both the goal of learning, the prerequisite for and the medium through which all learning occurs; whole activities — reading a book for escape, writing an apology to a friend — are greater than the sum of their parts; meaning and interpretation is central in all knowing). These assumptions directly challenge prevailing ideas that construct

157

learners as passive recipients of ready-made knowledge, that decompose activities (including teaching) into 'manageable' subskills and that use proficiency with those subskills as a basis for sorting and ranking people. At the same time, by recognizing an active learner whose hypotheses deserve respect, the assumptions that drive the work of the grassroots teachers' groups encourage sharing power and discourage ranking; i.e., they promote democratization in education.

A prime example of a group within this grassroots movement is s.m.i.l.e. (Support and Maintenance for Implementing Language Expression) in the greater Phoenix area. It has a newly created nonprofit corporate relative, the Center for Establishing Dialogue in Teaching and Learning, Inc. (CED). Both groups are based on the premises that: 1) state and district policies often impede rather than enhance learning and language development; 2) teachers already know more (and can learn even more) about language development and learning than do many who impose programs for teachers to follow; and 3) teachers can function as teachers for each other.

Since 1979, s.m.i.l.e. has offered semi-annual workshops on Saturday mornings, attended now by 600–800 teachers, administrators, and parents. After a keynote address by a noted educational leader (past speakers have included David Booth, Lucy Calkins, Ken Goodman, Yetta Goodman, Donald Graves, Jerry Harste, Frank Smith and Dorothy Watson), thirty or more teachers present individual hour-long workshops to share ways they have been working with holistic teaching in their classrooms (Christine, 1987). In 1982 at its workshops, s.m.i.l.e. began to sell books congruent with s.m.i.l.e. teachers' views on language and learning. The aim was to make it easier for teachers not close to a university bookstore to obtain texts such as Aronowitz and Giroux' *Education Under Seige*, Calkins' *The Art of Teaching Writing*, Goodman's *What's Whole in Whole Language*, Harste, Woodward and Burke's *Language Stories and Literacy Lessons*, Rosen's *And None of it was Nonsense*, Shannon's *Broken Promises*, Shor's *Freire for the Classroom*, Smith's *Insult to Intelligence*, and over fifty other titles. The hope was that such texts might help loosen the hold of opposing ideas prevalent in education. Additionally, members of s.m.i.l.e. have worked together as adjunct faculty, teaching a course on Whole Language at Arizona State University.

Four other groups in Arizona have modeled themselves after s.m.i.l.e., starting out with discussion/learning sessions for a small group which then organizes workshops for others in its own locality. These are WOW (Way Out West), WILD (Whole Integrated Language Development), GRIN (Greater Reservation Interdisciplinary Network) on the Navajo reservation, and RIMTALK located on the Mogollon Rim of the Grand Canyon. Two other groups of Arizona teachers have different primary activities but share s.m.i.l.e.'s general stance on language, learning, and teachers controlling their own professional lives. These are Tucson TAWL and Glendale SHARE (a group of holistic bilingual educators).

In 1985, Carol Christine, one of the teacher-founders of s.m.i.l.e., taught herself enough about written legal register to write two important documents on behalf of the founding of a new center; articles of incorporation and a legal application for nonprofit status. The state of Arizona approved these in 1986. The new nonprofit corporate center (CED) was initiated not only to relieve s.m.i.l.e. of the bookkeeping tasks involved in book sales but for two other more pressing reasons.

First, it would create an entity more capable of responding to increasing number of requests for in-service sessions in between the two yearly s.m.i.l.e. workshops. Second, it would divide at least some of s.m.i.l.e.'s former work along 'educational' and 'political' lines. That is, non-profit status would prohibit CED from engaging in 'political' activity such as lobbying for changes in state laws and campaigning for candidates for such positions as state superintendent of schools; but that work could now be done by s.m.i.l.e. since its load was lightened by having CED take over the professional development/in-service activity.

As might be expected, CED in-service differs from the usual top-down variety imposed by central administrators. The latter, compulsory and aimed at the presumed needs of a wide audience, rarely makes its theoretical positions salient. Instead, it usually concentrates on new ideas for subject-matter activities or on tips for controlling groups of children or for 'instruction' which often amounts to no more than managing the movement of children through pre-planned curricular packages. By contrast, attendance at CED in-service is voluntary; it is teacher-requested and offered to meet specific teachers' needs. In fact, CED-sponsored in-service is often conducted by teacher experts who are known in the community. It is attended primarily by teachers but also by parents and administrators (the latter have increased their participation significantly in the past two years). People who attend CED workshops frequently know the workshop giver; and they are certainly aware of the theoretical position on language and learning taken by the center. In electing to attend, they seek out practice associated with that theoretical position. They are thus more likely to walk away not with new activities or theory-blind 'tips', but with new ways of thinking.

While each grassroots teachers' group is somehow unique (few sell books, many offer in-service, some work only on local school problems, a few restrict themselves only to conducting child-study sessions, and so on), they share certain characteristics. First, members of these groups see teaching as a career rather than a job; they see 'teacher' as a major part of their identity. They are people who want control over who they become within their profession and how they will act as professionals. They are determined that they will not be defined by publishers' marketing notions or by bureaucrats' mandates.

Second, as one would expect given the makeup of the teaching ranks, most members are women. Nevertheless, given teachers' generally moderate voting patterns, most likely few would claim 'feminist' as a way of identifying themselves. Still, these women have created groups which embody principles remarkably like those proposed as feminist organizing principles (Stanley and Wise, 1983). For example, they are relatively small and nonhierarchical. Although responsibilities are frequently divided among members, there is shared control over topics to be dealt with, activities to be pursued, and ways to operate. TAWL groups (Teachers Applying Whole Language) are loosely organized (no dues, no officers) into a national group that holds a meeting in conjunction with the annual meetings of the National Council of Teachers of English and the International Reading Association; and a new international organization (Whole Language Umbrella) connects TAWL groups with some of the others. With these exceptions, the various grassroots teachers' groups are organizationally independent of each other. Decentralized and shaped according to local visions, the 'movement', then, is not only organizationally feminist but post-modernist in spirit. There are at least two other feminist organizational principles these groups share. In each, the individual teacher's experience and voice is heard as valid. And personal teaching experience is treated as part of a larger picture — often a political one.

The third feature the groups have in common is that they are consciously theoretical. They take an explicit position on the nature of learning (seeing it as holistic and as occurring primarily through productive activity rather than practice). They knowingly work from particular theoreticians' views (e.g., Piaget, Vygotsky, Dewey, Goodman, Carini, Freire). Indeed, the primary aim of working in this 'movement' relates to the fact that it is consciously theoretical. That aim is praxis — bringing theory and action together, improving education by resisting policies, programs, and materials that contradict holistic language and learning principles and that restrict teachers' autonomy. A by-product of this work is the teachers' own professional growth. In other words, by acting as the professionals they already are, teachers grow as professionals.

As mentioned at the outset, the activities of these groups constitute acts of resistance in Aronowitz and Giroux' (1985) terms. That is, the activities incorporate a 'language of possibility' (they propose and show what *can* be); they are 'intellectual' (they depend on a critical, creative questioning of authority while holding to principles); and they have the potential for changing oppressive structures through opening up opportunities for analyzing what is often avoided.

What is especially noteworthy, however, is that not only are these acts of resistance but they are acts of specified, detailed *curricular* resistance. They certainly do not constitute romanticized rebellion — making some grand, if futile, gesture. These teachers are engaged in a principled struggle over what they will teach as well as how they will teach it — and they are in it for the long haul. As they work, their theory becomes more solid, their strategies shift, their influence grows. Side by side with the deskilling that is now going by the name of increased professionalism is this professionalism that asks the right questions: Responsibility for what? Expert at what? Education for what? It is The Resistance. Its primary purpose is not to increase professionalism (which is a by-product) but to change educational contexts through praxis. To repeat — a brilliant light. May it shine ever brighter.

Chapter 11

Whole Language:
Making It A Whole Lot Better

Whole Language — a powerful answer to the question of how to educate for social justice — is still not the whole answer, at least not as it is currently and typically practiced. To explain requires first a delineation of just what it is that is not the whole answer, just what it is that can be made better.

The range of what goes by the name of Whole Language extends so far beyond the borders of the core meanings developed in this volume or in other Whole Language statements (e.g., Edelsky, Altwerger, and Flores, 1991; Goodman, 1986; Newman, 1985; Watson, 1989) that it is often difficult to distinguish living examples of what is labeled Whole Language from anything but the most traditional activity in education. However, in critiques of or comments on Whole Language, those who do not define themselves as Whole Language educators often seem to take the label at face value, so that any practice designated by someone somewhere as Whole Language is categorized as such by the critic/observer. Whole Language then becomes whatever anyone says it is. Self-designated Whole Language educators do not help. Some not knowing (not having well-worked out theoretical criteria), some not caring (having no more involvement than they would with any other fad), many not daring (afraid to alienate supporters or to create divisions), Whole Language educators rarely identify what is mislabeled as Whole Language. Critiques by outside observers who have set their sights on the wrong target along with (perhaps because of) nearly non-existent 'monitoring' by Whole Language educators are signs and consequences of the current status of Whole Language — its status as a *movement.*

That Whole Language has become a movement, even that it has become a buzz word (Edelsky, 1987), is a great boon to supporters (and, I believe, to teachers and students everywhere). The existence of a movement, popular enough to generate attendant buzz words, creates a more hospitable climate both for those who have battled for years to oppose oppressive traditional education and for those who are newly interested in experimenting with a different viewpoint. Whole Language as a buzz word gives people the sense that they are 'part of something larger' (Clarke, 1990); Whole Language as a movement confirms it.

But buzz words and movements not only can promote change; they can prevent it. Currently, the 'Whole Language' label is being affixed to everything from basals to a time slot in a teacher's schedule ('we "do" Whole Language on Tuesday afternoon') to any humanizing variation on the prevailing skills-based theme. No matter that there has been no change in underlying assumptions or framework; a new label announces that the change has already happened and implies promised benefits should be forthcoming. Application of the label — the *fait accompli* — short circuits further work at substantive change, without which, of course, the promise cannot be kept. With traditional instrumental (i.e., 'it works') discourse, the movement is then deemed a failure ('well, *that* didn't work'), making it even more difficult than before to change the educational enterprise.

Many of the most sincere, hardworking, gutsy educators are part of the Whole Language movement. So are people who have joined a bandwagon and who will jump off as soon as the next one rolls into town. So are those who are simply co-opting the label for private gain. This mix — the *movement* known as Whole Language — producing many instances of still skill-based practice that should not be categorized as Whole Language, is *not* what I mean when I say Whole Language is not the whole answer yet. Instead, it is Whole Language as a *perspective*-in-action — the core meaning of Whole Language — I am referring to.

There are many classrooms around North America and in the United Kingdom, though not as numerous as the movement makes it appear, in which the teacher has indeed succeeded in shifting to a Whole Language theoretical framework (a long process made easier by the collaborations and the more permissive climate enabled by the existence of a movement). In these classrooms, the teacher's perspective on language and language learning and her vision of a literacy and an education that empowers (Edelsky *et al.*, 1991) prevents the kind of distortions seen in other parts of the movement. Whole Language teachers who understand Whole Language *as a perspective* do *not* use literature to teach skills such as 'finding the main idea' or 'vocabulary building'; they do not plan social studies units consisting of thematized sets of 'creative activities' on trivial Disneyfied themes. They do not settle for a curriculum aimed only at private response and personal expression; they do not establish a curriculum that misses key opportunities for critical dialogue. Even so, *this* Whole Language — Whole Language as a *perspective* — is *still* not the whole answer, though it is becoming more so through recent beginning shifts in emphasis.

Whole Language as Potentially Liberatory Pedagogy

Stemming from their understanding that knowledge is not a given but is socially constructed, I have argued in this volume that Whole Language educators elevate to prominence problem-posing and analysis. Their classrooms are not places where 'critical thinking' has been reduced to a subskill, practiced on trivial hypothetical problems. Whole Language teachers understand that language is learned through actual use, through 'languaging'; further, they view this feature of learning as an excellent guide for other educational aims. Thus, science is best learned through 'sciencing', through doing science — working on problems as scientists would, including learning to ask multi- and inter-disciplinary questions of 'messy' phenomena that do not fall self-evidently into disciplinary domains. Such an understanding liberates the schedule from the ball and chain of drills and exercises. The

Whole Language appreciation of the social construction of knowledge and the value placed on critical thinking makes it likely that this freed up time will be devoted to topics and projects stemming from students' interests and providing opportunities for critique.

The Whole Language conception of reading as a transaction between a situated reader and a text in a context necessarily acknowledges readers' home discourses, schemas, and personal histories (including histories with other texts) as prime contributions on the reader's part. It overturns a faith in single interpretations that transcend history, the moral excellence of standard dialects, and single canonical traditions. Along with a view of learning as active, the idea of reading as transaction promotes pluralism and more democratic relationships (among students, teacher, and text) in the classroom. Putting students in the position of an involved, critical Subject *vis-à-vis* text and topic counters students' usual position of Object.

Moreover, by encouraging teachers to reclaim their professional autonomy and to overcome the barriers to education erected by basal and textbook publishers — an effort that often reveals to teachers, as nothing else in their experience has until then, just what the connections are between business interests and curricula — Whole Language subverts the usually unacknowledged, uncontested control of schools by the corporate sector.

But Whole Language is even more subversive than that. By refusing to sort students into high, medium and low reading groups and fast and slow tracks and by working to deemphasize (to the point of eliminating) tests used for sorting and ranking, Whole Language undermines some of education's major contributions to social stratification. Most significant of all is the key Whole Language premise: that language in use is whole, that it simultaneously dips into phonology (or graphics and othography), syntax, semantics, and pragmatics and that it is part of a Discourse (Gee, 1989a) — an 'identity kit' made up of words, acts, beliefs, gestures, attitudes and values. To learn it entails using it whole with other people who are also using it whole. To evaluate people's of language requires watching them use it — *whole*. This is in direct contradiction to the prevailing premise: that language in use is composed of separable components, that learning a language entails practicing its separate parts, that evaluating language ability is best (or even possibly) accomplished by testing people on their manipulation of separate parts.

What makes the Whole Language premise liberatory is not its content *per se* but its opposition — its opposition to this skills position — and what the opposition is used for and, therefore, in what Whole Language refuses to take part. The skills premise constitutes the underpinnings of a discriminatory arsenal. Conceiving of language as separable parts — teachable, learnable, assessable in separate parts — underlies the current technology of curriculum and materials development and testing that is used as a gate for sorting and ranking people and allotting differential access to particular cultural capital. In refuting through concrete practice (through eschewing skills-based exercises and skills-based means of assessment) the key premise of this oppressive technology, Whole Language attacks in actuality the entire arsenal of language-based weapons used against people so efficiently and so 'objectively'. If a principled, self-consciously theoretical whole language promotes pluralism and democracy, permits a curriculum of critique, and actually subverts structural inequality, why is it not the whole answer to questions of quality and equality in education?

What's Missing from Whole Language

Whole Language is not only a pedagogy that just happens to have political consequences; it is also a pedagogy with a political stance; i.e., Whole Language opposes social stratification and promotes an egalitarian social order. Though that stance has certainly been implicit in Whole Language principles from the beginning, it has rarely been emphasized in any sustained way. In fact, until very recently, it was usually not even explicitly mentioned. At the first Whole Language Umbrella Conference in St. Louis, in 1990, however, an entire strand of the conference was devoted to the topic of Whole Language's political stance. This is noteworthy for two reasons. First, it shows the evolving nature of Whole Language — that its emphasis is changing and will continue to change. And second, it begins to provide what has been omitted from Whole Language discussions. This omission — explicit statements about the political project of Whole Language and explicit discussion of the connection between its political stance and its theoretical positions on language and education — is the source of a significant gap in Whole Language. When people with a Whole Language perspective fail to explicate these connections, it is too easy for their theoretical positions to be used merely to create a 'kinder, gentler' *status quo*.

Thus, such Whole Language precepts as 'attend to language strengths' and 'students cannot be reduced to a test score' can be and usually are taken to be about individual uniqueness (which is also a Whole Language message) rather than about the occasionally explicit but always implicit Whole Language idea that a focus on language 'weaknesses' and on test or exercise responses promotes cultural imperialism and social inequality. Stressing language strengths (and assuming, axiomatically, that all people *have* language strengths) is more than a theoretical preference; it is a political tactic. It counters the prevailing political tactic of making it look like the knowledge that high status people have already learned outside of school as a function of their privileged status, knowledge that serves them well as they use it as a basis for further learning of class-biased knowledge inside of school (Gee, 1989a), is evidence of their superior innate ability.

When Whole Language educators critique tests only for bias or inauthenticity and fail to critique how they are used, the chances are great that the result will be improved means of evaluation but not improved uses; i.e., we will have richer and more theoretically defensible (and therefore even less assailable) means of assessment, but they will still be used for the same thing — for sorting and ranking. Or as another example, without explication of a political stance on equity, the Whole Language expectation of multiple interpretations of texts is left to mean simply a valuing of variety for its own sake. Similarly, the Whole Language position of welcoming and using not just the home language but the home discourse, with all its values, is frequently left untied to a clear political statement. That position is also rarely carried out in the classroom. Perhaps the imbalance between rhetoric and practice here is because of the difficulty of resolving the contradiction between a commitment, on the one hand, to promoting egalitarian relations in the classroom and, on the other, to honoring the values of cultures and families which do not all value those egalitarian relations in classrooms. Nevertheless, when such conflicts are glossed over and when the political stance of Whole Language is omitted from the discussion, it becomes too easy to confuse this profound desire — actualized or not — to minimize the educational advantage of the privileged with, again, a mere 'taste' for diversity.

For Whole Language to link the idea of multiple interpretations of texts to a conscious political awareness of the connection between Whole Language and equity issues and to a more elaborate theoretical understanding of how these interpretations relate to students' and teachers' gendered, classed, raced, ethnicitied positions (Gilbert, 1989) means grappling more seriously than it now does with the idea of language as a social semiotic. If such understandings were developed, they would reorder the curriculum in Whole Language classrooms. They would also highlight the tension involved between 'honoring the home discourse' and 'including more voices', voices which may be racist, classist, sexist (Ellsworth, 1989) and, thus, contradictory of what Whole Language stands for.

There are indeed scattered Whole Language teachers who work consciously and conscientiously not only at stocking the classroom with nonmainstream texts but also at raising the question of how gendered, raced, classed, ethnicitied positions went into the students' and the teacher's interpretation of a text and the question of what an author had to assume about the world to write what she wrote and how she came to make those assumptions. Broadening the in-school print environment is a common Whole Language effort. Regularly interrogating the class/gender/race/ethnic practices that generate seemingly individual interpretations is not. Though Whole Language implicitly permits such work regarding reading, it does little to actively encourage it. And it should.

The same is true for writing. Because published statements, coursework, and workshops rarely deal with Whole Language's underlying political project, because Whole Language relies heavily on the writing process movement's ideas for its direction in the teach of writing, and because writing process also usually omits explication of a political stance, writing in Whole Language classrooms tends to remain focused on personal expression, as Gilbert (in press) discussed. Few Whole Language teachers set up arrangements like Kimberley (1989) did with community publishing, wherein students have a chance to try to participate in and influence the out of school community — a chance to act upon the world with their writing. Whole Language does not preclude such writing; but it fails to promote it and, therefore, it misses opportunities to further its own political intent. (The writing process movement, Whole Language's guide regarding writing, also fails in this regard.)

Content study is another place in the curriculum where the absence of explicit statements about a Whole Language political stance is felt. In principled Whole Language practice (once again, as distinguished from practice that simply co-opts the label), teachers treat content seriously, not merely as entertainment or as glue to hold separate school subjects together (e.g., writing about dinosaurs, doing arithmetic problems about dinosaurs, reading about dinosaurs, and so on). But rarely does their inevitable shaping of the study include a nudge toward gender or race or class issues in relation to whatever the topic is. Rarely are children taught to ask: who benefits from this interpretation? from this 'fact'? from asking this question? It is understandable that teachers would be hesitant to pick blatantly political topics for study such as abortion or military aid to El Salvador. But without an awareness of the politics embedded in their own position, they are also not primed to take advantage of political teaching moments that crop up during 'neutral' academic study. (A Whole Language teacher of 10-year olds who does take advantage of such moments presented something of the sociopolitics of arithmetic during a discussion of a newspaper report on the dismantling of the Berlin Wall. She asked students whether one half million sounded bigger to them than five hundred thousand. They agreed. She then asked them why they thought the newspaper estimated the number of East Germans crossing over into West Germany the first days after the Wall came down as about one half million, while other reports of anti-nuclear rallies, numbered the demonstrators at five hundred thousand [Buchanen, 1989].) While Whole Language teachers work hard to figure out ways students can learn history by *doing* history, learn biology by *doing* biology, and so on, they get little direction from Whole Language statements in helping students see that doing history, biology, or any other academic inquiry is a social practice that can obscure as well as reveal, exclude and silence as well as include and articulate.

But just because Whole Language does not pay adequate attention to its own stance in favor of an equitable, democratic society, just because it does not make explicit the tie between that stance and its positions on language, curriculum and assessment, and just because, therefore, it rarely reaches its built-in liberatory potential does not mean its deconstructionist, post-structuralist, and 'critical' critics are right. Lumping Whole Language in with other 'holistic methodologies' or 'popular methodologies emphasizing individualism' and 'reading as process', Baker and Luke (in press), Gilbert (1989; in press), Luke (1989), Luke and Baker (in press), Willinsky (1987) and others claim that Whole Language is individualistic and Romantically personal, that it 'naturalizes' the individual 'self', obscuring the socially constructed character of 'selves' as well as the external interactional practices that constitute 'knowings' and 'readings'. The critique is partly correct. Whole Language *does* value individuals — their unique histories, interpretations and styles, but that is only part of the story about Whole Language values. The critique is also partly correct in another direction; Whole Language *does* omit sustained explicit political critique and therefore can be used to support as well as oppose dominant ideologies. But that too is only part of the story about Whole Language politics. As I discussed earlier, Whole Language subverts in actuality both mechanisms for social stratification and for corporate control over deskilled teachers. But there is yet another part of the story.

To appreciate that other part, critics would first have to distinguish Whole Language from other progressive educational alternatives and note the significant differences among them. One of those differences is the dominant historically situated contexts the various alternatives have been and are an alternative *to*. For instance, though the discursive practices of Whole Language, open education of the 1960s to 1970s, and early twentieth century Progressive Education are similar in some respects, they have different meanings because of their different contexts. And even Whole Language and 'writing process' (or Process Writing, as the movement is faddishly called) are different because writing process unseats nothing comparable to the powerful entrenched reading technology bucked by Whole Language. In other words, historical contexts shape the meanings of educational alternatives.

Moreover, to get the rest of the Whole Language story, critics must not only be careful to distinguish between Whole Language and other progressive educational alternatives; as I have tried to indicate, they also need to discriminate between activity that is merely called Whole Language from that which is theoretically framed as Whole Language. That is, currently, the critics observe the movement — a mixture of theoretical statements, consciously theory-driven practice, borrowed practices informed by skill-based theory, workshop advertisements, (mis)appropriations of the label in profit-making ventures (all representing contradictory assumptions or stances) — and pronounce it flawed.

Now it is certainly appropriate to evaluate Whole Language as a *movement*, but to equate that with Whole Language as a *perspective* (the conflux of ways of planning, interacting, and assessing, *consciously measured against particular theory*) promotes faulty conclusions. For example, the teachers Luke (1989) studied were all designated as Whole Language teachers by self-report or by the presence of supposedly Whole Language activities, *not* by evidence of a theoretical framework. Equity issues were not a major concern of these teachers. While principled Whole Language-*perspective* teachers may not make equity issues their *first* verbalized concern (for the unfortunate reasons I discussed above), my guess (based on my interactions with politically conscious Whole Language-perspective teachers in Phoenix, Tucson, Philadelphia, Albuquerque, Detroit and elsewhere) is they would not rank them last.

Not distinguishing movement from perspective also leads critics away from taking the perspective seriously enough to study it which, in turn, leads them toward making other mistakes. Like claiming that Whole Language is a methodology. Like ignoring the fact that a method is both action and belief, so that the 'same' method enacted by two people with different beliefs constitutes two different methods. Like criticizing Whole Language practices and then turning around and advocating what Whole Language advocates (Delpit, 1986; 1988). Like accurately perceiving that Whole Language uses a discourse of child-centeredness, but only to contrast it with curriculum-centeredness; and thus missing the Whole Language discourse of problem-centeredness, collaboration, and community (Newman, 1985). Like noting an emphasis in Whole Language on 'creativity' but failing to note competing Whole Language emphases: that learning is tied to communities; that there is a constant tension between idiosyncratic (but still historically constrained) invention and shared convention, between individual variation and social construction (Goodman, 1989). Like correctly identifying a Whole Language preference for incidental learning (of syntactic rules, for instance) but failing to identify the opposing Whole Language practice of explicit teaching — e.g., teaching about language conventions *during* editing and mini-lessons, directly pointing out features of literary discourse *during* on-going discussions of literature (K. Smith, 1990), and creating curricula which consciously interrogate everything from how language works to how government policies work (Edelsky *et al.*, 1991). Like rightfully analyzing how Whole Language's equation of the student writer with the published author omits an examination of the ways authors' works are social constructions (Gilbert, in press), but then missing one of the major Whole Language reasons for treating students as authors: to demystify in some small part, at least, the construction of texts. Like claiming that Whole Language romanticizes students as producers of original ideas and original texts, when in fact a Whole Language belief is that ideas and texts may be unique but not original, that all texts refer to, rely on, respond to other texts — that all texts are intertextual (Edelsky *et al.*, 1991).

The critics' mistakes and oversights, however, do not eliminate the need for educators with a Whole Language perspective to find ways to connect their theory-in-practice and their public pronouncements more directly to a fundamental political position. One step might be to augment the preferred reader response theory regarding interpreting texts with a theory of rhetoric, which includes an interest in how devices of language 'work' on interpretations (Eagleton, 1983) and, further, with a discourse theory which analyzes the 'work' of these language devices as social practice (Luke and Baker, in press). Another would be to find ways to integrate (not just tack on) critical sociology with Goodman's socio-psycholinguistic theory. Still another would be to explicate already existing connections and make new ones between Whole Language and critical theory in education (Gibson, 1986), between Whole Language and critical pedagogy (Ellsworth, 1989), and between Whole Language and theories of critical literacy (e.g., Gilbert, in press; Lankshire wth Lawler, 1987; Luke and Baker, in press; Shannon, 1989a, Shor and Freire, 1987).

But in no way should Whole Language be abandoned. Despite its omissions, its joint development by classroom teachers, teacher educators, and university researchers gives it special power. That collaboration has produced not only a theory with liberatory potential and not only a set of already existing present day progressive consequences, but also a theory-plus-curricular-implications with comprehensiveness, detail, and accessibility that are missing from the critiques and from alternate proposals. Whole Language as currently practiced does need some revision, and I have tried to signal directions for revision in this volume. Nevertheless, it is Whole Language classrooms (certainly not traditional classrooms premised on separate skills curricula and instruction, hierarchies, and single traditions) that have the most potential for promoting what both the critics and Whole Language educators want: justice and democracy.

References

ADAMS, R. (1985) 'Sex and background factors: Effect on ASAT scores', *Australian Journal of Education*, **29**, pp. 221–2.

ADELMAN, C. (1984) 'Review of C. RIVERA (Ed.) An Ethnographic/Sociolinguistic approach to Language Proficiency Assessment (Multilingual Matters No. 8) and of Language Proficiency and Academic Achievement (Multilingual Matters No. 10)', *CIRCE*, Urbana, IL, University of Illinois.

ALLEN, R.V. (1976) *Language Experiences in Communication*, Boston, MA, Houghton Mifflin.

ALTWERGER, B. and RESTA, V. (1986) 'Comparing standardized test scores and miscues', Paper presented at the International Reading Association Annual Convention, Philadelphia, PA.

ANDERSON, R., HIEBERT, E., SCOTT, J. and WILKINSON, I. (1985) *Becoming A Nation of Readers: The Report of the Commision on Reading*, Washington, DC, National Institute of Education.

APPLE, M. (1983) 'Work, gender, and teaching', *Teachers College Record*, **84**, pp. 611–28.

APPLE, M. (1989) 'The political economy of text publishing', in DECASTELL, S. *et al.* (Eds) *Language, Authority and Criticism*, London, Falmer Press, pp. 155–69.

ARCHBALD, D. and NEWMANN, F. (1988) *Beyond Standardized Testing: Assessing Authentic Academic Achievement in the Secondary School*, Reston, VA, National Association of Secondary School Principals.

ARONOWITZ, S. and GIROUX, H. (1985) *Education Under Seige: The Conservative, Liberal, and Radical Debate over Schooling*, South Hadley, MA, Bergin and Garvey.

ASHTON-WARNER, S. (1963) *Teacher*, New York, Bantam.

ATWELL, N. (1987) *In the Middle*, Upper Montclair, NJ, Boynton/Cook.

BAKER, C. and FREEBODY, P. (1989) *Children's First School Books: Introductions to the Culture of Literacy*, Cambridge, MA, Basil Blackwell.

BAKER, C. and LUKE, A. (1989, in press) 'Postscript: Discourses and practices', in LUKE, A. and BAKER, C. (Eds) *Toward a Critical Sociology of Reading Pedagogy: Papers of the XII World Congress on Reading*, Amsterdam, John Benjamins.

BARONE, T. (1990) 'On the demise of subjectivity in educational inquiry', Paper presented at American Educational Research Association Annual Convention, Boston.

BATESON, G. (1972) *Steps to an Ecology of Mind*, New York, Ballantine.

BAUDRILLARD, J. (1988) *Selected Writings*, POSTER, M. (Ed.), Cambridge, England Polity Press.

BECKER, A. (1988) 'Language in particular: A lecture', in TANNEN, D. (Ed.) *Linguistics in Context: Connecting Observation and Understanding*, Norwood, NJ, Ablex, pp. 17–36.

BENNETT, A. (1983) 'Discourses of power, the dialectics of understanding, the power of literacy', *Journal of Education*, **165**, pp. 53–74.

BERMAN, M. (1989) 'Why modernism still matters', *Tikkun*, **4**, 1, pp. 11–14; 81–86.

BIRKERTS, S. (1989) 'The nostalgia disease', *Tikkun*, **4**, 2, pp. 20–22; 117–8.

BLACK, J. and MARTIN, R. (1982) 'Children's concepts about writing at home and at school', Paper presented at National Council of Teachers of English Annual Convention, Washington, DC.

BLOOME, D. (1987) 'Reading as a social process in a middle school classroom', in BLOOME, D. (Ed.) *Literacy and Schooling*, Norwood, NJ, Ablex, pp. 123–49.

BLOOME, D. and BAILEY, F. (1990) 'From linguistics and education, a direction for the study of language and literacy: Events, particularity, intertextuality, history, material, and dialectics', Paper presented at National Conference on Research in English, Chicago.

BLUMER, H. (1969) *Symbolic Interactionism: Perspective and Method*, Englewood Cliffs, NJ, Prentice Hall.

BOGDAN, R. and BIKLEN, S. (1982) *Qualitative Research for Education*, Boston, Allyn and Bacon.

BOWLES, S. and GINTIS, H. (1977) *Schooling in Capitalist America: Educational Reform and the Contradictions of Economic Life*, New York, Basic Books.

BRANDT, D. (1989) 'The message is the massage: Orality and literacy once more', *Written Communication*, **6**, pp. 31–44.

BRESLIN, J. (1987) *Table Money*, New York, Penguin.

BRITZMAN, D. (1988) 'On educating the educators', *Harvard Educational Review*, **58**, pp. 85–94.

BRODKEY, L. (1987) Academic Writing as Social Practice, Philadelphia, Temple University Press.

BROPHY, J. (1979) 'Teacher behavior and student learning', *Educational Leadership*, **37**, pp. 33–38.

BROPHY, J. and EVERTSON, C. (1976) *Learning from Teaching: A Developmental Perspective*, Boston, MA, Allyn and Bacon.

BROWN, C. (1987) 'Appendix: Literacy in 30 hours: Paulo Freire's process in Northeast Brazil', in SHOR, I. (Ed.) *Freire for the Classroom*, Portsmouth, NH, Boynton/Cook and Heinemann, pp. 215–31.

BROWN, R. (1987) 'Literacy and accountability', *Journal of State Government*, **60**, pp. 68–72.

BROWNE, C. (1985) Personal communication.

BUCHANEN, J. (1989) Personal communication.

BUSSIS, A. and CHITTENDON, T. (1972) 'Toward clarifying the teacher's role', in NYGUIST, E. and HAWES, G. (Eds) *Open Education*, New York, Bantam, pp. 117–36.

CALKINS, L. (1983) *Lessons from a Child*, Exeter, NH, Heinemann.

CALKINS, L. (1986) *The Art of Teaching Writing*, Portsmouth, NH, Heinemann.

CAPLAN, J. (1990) 'The point is to change it', *The Nation*, August 13, pp. 173–5.

CARINI, P. (1982) *The School Lives of Seven Children: A Five Year Study*, Grand Forks, ND, North Dakota Study Group on Evaluation.

CAZDEN, C. (1979) 'Peekaboo as an instructional model: Discourse development at home and at school', *Papers and Reports on Child Language Development*, **17**, Department of Linguistics, Stanford University, Stanford, CA.

CAZDEN, C. (1983) 'Can ethnographic research go beyond the status quo?', *Anthropology and Education Quarterly*, **14**, pp. 33–41.

CAZDEN, C. (1989) 'Contributions of the Bakhtin circle to "communicative competence"', *Applied Linguistics*, 10, pp. 116–27.

CENTER FOR LANGUAGE IN SOCIAL LIFE (1987) 'Critical Language Awareness', CLSL Working Paper Series, No. 1, Department of Linguistics and Modern English Language, University of Lancaster, England.

CHALL, J. (1967) *Learning to Read: The Great Debate*, New York, McGraw-Hill.

CHOPIN, K. (1895/1972) *The Awakening*, New York, Avon.

CHRISTINE, C. (1987) 'Centering teaching and learning', Proposal to the Comprehensive Program Fund for the Improvement of Postsecondary Education, available from CED, 325 E. Southern, Tempe, AZ 85282.

CLANDININ, D.J. and CONNELLY, F.M. (1987) 'Teachers' personal knowledge: What counts as 'personal' in studies of the personal', *Journal of Curriculum Studies*, **19**, pp. 487–500.

CLARK, C. and PETERSON, P. (1986) 'Teachers' thought processes', in WITROCK, M. (Ed.) *Handbook of Research on Teaching*, 3rd edition, New York, Macmillan, pp. 255–96.

CLARKE, M. (1990) 'Some cautionary observations on liberation education', Language Arts, **67**, pp. 388–98.

COLLINS, J. and MICHAELS, S. (1986) 'Speaking and writing: Discourse strategies and the acquisition of literacy', in COOK-GUMPERZ, J. (Ed.) *The Social Construction of Literacy*, New York, Cambridge University Press, pp. 207–22.

CONDON, W. and SANDER, L. (1974) 'Neonate movement is synchronized with adult speech: Interactional participation and language acquisition', *Science*, **183**, pp. 99–101.

COOK, A. and MEIER, D. (n.d.) *Reading Tests: What Does That Score Mean?*, Grand Forks, ND, North Dakota Study Group on Evaluation.

COOK-GUMPERZ, J. (1986) 'Literacy and schooling: An unchanging equation?', in COOK-GUMPERZ, J. (Ed.) *The Social Construction of Literacy*, New York, Cambridge University Press, pp. 16–44.

CRAWFORD, J. (1987) 'Bilingual education: Language, learning and politics', *Education Week*, April 1, pp. 21–50.

CUMMINS, J. (1976) 'The influence of bilingualism on cognitive growth: A synthesis of research findings and an explanatory hypothesis', *Working Papers on Bilingualism*, **9**, pp. 1–43.

CUMMINS, J. (1979) 'Linguistic interdependence and the educational development of bilingual children', *Review of Educational Research*, **49**, pp. 222–51.

CUMMINS, (1980) 'The cross-lingual dimensions of language proficiency: Implications for bilingual education and the optimal age issue', *TESOL Quarterly*, **14**, pp. 175–88.

CUMMINS, J. (1981) 'The role of primary language development in promoting educational success for language minority students', in California State Department of Education, *Schooling and Language Minority Students: A Theoretical Framework*, Los Angeles, Evaluation, Assessment and Dissemination Center.

CUMMINS, J. (1982) Personal communication.

CUMMINS, J. (1984) 'Wanted: A theoretical framework for relating language proficiency to academic achievement among bilingual students', in RIVERA, C. (Ed.) *Language Proficiency and Academic Achievement*, Clevedon, Avon, England, Multilingual Matters, Ltd., pp. 2–19.

CUMMINS, J. (1986) 'Empowering minority students: A framework for intervention', *Harvard Educational Review*, **56**, pp. 18–36.

DECASTELL, S. and LUKE, A. (1986) 'Models of literacy in North American schools: Social and historical conditions and consequences', in DECASTELL, S. *et al.* (Eds) *Literacy, Society and Schooling*, Cambridge, England, Cambridge University Press, pp. 87–109.

DECASTELL, S., LUKE, A. and LUKE, C. (Eds) (1989) *Language, Authority and Criticism*, London, Falmer Press.

DEFORD, D. (1981) 'Literacy: Reading, writing, and other essentials', *Language Arts*, **58**, pp. 652–8.

DEFORD, D. (1985) 'Validating the construct of theoretical orientation in reading instruction', *Reading Research Quarterly*, **15**, pp. 351–67.

DEFORD, D. and HARSTE, J. (1982) 'Child language research and curriculum', *Language Arts*, **58**, pp. 590–600.

DELPIT, L. (1986) 'Skills and other dilemmas of a progressive black educator', *Harvard Educational Review*, **56**, pp. 379–85.

DELPIT, L. (1988) 'The silenced dialogue: Power and pedagogy in educating other people's children', *Harvard Educational Review*, 58, pp. 280–98.

DENHAM, C. and LIEBERMAN, A. (1980) *Time to Learn*, Washington, DC, National Institute of Education and California Commission for Teacher Preparation and Licensing.

DEYLE, D. (1986) 'Success and failure: A micro-ethnographic comparison of Navajo and Anglo students' perceptions of testing', *Curriculum Inquiry*, **16**, pp. 365–89.

DYSON, A. (1987) 'The social construction of written communication', *Technical Report No. 2*, University of California-Berkeley, Center for the Study of Writing.

DYSON, A. (1989) *The Multiple Worlds of Child Writers: A Study of Friends Learning to Write*, New York, Teachers College Press.

EAGLETON, T. (1983) *Literacy Theory*, Minneapolis, MN, University of Minnesota Press.

EDELSKY, C. (1978) '"Teaching" oral language', *Language Arts*, **55**, pp. 291–6.

EDELSKY, C. (1983) 'Segmentation and punctuation: Developmental data from a study of young children's writing', *Research in the Teaching of English*, **17**, pp. 135–56.

EDELSKY, C. (1986a) 'Review of C. RIVERA (Ed.) Language Proficiency and Academic Achievement, Multilingual Matters No. 10', *Language in Society*, **15**, pp. 123–8.

EDELSKY, C. (1986b) *Writing in a Bilingual Program: Había Una Vez*, Norwood, NJ, Ablex.

EDELSKY, C. (1987) 'Buzz words', Paper presented at the International Reading Association Annual Convention, Anaheim, CA.

EDELSKY, C. (1988) 'Living in the author's world; Analyzing the author's craft', *The California Reader*, **21**, pp. 14–17.

EDELSKY, C. (1989) 'Literacy education: Reading the word and the world', *English in Australia*, **89**, pp. 61–71.

EDELSKY, C., ALTWERGER, B. and FLORES, B. (1991) *Whole Language: What's the Difference?*, Portsmouth, NH, Heinemann.

EDELSKY, C. and DRAPER, K. (1989) 'Reading/"reading"; Writing/"writing"; Text/"text"', *Reading-Canada-Lecture*, **7**, pp. 201–16.

EDELSKY, C., DRAPER, K. and SMITH, K. (1983) 'Hookin' 'em in at the start of school in a "whole language" classroom', *Anthropology and Education Quarterly*, **14**, pp. 257–81.

EDELSKY, C. and HUDELSON, S. (1978) 'Acquiring a second language when you're not the underdog', Paper presented at Los Angeles Second Language Acquisition Research Forum, University of Southern California.

EDELSKY, C., HUDELSON, S., FLORES, B., BARKIN, F., ALTWERGER, B. and JILBERT, K. (1983) 'Semilingualism and language deficit', *Applied Linguistics*, **4**, pp. 1–23.

EDELSKY, C. and JILBERT, K. (1985) 'Bilingual children and writing: Lessons for all of us', *Volta Review*, **87**, pp. 57–72.

EDELSKY, C. and SMITH, K. (1984) 'Is that writing — or are those marks just a figment of your curriculum?', *Language Arts*, **61**, pp. 24–32.

ELLSWORTH, E. (1989) 'Why doesn't this feel empowering? Working through the repressive myths of critical pedagogy', *Harvard Educational Review*, **59**, pp. 297–324.

ELSASSER, N. (1988) personal communication.

EMMER, E., EVERTSON, C. and ANDERSON, L. (1980) 'Effective classroom management at the beginning of the school year', *The Elementary School Journal*, **80**, pp. 5–10.

ENRIGHT, S. (1986) '"Use everything you have to teach English": Providing useful input to young language learners', in RIGG, P. and ENRIGHT, S. (Eds) *Children and ESL: Integrating Perspectives*, Washington, DC, Teachers of English to Speakers of Other Languages, pp. 113–62.

ERICKSON, F. (1979) 'Mere ethnography: Some problems in its use in educational practice'. *Anthropology and Education Quarterly*, **10**, pp. 182–8.

ERICKSON, F. (1984) 'School literacy, reasoning, and civility: An anthropologist's perspective'. *Review of Educational Research*, **54**, pp. 525–46.

ERICKSON, F. (1986) 'Tasks in times: Objects of study in a natural history of teaching', in ZUMWALT, K. (Ed.) *Improving Teaching, ASCD Yearbook*, Alexandria, VA, Association for supervision and Curriculum Development, pp. 131–47.

ERVIN-TRIPP, S. (1970) 'Structure and process in language acquisition', in ALATIS, J. (Ed.) *Bilingualism and Language Contact: Anthropological, Linguistic, Psychological and Social Aspects, Monograph Series on Languages and Linguistics (GURT), No. 23*, Washington, DC, Georgetown University Press, pp. 313–53.

EVERTSON, C. and ANDERSON, L. (1978) Beginning School, Austin, TX, The Research and Development Center for Teacher Evaluation, University of Texas.

EVERTSON, C. and EMMER, E. (1982) 'Effective management at the beginning of the school year in junior high classes', *Journal of Educational Psychology*, **74**, pp. 485–98.

FERREIRO, E. and TEBEROSKY, A. (1982) *Literacy Before Schooling*, Exeter, NH, Heinemann.

FILLMORE, L.W. (1976) 'The second time around: Cognitive and social strategies in second language acquisition', PhD dissertation, Stanford University, Stanford, CA.

FILLMORE, L.W. (1978) 'Directionality in second language acquisition', Paper presented at Los Angeles Second Language Acquisition Research Forum, University of Southern California.

FINGERET, A. (1987) Talk given at Literacy Assistance Center, New York, February 13.

FIORE, K. and ELSASSER, N. (1982) ' "Strangers no more": A liberatory literacy curriculum', *College English*, **44**, pp. 115–28.

FISHMAN, J. (1976) *Bilingual Education: An International Sociological Perspective*, Rowley, MA, Newbury House.

FLORIO, S. (1980) 'Very special natives: The evolving role of teachers as informants in educational ethnography', Paper presented at Fifth Annual College of Education Symposium, University of Delaware.

FLORIO, S. and CLARK, C. (1982) 'The functions of writing in an elementary classroom'. *Research in the Teaching of English*, **16**, pp. 115–30.

FRASER, N. (1989) *Unruly Practices: Essays on Gender, Discourse and Power*, Chicago, University of Chicago Press.

FREIRE, P. (1970) *Pedagogy of the Oppressed*, New York, Seabury Press.

FROMKIN, V. and RODMAN, R. (1983) *An Introduction to Language*, New York, Holt, Rinehart and Winston.

GARFINKEL, H. (1967) *Studies in Ethnomethodology*, Englewood Cliffs, NJ, Prentice Hall.

GEE, J. (1987) 'What is literacy?', *Teaching and Learning: The Journal of Natural Inquiry*, **2**, pp. 3–11.

GEE, J. (1989a) 'Literacy, discourse, and linguistics: Introduction', *Journal of Education*, **171**, pp. 5–17.

GEE, J. (1989b) 'What do English teachers teach? (or why isn't the Pope a bachelor?'), *Journal of Education*, **171**, pp. 135–47.

GEE, J. (1989c) 'What is literacy', *Journal of Education*, **171**, pp. 18–25.

GEE, J. (1991) *Social Linguistics and Literacies*, London, Falmer Press.

GELB, S. (1990) personal communication.

GENERAL ACCOUNTING OFFICE (1987) *Bilingual Education: A New Look at the*

Research Evidence, Washington, DC, United States Government Printing Office.

GENISHI, C. (1976) 'Rules for code switching in young Spanish-English speakers', PhD dissertation, University of California, Berkeley.

GIACCOBBE, M. (1989) Workshop presented for Center for Establishing Dialogue between Teaching and Learning, Temple, AZ.

GIBSON, R. (1986) *Critical Theory and Education*, London, Hodder and Stoughton.

GILBERT, P. (1989) 'Personally (and passively) yours: Girls, literacy and education', *Oxford Review of Education*, **15**, pp. 257–65.

GILBERT, P. (in press) 'Writing pedagogy: Personal voices, truth telling and 'real' texts', in LUKE, A. and BAKER, C. (Eds) *Toward a Critical Sociology of Reading: Papers from the Twelfth World Congress of Reading*, Amsterdam, John Benjamins.

GILMAN, C. (1892/1973) *The Yellow Wallpaper*, Old Westbury, NY, The Feminist Press.

GIROUX, H. (1984) 'Rethinking the language of schooling', *Language Arts*, **61**, pp. 33–40.

GIROUX, H. and McLAREN, P. (1986) 'Teacher education and the politics of engagement: The case for democratic schooling', *Harvard Educational Review*, **56**, pp. 213–38.

GITLIN, A. (1980) 'Understanding the work of teachers', Doctoral dissertation, Madison, WI, University of Wisconsin.

GITLIN, A., SIEGEL, M. and BORU, K. (1989) 'The politics of method: From leftist ethnography to educative research', *Qualitative Studies in Education*, **2**, pp. 237–53.

GLADWIN, H. (1985) 'In conclusion: Abstraction versus "how it is"', *Anthropology and Education Quarterly*, **16**, pp. 207–13.

GLASER, B. (1978) *Theoretical Sensitivity*, Mill Valley, CA, Sociology Press.

GOFFMAN, E. (1959) *The Presentation of Self in Everyday Life*, Garden City, NY, Doubleday Anchor Books.

GOLLASCH, F. (1982) *Language and Literacy: The Selected Writings of Kenneth S. Goodman, Volumes 1 and 2*, London, Routledge and Kegan Paul.

GOODMAN, K. (1969) 'Analysis of oral reading miscues: Applied psycholinguistics', *Reading Research Quarterly*, **5**, pp. 9–30.

GOODMAN, K. (1984) 'Unity in reading', in PURVES, A. and NILES, O. (Eds) *Becoming Readers in a Complex Society, 83rd Yearbook of the National Society for the Study of Education*, Chicago, National Society for the Study of Education, pp. 79–114.

GOODMAN, K. (1986) *What's Whole in Whole Language?* Portsmouth, NH, Heinemann.

GOODMAN, K. (1989) 'Whole language research: Foundations and development', *Elementary School Journal*, **90**, pp. 207–22.

GOODMAN, K. and GOODMAN, Y. (1978) 'Reading of American children whose language is a stagle rural dialect of English or a language other than English', *Final Report, Project NIE C–00–3–0087*, Washington, DC, National Institutes of Education.

GOODMAN, K. and GOODMAN, Y. (1981) 'A whole-language comprehension-centered view of reading development', Occasional Paper No. 1, Program in Language and Literacy, University of Arizona, Tucson.

GOODMAN, K., FREEMAN, Y., MURPHY, S. and SHANNON, P. (1988) *Report Card on Basal Readers*, Katonah, NY, Richard C. Owen Publishers.

GOODMAN, K., GOODMAN, Y. and FLORES, B. (1979) *Reading in the Bilingual Classroom: Literacy and Biliteracy*, Rosslyn, VA, National Clearinghouse for Bilingual Education.

GOODMAN, Y. (1980) Personal communication.

GOODMAN, Y. (1985) '"Kidwatching": Observing children in the classroom', in JAGGAR, A. and SMITH-BURKE, M. (Eds) *Observing the Language Learner*, Newark, DE, International Reading Association, pp. 9–19.

GOODMAN, Y., WATSON, D. and BURKE, C. (1987) *Reading Miscue Inventory*, New York, Richard C. Owen Publishers.

GRAFF, H. (1986) 'The legacies of literacy: Continuities and contradictions in Western society and culture', in DECASTELL, S. *et al.* (Eds) *Literacy, Society and Schooling*, Cambridge, England, Cambridge University Press, pp. 61–86.

GRAFF, H. (1987) *The Legacies of Literacy*. Bloomington, IN, Indiana University Press.

GRAVES, D. (1978) 'We won't let them write', *Language Arts*, **55**, pp. 635–40.

GRAVES, D. (1979) Colloquium, University of Arizona, Tucson.

GRAVES, D. (1983) *Writing: Teachers and Children at Work*, Exeter, NH, Heinemann.

GREEN, J. and WALLAT, C. (1981) 'Mapping instructional conversation — a sociolinguistic ethnography', in GREEN, J. and WALLAT, C. (Eds) *Ethnography and Language in Educational Settings*, Norwood, NJ, Ablex, pp. 161–205.

GROSJEAN, F. (1982) *Life with Two Languages: An Introduction to Bilingualism*, Cambridge, MA, Harvard University Press.

GROSS, R. and GROSS, B. (1969) *Radical School Reform*, New York, Simon and Schuster.

HAKUTA, K. (1986) *Mirror of Language: The Debate on Bilingualism*, New York, Basic Books.

HALE, R. and POTOK, A. (1981) 'Sexual bias in the Slosson Intelligence Test', *Diagnostique*, **6**, pp. 3–7.

HALLIDAY, M.A.K. (1977) *Learning How to Mean*, New York, Elsevar North-Holland.

HALLIDAY, M.A.K. (1978) *Language as Social Semiotic: The Social Interpretation of Language and Meaning*, Baltimore, MD, University Park Press.

HALLIDAY, M.A.K. (1985) *An Introduction to Functional Grammar*, Baltimore, MD, Edward Arnold.

HALLIDAY, M.A.K. (1990) 'Linguistic perspectives on Literacy: A systemic-functional approach', Paper presented at the Inaugural Australian Systemics Network Conference, Geelong, Victoria, Deakin University.

HANSEN, J. (1987) *When Writers Read*, Portsmouth, NH, Heinemann.

HARMAN, S. (1982) 'Model airplanes and flowers: The logic of special education', *Outlook*, **43**, pp. 48–55.

HARSTE, J. (n.d.) 'A profession at risk', Bloomington, IN, Indiana University, unpublished manuscript.

HARSTE, J. (1980) 'Examining instructional assumptions: The child as informant', *Theory Into Practice*, **19**, 170–8.

HARSTE, J. (1989) 'The basalization of American reading instruction: One researcher responds', *Theory Into Practice*, **28**, pp. 265–73.

HARSTE, J. and BURKE, C. (1977) 'A new hypothesis for reading teacher research: Both teaching and learning of reading are theoretically based', in PEARSON, P.D. (Ed.) *Reading: Theory, Research, and Practice, 26th Yearbook of the National Reading Conference*, St. Paul, MN, Mason.

HARSTE, J., BURKE, C. and WOODWARD, V. (1982) 'Children's language and world: Initial encounters with print', *Final Report, NIE Project G–79–0132*. Washington, DC, National Institutes of Education.

HARSTE, J., BURKE, C. and WOODWARD, V. (1983) 'The young child as writer-reader, and informant', *Final Report, NIE Project G–80–0121*.

HARSTE, J., WOODWARD, V. and BURKE, C. (1984) *Language Stories and Literacy Lessons*, Exeter, NH, Heinemann.

HATCH, E. (1978) 'Discourse analysis and second language acquisition', in HATCH, E. (Ed.) *Second Language Acquisition*, Rowley, MA, Newbury House, pp. 401–35.

HATTON, E. (1989) 'Levi-Strauss's *bricolage* and theorizing teachers' work', *Anthropology and Education Quarterly*, **20**, pp. 74–96.

HEARN, J. (1982) 'Notes on patriarchy: Professionalization and the semi-professions', *Sociology*, **16**, pp. 184–202.

HEATH, S.B. (1982) 'What no bedtime story means: Narrative skills at home and school', *Language in Society*, **11**, pp. 49–78.

HEATH, S.B. (1983) *Ways with Words: Language, Life, and Work in Communities and Classrooms*, Cambridge, England, Cambridge University Press.

HIERONYMUS, A., HOOVER, H. and LINDQUIST, E. (1983) *Iowa Test of Basic Skills, Level B*, Chicago, Riverside Publishing Company.

HOFFMAN, B. (1962) *The Tyranny of Testing*, New York, Crowell-Collier Press.

HORTON, M. (1990) *The Long Haul*, New York, Doubleday.

HUDELSON, S. (1978) 'Videotape analysis: Beto at the sugar table', Unpublished manuscript, Arizona State University, Tempe, AZ.

HUDELSON, S. (1981–82) 'An investigation of children's invented spelling in Spanish', *NABE Journal*, **9**, pp. 53–68.

HUDELSON, S. (1984) 'Kan yu ret an rayt en ingles: Children become literate in English as a second language', *TESOL Quarterly*, **18**, pp. 221–38.

HUDELSON, S. (1985) 'Janice: Becoming a writer of English', ERIC Document ED 249 760.

HUDELSON, S. (1986) 'ESL children's writing: What we've learned, what we're learning', in RIGG, P. and ENRIGHT, D.S. (Eds) *Children and ESL: Integrating Perspectives*, Washington, DC, Teachers of English to Speakers of Other Languages, pp. 23–54.

HUDELSON, S. (1987) 'The role of native language literacy in the education of language minority children', *Language Arts*, **64**, 827–41.

HUDSON, S. (1988) 'Children's perceptions of classroom writing: Ownership within a continuum of control', in RAFOTH, B. and RUBIN, D. (Eds) *The Social Construction of Written Communication*, Norwood, NJ, Ablex, pp. 37–69.

References

HUNT, R. (1989) 'A boy named Shawn, a horse named Hans: Responding to writing by the Herr von Osten method', in ANSON, C. (Ed.) *Writing and Response: Theory, Practice, and Research*, Urbana, IL, National Council of Teachers Of English, pp. 80–100.

HURSTON, Z.N. (1979) *I Love Myself When I Am Laughing*, Old Westbury, NY, The Feminist Press.

HYMES, D. (1970) 'The ethnography of speaking', in FISHMAN, J. (Ed.) *Readings in the Sociology of Language*, The Hague, Mouton, pp. 99–138.

HYMES, D. (1972a) 'Introduction' in CAZDEN, C., HYMES, D. and JOHN, V. (Eds) *Functions of Language in the Classroom*, New York, Teachers College Press, pp. xi–lvii.

HYMES, D. (1972b) 'The scope of sociolinguistics', in SHUY, R. (Ed.) *Sociolinguistics, GURT Number 25*, Washington, DC, Georgetown University Press, pp. 313–33.

HYMES, D. (1980a) 'Functions of speech: An evolutionary approach', *Language and Ethnography Series, Language in Education: Ethnolinguistic Essays*, Washington, DC, Center for Applied Linguistics, pp. 1–18.

HYMES, D. (1980b) 'Speech and language: On the origins and foundations of inequalities among speakers', *Language and Ethnography Series, Language in Education: Ethnolinguistic Essays*, Washington, DC, Center for Applied Linguistics, pp. 19–61.

HYMES, D. (1985) 'Preface', in WOLFSON, N. and MANES, J. (Eds) *Language of Inequality*, Berlin, Mouton, pp. v–viii.

ILLICH, I. (1970) *Deschooling Society*, New York, Harper and Row.

ISAAC, J. (1989) 'Why postmodernism still matters', *Tikkun*, 4, 4, pp. 118–22.

ITOH, H. and HATCH, E. (1978) 'Second language acquisition: A case study', in HATCH, E. (Ed.) *Second Language Acquisition*, Rowley, MA, Newbury House, pp. 76–88.

JENNINGS, K. and JENNINGS, S. (1974) 'Tests and experiments with children', in CICOUREL, A. (Ed.) *Language Use and School Performance*, New York, Academic Press, pp. 248–99.

JILBERT, K. (1989) Personal communication.

JOHNSTON, P. (1984) 'Assessment in reading', in PEARSON, P.D. (Ed.) *Handbook of Reading Research*, New York, Longman, pp. 147–82.

JOHNSTON, P. (1985) 'Understanding reading disability: A case study approach', *Harvard Educational Review*, 55, pp. 153–77.

JOHNSTON, P. (1990) 'Toward a more naturalistic approach to the assessment of the reading process', in LEGG, S. and ALGINA, J. (Eds) *Cognitive Assessment of Language and Math Outcomes*, Norwood, NJ, Ablex, pp. 92–143.

JHONSTON, P. (in press) 'Steps toward a more naturalistic approach to the assessment of the reading process', in ALGINA, J. (Ed.) *Content-based Educational Assessment*, Norwood, NJ, Ablex.

JORDAN, J. (1985) *On Call: Political Essays*, Boston, South End Press.

KAMLER, B. (1980) 'One child, one teacher, one classroom: The story of one piece of writing', *Language Arts*, 57, pp. 680–93.

KIMBERLY, K. (1989) 'Community publishing', in deCASTELL, S. *et al.* (Eds) *Language, Authority and Criticism*, London, Falmer Press, pp. 184–94.

KINGSTON, M.H. (1976) *Woman Warrior*, New York, Knopf.

KRASHEN, S. (1982) *Principles and Practice in Second Language Acquisition*, Hayward, CA, Alemany Press.

KRASHEN, S. (1988) 'Do we learn to read by reading?: The relationship between free reading and reading ability', in TANNEN, D. (Ed.) *Linguistics in Context: Connecting Observation and Understanding*, Norwood, NJ, Ablex, pp. 269–98.

LABORATORY OF COMPARATIVE HUMAN COGNITION (1982) 'A model system for the study of learning difficulties', *Quarterly Newsletter of the Laboratory of Comparative Human Cognition*, **4**, pp. 39–66.

LABORATORY OF COMPARATIVE HUMAN COGNITION QUARTERLY EDITORS (1988) 'Introduction: Comparing Piaget and Vygotsky', *LCHC Quarterly*, **10**, pp. 98–99.

LABOV, W. (1970) 'The logic of non-standard English', in WILLIAMS, F. (Ed.) *Language and Poverty*, Chicago, Markham, pp. 153–89.

LAKOFF, G. and JOHNSON, M. (1980) *Metaphors We Live By*, Chicago, University of Chicago Press.

LAMBERT, W. and TUCKER, G. (1972) *Bilingual Education of Children: The St. Lambert Experiment*, Rowley, MA, Newbury House.

LAMOREAUX, L. and LEE, D. (1943) *Learning to Read through Experience*, New York, Appleton Century Crofts.

LANGER, J. (1986) 'Literacy instruction in American schools: Problems and perspectives', in STEIN, N. (Ed.) *Literacy in American Schools: Learning to Read and Write*, Chicago, University of Chicago Press.

LANKSHIRE, C. with LAWLER, M. (1987) *Literacy, Schooling and Revolution*, New York, Falmer Press.

LEONTEV (1978) *Activity, Consciousness, and Personality*, Englewood Cliffs, NJ, Prentice Hall.

LINDFORS, J. (1987) *Children's Language and Learning*, 2nd edition, Englewood Cliffs, NJ, Prentice Hall.

LUCAS, C. (1976) 'Humanism and the schools: The open education movement', in LUCAS, C. (Ed.) *Challenge and Choice in Contemporary Education*, New York, Macmillan, pp. 169–91.

LUKE, A. (1989) 'Curriculum theorizing and research as "reading practice": An Australian perspective', Paper presented at American Educational Research Association Annual Convention, San Fransisco.

LUKE, A. (1990) Personal communication.

LUKE, A. (in press) 'From psychology to linguistics in the production of the literate: Metanarrative and the politics of schooling', in CHRISTIE, F. (Ed.) *Literacy in Social Processes*, Woodanga, New South Wales, Literary Technologies.

LUKE, A. and BAKER, C. (in press) 'Toward a critical sociology of reading pedagogy: An introduction', in LUKE, A. and BAKER, C. (Eds) *Toward a Critical Sociology of Reading Pedagogy: Papers of the Twelfth World Congress on Reading*, Amsterdam, John Benjamins.

LUKE, A. and BAKER, C. (Eds) (in press) *Toward a Critical Sociology of Reading Pedagogy: Papers of the Twelfth World Congress on Reading*, Amsterdam, John Benjamins.

LUKE, A. FREEBODY, P. and GILBERT, P. (in press) 'What counts as reading in the secondary school classroom: The selective tradition of reading practices and positions', in WATSON, K. and SAWYER, W. (Eds) *Teaching English: The State of the Art*, Sydney, Australian Association for Teachers of English.

LYOTARD, J. (1984) *The Postmodern Condition: A Report on Knowledge*, Manchester, Manchester University Press.

MACKAY, R. (1973) 'Conceptions of children and models of socialization', in DREITZEL, H. (Ed.) *Childhood and Socialization*, New York, MacMillan.

MARTIN-JONES, M. and ROMAINE, S. (1984) 'Semilingualism: A half-baked theory of communicative competence', Paper presented at the Nordic Symposium on Bilingualism, Uppsala, Sweden.

MCCORMICK, W. (1979) 'Teachers can learn to teach more effectively', *Educational Leadership*, **29**, pp. 59–60.

MCDERMOTT, R. (1977) 'Social relations as contexts for learning in school', *Harvard Educational Review*, **47**, pp. 198–213.

MCDERMOTT, R. (1987) 'The explanation of minority school failure, again', *Anthropology and Education Quarterly*, **18**, pp. 361–4.

MCLEOD, A. (1986) 'Critical literacy: Taking control of our own lives', *Language Arts*, **63**, pp. 37–50.

MEHAN, H. (1978) 'Structuring school structure', *Harvard Educational Review*, **48**, pp. 32–64.

MEHAN, H. (1979) *Learning Lessons*, Cambridge, MA, Harvard University Press.

MEHAN, H. and WOOD, H. (1975) *The Reality of Ethnomethodology*, New York, Wiley.

MEIER, D. (1981) 'Why reading tests don't test reading', *Dissent*, **28**, pp. 457–66.

MINICK, N. (1985) 'L.S. Vygotsky and Soviet activity theory', Unpublished doctoral dissertation, Northwestern University, Evanston, IL.

MOLL, L. (1981) 'The microethnographic study of bilingual schooling', Paper presented at Ethnoperspectives Conference on Bilingual Education, Eastern Michigan University, Ypsilanti, Michigan.

MONAGHAN, E. and SAUL, W. (1987) 'The reader, the scribe, the thinker: A critical look at the history of American reading and writing instruction', in POPKEWITZ, T. (Ed.) *The Formation of School Subjects*, London, Falmer Press, pp. 85–122.

MORGAN, T. (1990a) 'Reorientations', in HENRICKSEN, B. and MORGAN, T. (Eds) *Reorientations: Critical Theories and Pedagogies*, Urbana, IL, University of Illinois Press, pp. 3–27.

MORGAN, T. (1990b) Personal communication.

MORRISON, A. (1982), Personal communication.

MOSKOWITZ, G. and HAYMAN, J. (1976) 'Success strategies of inner city teachers: A year-long study', *Journal of Educational Research*, **69**, pp. 283–9.

MOSS, R. and STANSELL, J. (1983) 'Wof stew: A recipe for growth and enjoyment', *Language Arts*, **60**, pp. 346–50.

NEILL, A.S. (1960) *Summerhill: A Radical Approach to Child-rearing*, New York, Hart.

NESPOR, J. (1987) 'The role of beliefs in the practice of teaching', *Journal of Curriculum Studies*, **19**, pp. 317–28.

NEWMAN, J. (1985) *Whole Language: Theory in Use*, Portsmouth, NH, Heinemann.

NYGUIST, E. and HAWES, G. (1972) *Open Education: A Sourcebook for Parents and Teachers*, New York, Bantam.

OAKES, J. (1985) *Keeping Track: How Schools Structure Inequality*, New Haven, CT, Yale University Press.

OGBU, J. (1987) 'Variability in minority school performance: a problem in search of an explanation', *Anthropology and Education Quarterly*, **18**, pp. 312–34.

OLLER, J. (1978) , 'The language factor in the evaluation of bilingual education', in ALATIS, J. (Ed.) *International Dimensions of Bilingual Education, GURT 1978*, Washington, DC, Georgetown University Press, pp. 410–22.

OLLER, J. (1980) Guest lecture, notes from S. KRASHEN's class, Second Language Acquisition, Linguistic Society of America/Teachers of English to Speakers of Other Languages Summer Institute, Albuquerque, NM, July 24.

ORASANU, J., McDERMOTT, R., BOYKIN, A. and THE LABORATORY FOR COMPARATIVE HUMAN COGNITION (1977) 'A critique of test standardization', *Social Policy*, **8**, pp. 61–67.

OWEN, D. (1985) *None of the Above: Behind the Myth of Scholastic Aptitude*, Boston, Houghton Mifflin.

PEAL, E. and LAMBERT, W. (1962) 'The relation of bilingualism to intelligence', *Psychological Monographs*, **76**, pp. 1–23.

PELLER, G. (1987) 'Reason and the mob: The politics of representation', *Tikkun*, **2**, 3, pp. 28–31; 92–95.

PETERSON, R. (1981) 'Language experience: A methodic approach to teaching literacy', *Georgia Journal of Reading*, **7**, pp. 15–23.

PETERSON, R. and EEDS, M. (1990) *Grand Conversations: Literacy Studies in Action*, Richmond Hill, Ontario, Scholastic-Tab.

PRATT, M.L. (1977) *Toward a Speech Act Theory of Literary Discourse*, Bloomington, IN, Indiana University Press.

PRATT, M.L. (1985) 'Scratchings on the face of the country; or, what Mr. Barrow saw in the land of the Bushman', *Critical Inquiry*, **12**, pp. 119–43.

RAIMES, A. (1983) 'Tradition and revolution', *TESOL Quarterly*, **17**, pp. 535–52.

READ, C. (1975) *Children's Categorization of Speech Sounds*, Urbana, IL, National Council of Teachers of English.

RIVERA, C. (1984) (Ed.) *Language Proficiency and Academic Achievement*, Clevedon, Avon, England, Multilingual Matters.

RODRIGUEZ, R. (1981) *Hunger of Memory: The Education of Richard Rodriguez, An Autobiography*, Boston, Godine.

ROSENBLATT, L. (1978) *The Reader, the Text, the Poem*, Carbondale, IL, Southern Illinois University Press.

ROSENBLATT, L. (1985) 'Transaction versus interaction — A terminological rescue operation', *Research in the Teaching of English*, **19**, pp. 96–107.

ROSENSHINE, B. (1971) *Teaching Behaviors and Student Achievement*, Windsor Berkshire, England, National Foundation for Educational Research in England and Wales.

ROSIER, P. and HOLM, W. (1979) *The Rock Point Experience: An Experiment in Bilingual Education*, Washington, DC, Center for Applied Linguistics.

RYAN, J. and SACKERY, C. (1984) *Strangers in Paradise: Academics from the Working Class*, Boston, South End Press.

SAMUDA, R. (1975) *Psychological Testing of American Minorities: Issues and Consequences*, New York, Harper and Row.

SANFORD, J. and EVERTSON, C. (1980) *Beginning the School Year at a Low SES Junior High: Three Case Studies*, Austin, TX, The Research and Development Center for Teacher Evaluation, University of Texas.

SAVILLE-TROIKE, M. (1988) 'From context to communication: Paths to second language acquisition', in TANNEN, D. (Ed.) *Linguistics in Context: Connecting Observation and Understanding*, Norwood, NJ, Ablex, pp. 249–68.

SCHON, I. (1978) *Books in Spanish for Children and Young Adults*, Metuchen, NJ, Scarecrow Press.

SCHOOLBOYS OF BARBIANA (1970) *Letter to a Teacher*, New York, Random House.

SCHULZ, J. (1975) 'Language use in bilingual classrooms', Unpublished manuscript, Graduate School of Education, Harvard University, Cambridge, MA.

SCHUTZ, A. (1962) *Alfred Schutz: Collected Papers*, NATANSON, M. (Ed.), The Hague, Nartinus Nijhoff.

SCRIBNER, S. and COLE, M. (1978) 'Literacy without schooling: Testing for intellectual effects', *Harvard Educational Review*, **48**, pp. 448–61.

SCRIBNER, S. and COLE, M. (1981) 'Unpackaging literacy', in WHITEMAN, M. (Ed.) *Writing: The Nature, Development, and Teaching of Written Communication, Volume 1, Variation in Writing*, Hillsdale, NJ, Lawrence Erlbaum, pp. 71–88.

SHANNON, P. (1985) 'Reading instruction and social class', *Language Arts*, **62**, pp. 604–13.

SHANNON, P. (1989a) *Broken Promises: Reading Instruction in Twentieth Century America*, Granaby, MA, Bergin and Garvey.

SHANNON, P. (1989b) 'The struggle for control of literacy lessons', *Language Arts*, **66**, pp. 625–34.

SHAVELSON, R. and STERN, P. (1981) 'Research on teachers' pedagogical thoughts, judgments, decisions, and behaviour', *Review of Educational Research*, **51**, pp. 455–98.

SHOR, I. (1990) 'Liberation education: An interview with Ira Shor', *Language Arts*, **67**, pp. 342–53.

SHOR, I. and FREIRE, P. (1987) *A Pedagogy for Liberation*, South Hadley, MA, Bergin and Garvey.

SHUCK, J. (1990) Personal communication.

SHULMAN, L. (1987) 'Knowledge and teaching: Foundations of the new reform', *Harvard Educational Review*, **57**, pp. 1–22.

SHUY, R. (1981) 'What the teacher knows is more important than text or test', *Language Arts*, **58**, pp. 919–30.

SILBERMAN, C. (1970) *Crisis in the Classroom: The Remaking of American Education*, New York, Vintage Books.

SIMON, R. and DIPPO, D. (1986) 'On critical ethnographic work', *Anthropology and Education Quarterly*, **17**, pp. 195–202.

SKUTNABB-KANGAS, T. and TOUKOMAA, P. (1976) *Teaching Migrant Children's Mother Tongue and Learning the Language of the Host Country in the Context of the Socio-Cultural Situation of the Migrant Family*, Helsinki, The Finnish National Commission for UNESCO.

SMITH, F. (1973) 'Twelve easy ways to make learning to read difficult', in SMITH, F.

(Ed.) *Psycholinguistics and Reading*, New York, Holt, Rinehart and Winston, pp. 183–96.

SMITH, F. (1981) 'Demonstrations, engagement, and sensitivity', *Language Arts*, **58**, pp. 103–12.

SMITH, F. (1982a) *Understanding Reading*, 3rd edition, New York, Holt, Rinehart and Winston.

SMITH, F. (1982b) *Writing and the Writer*, New York, Holt, Rinehart and Winston.

SMITH, F. (1984) 'The creative achievement of literacy', in GOELMAN, H., OBERG, A. and SMITH, F. (Eds) *Awakening to Literacy*, Exeter, NH, Heinemann, pp. 143–53.

SMITH, F. (1986) *Insult to Intelligence: The Bureaucratic Invasion of Our Classrooms*, New York, Arbor House.

SMITH, K. (1990) 'Entertaining a text: A reciprocal process', in SHORT, K. and PIERCE, K. (Eds) *Talking About Books*, Portsmouth, NH, Heinemann, pp. 17–32.

SOTO, P. (1973) *Spiks*, New York, Monthly Review Press.

SPOLSKY, B. and IRVINE, P. (1982) 'Sociolinguistic aspects of the acceptance of literacy in the vernacular', in BARKIN, F., BRANDT, E. and ORNSTEIN-GALICIA, J. (Eds), *Bilingualism and Language Contact: Spanish, English and Native American Languages*, New York, Teachers College Press, pp. 73–79.

STANLEY, L. and WISE, S. (1983) *Breaking Out: Feminist Consciousness and Feminist Research*, Boston, Routledge and Kegan Paul.

STERLING, R. and WOLFE, M. (1990) 'Portfolio assessment', Workshop presented at the Wyoming Conference on English, Laramie, WY.

STREET, B. (1984) *Literacy in Theory and Practice*, Cambridge, England, Cambridge University Press.

SULZBY, E. (1990) Personal communication.

SWAIN, M. (1981) 'Time and timing in bilingual education', *Language Learning*, **31**, pp. 1–16.

SWAIN, M. (1985) 'Communicative competence: Some roles of comprehensible input and comprehensible output in its development', in GASS, S. and MADDEN, C. (Eds) *Input in Second Language Acquisition*, Rowley, MA, Newbury House, pp. 235–56.

SZWED, J. (1981) 'The ethnography of literacy', in WHITEMAN, M. (Ed.) *Writing: The Nature, Development and Teaching of Written Communication, Volume I*, Hillsdale, NJ, Erlbaum, pp. 13–24.

TAYLOR, D. (1989) 'Toward a unified theory of literacy learning and instructional practices', *Phi Delta Kappan*, **71**, pp. 184–93.

TAYLOR, S. (1989) 'Empowering girls and young women: The challenge of the gender-inclusive curriculum', *Journal of Curriculum Studies*, **21**, pp. 441–56.

TAYLOR, S. (in press) 'Feminist classroom practice and cultural politics: Some further thoughts about "girl number twenty" and ideology', *Discourse*.

TEALE, W. (1982) 'Toward a theory of how children learn to read and write naturally', *Language Arts*, **59**, pp. 555–70.

TIERNEY, R. and PEARSON, P.D. (1983) 'Toward a composing model of reading', *Language Arts*, **60**, pp. 568–80.

TIKUNOFF, W. (1982) *An Emerging Description of Successful Bilingual Instruction:*

Executive Summary of Part 1 of the SBIF Descriptive Study, San Francisco, Far West Laboratory for Educational Research and Development.

TIKUNOFF, W., WARD, B. and DASHO, S. (1978) 'Volume A: Three Case Studies', *Report No. A78–7*, San Francisco, Far West Laboratory for Educational Research and Development.

TITTLE, C. (1973) 'Sex bias in tests', *Phi Delta Kappan*, **55**, pp. 118–9.

TORBE, M. (1988) 'Reading meanings: A discussion of the social definition of literacy in relation to school and its approaches to reading for meaning', Paper presented at Post-World Reading Congress Symposium, Brisbane.

TORRES, M. (1988) 'Attitudes of bilingual education parents toward language learning and curriculum and instruction', *NABE Journal*, **12**, pp. 171–85.

TOUKOMAA, P. and SKUTNABB-KANGAS, T. (1977) *The Intensive Teaching of the Mother Tongue to Migrant Children of Pre-School Age and Children in the Lower Level of Comprehensive School*, Helsinki, The Finnish National commission for UNESCO.

TRABASSO, M. (1981) 'On the making of inferences during reading and their assessment', in GUTHRIE, J. (Ed.) *Comprehension and Teaching*, Newark, DE, International Reading Association, pp. 56–76.

TROIKE, R. (1981) 'Synthesis of research on bilingual education', *Educational Leadership*, **14**, pp. 498–504.

TROIKE, R. (1984) 'SCALP: Social and cultural aspects of language proficiency', in RIVERA, C. (Ed.) *Language Proficiency and Academic Achievement*, Clevedon, Avon, England, Multilingual Matters, pp. 44–54.

TRUEBA, H. (1988) 'Culturally based explanations of minority students' academic achievement', *Anthropology and Education Quarterly*, **19**, pp. 270–87.

UNESCO (1953) *The Use of Vernacular Languages in Education*, Paris, UNESCO.

US COMMISSION ON CIVIL RIGHTS (1975) *A Better Chance to Learn: Bilingual/ Bicultural Education*, Washington, DC, US Commission on Civil Rights Clearinghouse, Publishing No. 51.

VEATCH, J., SAWICKI, F., ELLIOTT, G., BARNETTE, E. and BLAKEY, J. (1973) *Key Words to Reading: The Language Experience Approach Begins*, Columbus, OH, Charles Merrill.

VILLANUEVA, V. (1988) 'A rhetorically critical literacy', *Information Update*, **4**, 3, New York, Literacy Assistance Center, pp. 3–4.

VYGOTSKY, L. (1978) *Mind in Society*, Cambridge, MA, Harvard University Press.

WALD, A. (1989) 'Hegemony and literary tradition in the United States', in DECASTELL, S. *et al.* (Eds) *Language, Authority and Criticism*, London, Falmer Press, pp. 3–16.

WALKER, A. (1982) *The Color Purple*, New York, Pocket Books.

WATSON, D. (1989) 'Defining and describing whole language', *Elementary School Journal*, **90**, pp. 129–41.

WEBSTER, R., MCLNNIS, E. and CROVER, L. (1986) 'Curriculum biasing effects in standardized and criterion-referenced reading achievement tests', *Psychology in the Schools*, **23**, pp. 205–13.

WEINSTEIN, R. (1976) 'Reading group membership in first grade: Teacher behaviors and pupil experience over time', *Journal of Educational Psychology*, **68**, pp. 103–16.

WEINSTEIN-SHR, G. (1989, in press) 'Literacy and social process: A community in transition', in STREET, B. (Ed.) *Cross-cultural Approaches to Literacy*, Cambridge, England, Cambridge University Press.

WELLS, G. (1977) 'Language use and educational success: An empirical response to Joan Tough's "The development of meaning"', *Research in Education*, **18**, pp. 9–34.

WELLS, G. (1979) 'Describing children's learning: Development at home and at school', *British Educational Research Journal*, **5**, pp. 75–89.

WELLS, G. (1981) *Learning Through Interaction: The Study of Language Development*, New York, Cambridge University Press.

WELLS, G. and RABAN, E. (n.d.) 'Children learning to read', *Final Report: Grant HR 3797/1*, Social Science Research Council, Research Unit, 19 Berkeley Square, Bristol, England.

WEXLER, P. (1987) *Social Analysis of Education: After the New Sociology*, London, Routledge and Kegan Paul.

WILDE, J. (1988) 'The written report: Old wine in new bottles', in NEWKIRK, T. and ATWELL, N. (Eds) *Understanding Writing*, Portsmouth, NH, Heinemann, pp. 179–90.

WILLES, M. (1981) 'Learning to take part in classroom interaction', in FRENCH, P. and MACLURE, M. (Eds) *Adult-Child Conversation*, New York, St. Martin's Press, pp. 73–95.

WILLIAMS, R. (1989) ' Hegemony and the selective tradition', in DECASTELL, S. *et al.* (Eds) *Language, Authority and Criticism*, London, Falmer Press, pp. 56–60.

WILLINSKY, J. (1987) 'The seldom-spoken roots of the curriculum: Romanticism and the New Literacy', *Curriculum Inquiry*, **17**, pp. 267–91.

WOLFE, J. (1988) Personal communication.

WOODS-ELLIOTT, C. and HYMES, D. (n.d.) 'Issues in literacy: Different lenses', unpublished manuscript.

Index

The Falmer Press

Related Titles

The Labyrinths of Literacy:
Reflections on Literacy Past and Present
Harvey J. Graff, *University of Texas at Dallas, USA*

'... *Yet another book from Falmer Press that breaks new ground ... Readers who don't want their current assumptions about literacy's place in the world to be challenged should not read this book. Those who want to engage with a text, tussling with and reflecting upon important philosophical, historical and social issues should buy this book.*' **Discourse Processing Forum**

'... *throws up many important new points and questions accepted "truths", thus making a valuable contribution to the development and understanding of the subject.*' **History of Education**

275pp
Cloth ISBN 1 85000 163 4
Paper ISBN 1 85000 164 2

Literacy, Textbooks, and Ideology:
Postwar Literacy Instruction and the Mythology of Dick and Jane
Allan Luke, *James Cook University of North Queensland, Australia*

'... *of considerable interest not only to those involved in the critical curriculum community, but to all those who care about reading and literacy instruction, textbooks, and the politics of the classroom.*'
Michael W. Apple, Teachers College Record

'*Luke's work sets new standards in scholarly commentary on school texts and provides a new, improved methodology for analysis which makes previous attempts to explain texts of the past seem very thin indeed.*' **Garth Boomer, Australian Journal of Reading**

Literacy, Schooling and Revolution
Colin Lankshear, *University of Auckland, New Zealand* with Moira Lawler

'*What makes this book valuable is not only its exceptionally useful conceptual and political clarification of what literacy has meant and might actually mean in the search for what Marcus Raskin has called "the common good". The volume goes considerably further. It provides us with a series of detailed pictures of significant historical and contemporary struggles to engage in "proper literacy".*'
Michael W. Apple, University of Wisconsin-Madison, USA

'*A challenging introduction to the politics literacy.*' **Curriculum Perspectives, Australia**

'*... provides a sombre background to the underlying question; "What is all this education for?"* '
Times Educational Supplement

'*The authors challenge assumptions and practices that are no longer useful; they also point the way to a more just and equitable society. It's a fine, powerful and timely book.*' **New Zealand Listener**

Winner of the 1988 American Educational Studies Association Critics Choice Award

274pp
Cloth ISBN 1 85000 239 8
Paper ISBN 1 85000 589 3

Language and Literacy in the Primary School
Edited by Margaret Meek, *University of London Institute of Education, UK* and Colin Mills, *Worcester College of Higher Education, UK*

'*... represents the most important collection so far available of views reflecting a new and influential way of looking at literacy development.*' **David Wray, LINKS**

310pp
Cloth ISBN 1 85000 352 1
Paper ISBN 1 85000 357 2

Language, Authority and Criticism:
Readings on the School Textbook
Edited by Suzanne de Castell, *Simon Fraser University, Canada* and Allan and Carmen Luke, *James Cook University of North Queensland, Australia*

'*... essential background reading to any study of the role of interactively produced texts in education. Coupled with other books in the series such as* Literacy, Textbooks and Ideology, *it should form an important part of the library of all educators.*' **Bob Young, Australian Journal of Educational Studies**

'*... a useful and important study of the process by which textbooks are made, marketed, and utilized.*' **Interchange**

'*... These essays look at the content, form, production and language of textbooks. They raise pertinent questions about insidious censorship and the authority mistakenly still given to some textbooks.*' **Times Educational Supplement**

322pp
Cloth ISBN 1 85000 365 3
Paper ISBN 1 85000 366 1